My Most-Wanted
Marijuana Mom

D0100603

My Most-Wanted Marijuana Mom

*Growing Up
in a Smuggling Family*

DAVID MICHAEL MCNELIS

Exposit

Jefferson, North Carolina

LIBRARY OF CONGRESS CATALOGUING-IN-PUBLICATION DATA

Names: McNelis, David Michael, author.
Title: My most-wanted marijuana mom : growing up
in a smuggling family / David Michael McNelis.
Description: Jefferson, North Carolina : Exposit Books, 2018 | Includes index.
Identifiers: LCCN 2018004248 | ISBN 9781476673080 (softcover : acid free paper) ∞
Subjects: LCSH: McNelis, David Michael. | Women drug
dealers—United States—Biography. | Children of criminals—United
States—Biography. | Drug traffic—United States.
Classification: LCC HV5805.M3866 A3 2018 | DDC 364.1/3365092 [B] —dc23
LC record available at https://lccn.loc.gov/2018004248

BRITISH LIBRARY CATALOGUING DATA ARE AVAILABLE

ISBN (print) 978-1-4766-7308-0
ISBN (ebook) 978-1-4766-3311-4

Front cover image of Judy "Haas" McNelis, circa 1985
in federal prison; marijuana leaf © 2018 traffic_analyzer/iStock

Printed in the United States of America

Exposit is an imprint of McFarland & Company, Inc., Publishers
Jefferson, North Carolina

Exposit
*Box 611, Jefferson, North Carolina 28640
www.expositbooks.com*

To Violet Marie Haas, aka "Bummy," for first introducing me to the magnificent world of reading. Books forever changed my life and allowed me to survive life's rough spots…

To Mom, for never giving up during the darkest hours and showing what it means to be a positive thinker. Life with you had its trials, but it surely has been an adventure…

To Jesus, for giving me life and answering all my prayers…

And finally, to my lovely wife Christine and my sons Zachary and Jagger, for all your support and understanding while I was writing this book. You guys rock! You are my world and I love you more than words can say.

Table of Contents

Prologue

It went down on a day much like any other, as routine and casual as a trip to the neighborhood supermarket. But this was murder. Bloody, undignified, and … permanent. The victim was found lying face down in a water-filled ditch off the roadside, stinking of urine and feces, with two bullets in the brain and his fly open. Not a pretty sight.

The last time I saw Frank Marrs alive was the afternoon he'd picked up the $25,000 he had earned a few weeks earlier. He was a highly trained and skilled pilot who formerly flew for Eastern Airlines and this money represented less than a day's measure of his time.

"Can't get paid like this hauling people," he often chuckled. That was true. Only I'm sure he didn't intend to wind up worm food.

Frank had arrived at our rented beach house in West Palm Beach as I was munching cereal and Mom was making tea. Earl Grey, her favorite. I could smell the bergamot as she tended the steaming cups. Frank hustled in with a quick "Hello" and a smiling nod, and then grabbed the plain brown paper bag that was sitting on a nearby chair and dumped its contents on the kitchen table. He quickly counted the money, mostly bundles of twenties and tens, and thanked Mom with a brief hug and a peck on the cheek. Neither of us was surprised: Frank was used to getting paid in cash and I had seen far greater sums in the past. Gathering up the cash, Frank stuffed it in a small leather satchel he'd brought to carry the cash and explained that he couldn't stay for tea because John and Gary were waiting in the van. They were going to "check out a strip."

This was nothing unusual. A *cool* strip only stayed cool for awhile. After a few trips, a strip would be unceremoniously dropped as a primary landing or drop-site. Overuse was too risky and unnecessary. The wrong people could have noticed something that had to remain private.

Emergencies didn't count, in a pinch almost anyplace would do, but keeping an eye out for potential sites was a never-ending job. A job Gary Childers, the man responsible for "catching" the load, seemed not to mind all that much. After all, he had a substantial stake in a trip's success and would do just about anything to feel like a big shot. John Parella—who Frank knew and trusted primarily because of his association with Gary—came along for the ride.

Frank pecked Mom on the cheek and shook my hand and smiled. He gripped his satchel casually in one hand and waved with the other as he was walking out the door. As he climbed into Gary's van he exclaimed happily, "Let's grab a beer first."

It would be more than seven years before I would hear exactly what had happened to Frank straight from the mouths of his killers as they testified under oath in a capital murder trial in south Florida. My mother's murder trial. How could this happen?

Frank, Gary, and John had left our house and more or less blew the rest of the day "cruising around, drinking beer and bullshitting," as they put it. They were killing time in order to examine the strip around dusk when they would attract the least attention, as the most desirable strips were always located on private property belonging to strangers or public land accessible to anybody. And besides, it didn't hurt to see a strip in poor visibility since conditions were hardly ever perfect. The beer flowed freely and then it was time.

The strip, according to Gary's directions, was located in rural Palm Beach County, less than a 45-minute drive from West Palm Beach. Frank knew the area to be rich in possibilities; isolated and private, it had only a small number of large trees and a great many wide-open deserted level fields. The few roads and highways in the area carried little traffic and could be used as emergency runways in a pinch. Snakes and alligators were the movers and shakers out there and they didn't care what went on as long as you kept out of their way.

"Almost there," Gary belched from the driver's seat. "Want another?" He pointed at the cooler between the captain's chairs while looking back at John, who shook his head slowly and seriously. His lifeless eyes betrayed no emotion.

"What about you, Frank, you ready for another one?" Gary chortled while slugging the last of his can. Gary loved beer and it showed. He carried a 50-pound spare tire around his waist as proudly as an expectant mother. He also hated to drink alone, especially that evening. "Whaddaya say?"

"What I need is to take a piss," John answered for Frank.

"Same here." Frank was relieved. It was hard to keep up with Gary's 275 pounds of beer-guzzling power.

"You got it."

Gary eased the van to the shoulder and John and Frank stepped out, stretching their arms and shaking their legs to restore circulation. No cars were in sight and there was no sound except the wind blowing across the dirt road, the idling van, and some brown water flowing sluggishly in a nearby drainage ditch. A commercial airliner, probably bound for Miami, thundered far overhead. Then things moved real fast.

Frank had just unzipped his fly and was beginning to relieve himself when John, with a swift and steady hand, drew his "sweetheart" from beneath his windbreaker and leveled it at the back of Frank's tousled head. She was a .38 snub-nose revolver, made for up-close work, the way Parella liked it. Proximity allowed for accuracy and hollow-point bullets assured a complete job, for John had learned from past mistakes and wanted no problems here.

"Pop…. Pop." A silencer wasn't needed. For all practical purposes they were in the middle of nowhere. Parella tucked the pistol back in his waistband.

Frank Marrs hardly resembled himself anymore, resting in a puddle of his own urine and twitching ever so slightly, eyes skyward in a blank stare. Both slugs had entered his skull behind his left ear and fragmented inside the cranial cavity before violently exiting in pieces amid a shower of brains and blood.

"Stupid son of a bitch," Parella muttered, as he spit on what had only moments before been a father, a husband, and a damned good pilot. Then together they rolled Frank's body in a piece of carpet from Gary's van and pushed the corpse into a nearby drainage ditch. The murder had only taken a minute. Without a backward glance, they climbed back into the van.

"What should we do with this?" Gary held up Frank's jacket. Parella snatched it from his hand and angrily threw it out the window.

"Let's get the fuck out of here. Now! Or you'll be joining the flyboy," growled Parella. He began counting the contents of Frank's satchel, stacking the bills in his lap as he divvied up the cash.

Gary floored it. "How 'bout a beer?" he asked nervously.

"Sure."

The two cold-blooded killers smiled, evidently satisfied with their day's work. According to court testimony given many years later, they felt they had pulled off the perfect murder. And they did get away with it for quite some time. But the pendulum of retribution was merely waiting to swing in the opposite direction, patiently biding its time to indiscriminately crush everyone and anyone in its path.

In fact, my mom, Judy "Haas" McNelis, ultimately wound up being tried for capital murder in the horrific death of her friend and smuggling associate, Frank Marrs, for he was one of several pilots she employed in her international marijuana smuggling operation, dubbed the "Haas Organization" by U.S. federal authorities.

That was the name I heard the feds, as well as the press, use when they described Mom's "$267 million-a-year" smuggling enterprise and placed her on both the FBI's and U.S. Marshals' "Most-Wanted" lists. But what did they really know?

Did Mom, a laid-back divorcee with a hippie mind-set, two young children, a beat-up old car, and no money, purposely set out to become one of the largest and most successful marijuana smugglers in American history? In fact, can anyone plan such an eventuality, or does it simply occur by mere happenstance?

Well, I was there and this is the true story of what really happened.

I was just an innocent teenager living much like any other kid. A student, musician, Eagle Scout. But Mom was, for a few years in the late 70s and early 80s, exactly what the authorities said in one respect. She was a marijuana smuggling "queenpin" back in the heyday of such activity when few contemporaries existed. I was there and I saw or heard firsthand nearly everything that went down. I was there when times were tough right after Mom and Dad's divorce and there when money flowed like water. I was there when our family was united and there when betrayal was running rampant. I was also there as this incredible and sometimes inconceivable parade of individuals—smugglers, dealers, killers, cops, pilots, feds, and fishermen—passed through my life and home, invariably causing me to bear witness to the events I now expose in this book. And I was there when everything finally exploded into chaos. I was there like the proverbial fly on the wall.

1

Saturday Night in Buckeye

To really know what happened is to know how and where it all started, and it all started outside a tiny, tumbleweed-infested town in the middle of the Arizona desert. The town was Buckeye, and in 1971 it was literally in the middle of nowhere. Summer daytime temperatures of 115° weren't unusual in the least—you just got used to it or moved away. But the living was cheap there, lots of open space and plenty of room to dream. Just what I needed, as I was a "Dreamin' Man" then, as Neil Young once titled a song. I just didn't know it yet. Mom just needed a cheap place to take our little family to live.

The divorce had finally sunk in. I was seven years old and had held on, week after week, hoping that Mom and Dad would work it out and reconcile. I didn't blame myself since I knew it was up to them to get it together or not. Sink or swim. They sank. Mom and Dad just weren't compatible. At the time I couldn't see it. Nowadays, I simply can't imagine two people more fundamentally different than my parents. Yin and yang. They were, and still are, for that matter, total polar opposites.

In better times, our typical 1970s nuclear family had lived in a large red-brick house in Parker, Arizona, that had been our home since I'd started kindergarten, and I'd had a lot of good times there and at least one that I really couldn't wrap my little five-year-old brain around until much later. Mom and Dad had gone out for the evening and my teenage babysitter had fallen asleep in Dad's La-Z-Boy, kicked back in full recline. I was playing cowboy and crawling around on the carpeted floor wearing a Stetson, a badge, and a gun-belt with two Colt cap-guns, fully loaded. And when I finally crawled around to the foot of the chair and happened to look up, I saw a sight unlike anything I had ever seen before. It appeared to be some sort of strange dark furry creature, and it was nestled right in my babysitter's crotch! I could see it clearly because she wore no panties under her short dress. Thank God I was armed and knew what to do, for I immediately drew both pistols and fired away, caps blazing. I had aimed carefully and must have hit it, but the tiny animal had never moved. I found it odd that my babysitter never woke up until shortly before Mom and Dad got home. Oh well, at least I knew I had saved her from the little critter, and that was enough for me. Yes, I had loved that house and was going to miss living there, but the divorce was inevitable and I said goodbye. Dad found new digs (at times even staying at my grandparents' in their guesthouse while he tried to reconcile with Mom) and Mom, Melanie and I moved into a small two-room house next to a dried-up river and two enormous mesquite trees. My younger sister Melanie didn't like what she saw. I wholeheartedly agreed.

The house was run down to say the least. Poorly insulated, it leaked from every door and window during (thankfully) infrequent rains, and it needed paint in a frightful way. But it was a home and cheap. I didn't know it then, but Mom always had a talent for finding things cheap or free, and this place fit the bill in that regard. But heck, I remember that place was cold. Far too cold for what most think of when they think of the desert in winter.

People think of the desert and automatically think heat, but the desert at night was different. At night the temperatures dropped, often dramatically, causing me and Melanie to burrow under as many blankets as possible. There was no heat in the house except for a fireplace in the living room which took considerable effort to get going. In my new role as the "man of the house," the responsibility was mine.

First I'd gather the firewood, which was not easy in the desert. Sometimes I got lucky and found a fallen mesquite or palo verde tree. Other times, much less often, Mom bought half a cord or whatever quantity she could afford. Then, with numb hands and a dull hatchet, I'd split the lighter pine if we had any. And finally, with any luck, 20 minutes later when I felt as though frostbite was surely setting in, I'd start to thaw out. It was a lot to do before catching the bus for school. I usually passed on the whole ordeal unless it was desperately cold. Besides, a fire could, and often did, attract desert creatures of the night.

Our first nocturnal visitor of note must have been cold and looking for a warm abode, as it was a bright moonlit night and cold enough to warrant a blazing fire and a huge stack of wood in the center of our only living space. The three of us spent the night comfortably enough, and it wasn't until early the next morning that I discovered a sidewinder rattlesnake wedged beneath the front door, half its sinuous body inside, half outside. It was in fine shape otherwise, only a little sluggish from the cold half of its body. Mom used that to her advantage and neatly severed its head with a garden hoe. Too bad, I thought, feeling sorry for the snake. At least it was an honest adversary that used the front door. The future would bring many other snakes of the human variety that didn't.

If it wasn't cold, then it was the infernal sun! The three of us, native Arizonans all, endured that first summer's heat with the negligible help of a noisy second-hand window AC until it broke. Then we survived with a fan alone. It was sweltering indoors. Thank heavens for shade and low humidity. Nature's air-conditioning for poor people.

The desert was a starkly beautiful place in many ways, and our newly down-sized family slowly adapted to our new life. The dusky brown hues that dominated the scenery all day gradually transformed into dazzling shades of golden yellows, oranges, and reds toward sunset. Everything seemed magnified, like you could see forever.

Springtime brought a flourish of flowers like I had never seen in town. The desert had long since learned to make the best of any opportunity during favorable weather and times of plenty. That was lesson number one, and I took it with me when I eventually moved from the desert. When rain came, as it did rarely, it came with a vengeance as if to wash away what nature created. On those occasions, the riverbed next to our home would briefly fill and flow sluggishly. And with the water came life. But I soon realized the desert face was only a mask. It was teeming with life just beneath its surface, especially after dark.

And I, as most any seven-year-old boy would be inclined, made it my point in life to seek out that wildlife and explore the desert. I had my best friend at my side and I was armed for protection. It didn't matter to me that my best friend was a nine-pound dachshund named Rudi or that my gun was a Daisy Red Rider that shot only BBs. Life was good because there was always an adventure on the horizon, at least the four-legged variety. No, I'm not talking about furry little indoor animals that don't move when you shoot at them; I'm talking about coyotes.

One fall morning, as I waited for the school bus alone, I noticed a lone coyote peering at me from between a thicket of tumbleweeds across the road. He appeared enormous and wildly fierce in my young mind and I was more than a little afraid. Was he just curious, or hungry, ready to attack me for his next meal? I stared hard, but it was hard to tell. Should I run away? Or should I remain standing, frozen solid, where I was until the beast lost interest? If only I had my trusty Red Rider! Probably by default, I remained still and silent, eyes locked with the coyote until it cooperated with my unspoken prayers, slinking away with the tireless gait of a wild animal.

The lesson learned from that day? When in doubt, it is best to keep quiet, period. Although I didn't know it at the time, silence would serve me well in my future life. A life filled with crazy, competitive, dysfunctional weirdoes, most of whom were wilder than any coyote and I have to admit right here that a few were actually members of my family.

My Uncle Rod was one of the craziest, and I think maybe Vietnam was at least partly to blame. I guess the most accurate term to describe his condition would be "post-traumatic stress syndrome," or PTSD. World War II-era folks would probably label it "shellshock," and it could have been plain old substance abuse, but anyway you sliced it, lunacy was Rod's norm. Some of his habits would easily qualify him to be a card-carrying member of the Addams Family. Here are just a few examples of what I am talking about.

He collected live black widow spiders and various breeds of scorpions by the dozens which he stored in glass jars he kept on the mantle in his living room. On many nights as I slept over at Aunt Nancy's, Rod's wife and Mom's younger sister, I remember hearing the eerie tinkling and scratching of armored claws and stingers against the glass and thinking to myself, "What sort of person would bring such pests into their home?" I knew I wouldn't.

My two younger cousins, Allison and Amy, couldn't agree more. They detested the vermin, as did Aunt Nancy, yet there seemed to be a never-ending supply. As they died off, Rod would simply overturn a few rocks in the yard and … voilà! The scorpions would dance, their poisonous stingers held high and ready as Rod nonchalantly, even carelessly, gathered them bare-handed and deposited them in his awful jars. Black widows weren't scarce either, as they frequently collected beneath the hood of the propane tank in the backyard. It was an easy harvest and Rod had his "pets." Unfortunately, this wasn't all.

Uncle Rod was a major gun nut. Twenty-four hours a day, seven days a week, it seemed, he handled guns, collected guns, and traded guns. He constantly cleaned them with an almost religious fervor. But most of all, he absolutely loved to shoot them—anywhere and everywhere. And, as I soon learned, no place was off limits or out of bounds.

One typical evening, as everyone watched TV in the living room, Rod evidently ran into a problem. Something had jammed the firing mechanism of a .45 automatic he was cleaning, and boy, was he pissed. Yet, a few more seconds cursing and prying seemed to clear the problem, and he was soon grinning a somewhat maniacal smile once more. For, like I said, Uncle Rod knew and loved his guns better than a glutton loves a smorgasbord.

His next step? Well, the gun needed test-firing, of course! "Gotta be sure it's ready," he had told me more than once. And the sooner, the better, he must have believed, for without any word of warning and within the space of five seconds, he slammed a clip home, chambered a round, and "BOOM, BOOM, BOOM, BOOM, BOOM" added a decoration of five bullet holes to the living room wall.

The gun's roar was deafening, the small room magnified the sound and we kids were impressed to say the least. That was the first time in my life I heard live gunfire at very close range and I can't say the ringing it left in my ears was pleasurable. I wonder now, looking back, if it was the last sound Frank Marrs heard, or was there only a sudden silence at the end of his life?

Rod, gun in hand, took a long drag off a roach which smoldered at the tip of a rattlesnake-head clip as I sat in dumb silence, ears still buzzing, and watched the bluish-white marijuana smoke curl around his head. He coughed out an even thicker cloud and smiled with evident satisfaction.

"Sweet," he muttered.

If there was anything Rod enjoyed as much as guns, it would be drugs, and marijuana was one of his favorites. He liked to stay high constantly, and it was probably just as well since pot tended to slow him down and quell some of the demons that had followed him home from Vietnam. Smoking grass was a sort of ceremony, one that Rod took seriously, and steady celebration called for a steady supply which he harvested from plants he grew in a closet under artificial lights. Among friends, he was always quick to point out the obvious advantages of growing your own.

"I start with nothing but a few seeds, some buckets and lights and a little luck and in two months I'm smoking tops, and in five I've got some real sweet shit. Doesn't cost me but a little time and a little juice and I'm smoking for free. Cops don't have a clue."

Uncle Rod was constantly pestering Aunt Nancy and Mom to help him expand his little "garden" so he could raise enough pot to sell. He was sick and tired of, as he put it, "being broke in this one-horse town." He also knew that one type of green could be quickly turned to green of another kind.

Mom and Aunt Nancy certainly weren't unaware of this either. And hell yes! They could surely use a few bucks to take us kids on a long-overdue shopping spree. Both had been through recent divorces. Money was in very short supply and kids needed school clothes. Mom's old Chevy truck was a pile of junk that barely ran and had bald tires. Seemingly endless planning and animated talking, amid clouds of pot smoke, took place toward the end of that year and the general gist of it was simple. "It's the early 1970s and we're free! Besides, it's only grass. It's harmless. Everyone's smoking it…." Blah, blah, blah, and on and on it went. I was seven years old. Mom and Nancy were only in their late 20s. Still kids themselves, really.

Rod's excitement soon caught and spread like wildfire and it wasn't too long before the three were itching to start. Growing pot not only sounded like a great idea, it was the only logical thing to do in their minds. And they had a hidden trump card to boot, for Mom had always been the proud owner of a green thumb the size of Texas.

2

Kindergarten for Grownups

The plan was pretty simple. And it had to be, for the trio truly had no real experience in such a venture other than Uncle Rod's minor dabbling in his closet. Much like children starting kindergarten, this was all new territory and would require a concentration of effort if they were going to grow enough marijuana to become comfortably wealthy, meaning nice homes, cars, and a few toys for everyone. The works. But there was some disagreement early on. Such as the grow location.

Rod preferred indoor growing in a controlled environment and felt it was both easier and quicker. He had an operation up and running; it only needed to be enlarged. He suggested they buy more lights and buckets and let the kids share a room to gain the necessary extra space.

Mom and Nancy weren't so sure. I knew they didn't like the idea of sitting on that much weed in a house full of children. The three bickered back and forth for practically a week before they ultimately decided to grow the "herb" (Mom's favorite pet term for marijuana) outdoors along the Hassayampa River, because that location provided at least some partial cover from the mesquite and palo verde trees that grew thick in the area as well as a close and plentiful water supply. Furthermore, it was close to home—less than a mile away from Nancy and Rod's place.

The decision to grow outdoors was mostly Mom's idea and she had pushed hard until she got her way. Mom felt more comfortable growing things according to natural light cycles and scoffed at the idea of grow lights. Besides, she thought there just wasn't enough space indoors to do the job right. The dozen or so plants Rod had been growing were okay, but Mom always thought big in practically every regard, and gardens were no exception. To generate big money they would need serious growing space, not limited to a small room and a couple of puny closets.

Then there was the final argument, and possibly the single most important consideration Mom echoed relentlessly. I remember it as the one that impressed Rod the most and eventually swayed him.

"What will you do if the cops come knocking at the door, for any reason, and smell something? What then?" I heard Mom ask.

"What if this! What if that! Who gives a shit? It ain't gonna happen. No way."

"But why take a chance? Why sit on the plants if we don't have to? If they're found in the desert, they're nobody's, and we move on. Think about that. Think hard."

That was the last straw. Rod had heard enough. He'd always been the paranoid type ever since being thrown as a teenager into a jungle hell half a world away. Under-trained and unprepared, it was easy for him to wonder, "Why in the hell am I here?" As to *how* he got there, the answer to that question was clear in his mind. The government. The *establishment*. Authority. No, sir, Uncle Sam was no friend of his. He was more an enemy, definitely not to be trusted, and the thought of out-witting his authority was an appealing idea. So outdoors it would be.

They initially decided on a hundred plants, and then quickly upped the number to 300. That seemed a good round number for splitting three ways and Mom figured this number of plants would be about the most they could feasibly handle. She was right. I'm sure the whole operation would have been a breeze except for the never-ending watering the plants required. After all, it was a desert garden, and they weren't allowed to forget it for a moment. More often than not, on particularly hot days, watering had to be done twice daily. This would have been a nearly impossible task without a close water supply.

In that regard, the nearby Hassayampa River was a savior. It was hardly bigger than a medium-sized stream and not deep, but without it precious water would have to be hauled by hand or small cart (anything motorized would tend to attract unwanted attention) through rough desert terrain. As it was, they planted the seedlings within a few yards of the river, staggering them at intervals of about 25 paces among the scattered trees. Being that close, watering was easy. A small bucket did nicely. Yet it was still a chore and they split the duty three ways.

Mom took over the job as the lead gardener early on. Rod was a little out of his element without grow lights and fertilizer and didn't seem to mind. Mom had the ever-present sun, the river, and the desert soil, which was virgin rich. Water had been the only missing ingredient needed to release the latent nutrients.

The plants grew quickly, like ... well ... the weeds they really were, I guess.

In the span of four months they grew from two-inch seedlings with four leaves apiece to virtual bushes nearly waist high. The indigenous trees and scrub provided just enough cover and the marijuana plants blended in with the scenery well enough that it would require a lot of luck or a skilled eye to pick them out.

There were losses—some plants completely disappeared without so much as a root stem to mark their place—but there was little cause for concern. Mom had expected this and blamed the loss on some cannabis-loving wild animal. Nancy agreed. Rod, consistent with his paranoia, felt it might be someone ripping him off. In my child's mind, I thought about the possibility of coyotes being the culprits. They always seemed hungry to me. Anyway, the loss of a few plants was insignificant. There would be more than enough survivors to sell and provide a healthy boost for Rod's personal stash besides.

As the fall days grew shorter and the time of harvest approached (marijuana naturally begins to bud as the daylight hours diminish), Mom, Nancy, and Rod began counting the money. Of course they didn't have it yet, but it was great fun to dream. And dream they did. There was also a lot of talk about getting out of Buckeye.

They figured that each plant would yield about a half-pound of salable pot. Assuming that 250 plants survived to be harvested, they could count on 125 pounds to sell. And that, according to Rod, could be sold to his "'Nam buddy" Michael for around $250 a pound. Nancy whipped out a pencil and calculated rapidly.

"That's over ten grand each!"

"And that's just for starters, baby!" Rod was clearly in one of his better moods as he huffed and puffed on his ever-present joint.

We kids heard the adults' blatant cash talk and it sounded like a million dollars to us. I couldn't comprehend that much money. Wow! Even Dad had only earned a few hundred dollars or so a week as a banker. And we sure perked up even more when they began discussing the many ways of spending the windfall.

Nancy started in right away promising my cousins, Amy and Allison, new clothes and toys. Lucky them. I didn't care much for clothes, but the talk of toys was thrilling. For my part, I could sure use a new Red Rider BB gun.

Mom said she wanted to catch up on our utilities (they were always getting turned off) and our rent (we were always a month or two behind). Luckily, since our home was such a dive it was also cheap and the landlord was lenient, thank God. From the beginning of the divorce we'd survived primarily from the support provided by my grandparents. Dad was still in the picture at the time, but fighting an uphill battle to stay in touch with Melanie and me.

Besides my grandparents and their crucial support, it also helped that we had a productive vegetable garden, a couple dozen chickens, and several milk-producing goats. Mom also did a little custom sewing on the side which earned a few bucks here and there. It was more than tight money-wise at our home, and I hated to see Mom worry so much. She didn't seem to be poised to go on a spending spree with her share. Oh well, I thought. Easy come, easy go. But my sister Melanie didn't want to give up without a fight.

"I want clothes too, Mom, please … please!"

"Sure, honey." Mom was, and still is, a materially generous person.

Even at the tender age of five years old, Melanie knew how to pull Mom's strings.

She knew the score. We were only going through the motions anyway. There was no money now—no reason to get excited. It would be another couple months yet before everyone could go spend-crazy. In 60 days and with a little luck this rag-tag bunch of amateur pot growers was destined to be sitting on a domestic load of quality marijuana. Against the odds and despite the haphazard organization, they were about to pull off a major coup. Too bad it had to end like it did.

I wish I could say the plants withered in the heat or were eaten by a roving band of mutant jack-rabbits or something else … anything else … but the fact was that Uncle Rod fell victim to a severe case of genuine old-fashioned paranoia. That is, paranoia with a capital "P."

The fiasco began with a phone call in the middle of the night. Mom quickly answered the phone in order not to wake us, but it was too late. I was awake in bed, under the covers reading by flashlight as was my habit. I sprang out of bed and stood in the doorway of my shared bedroom, straining to hear what was going on. It was Aunt Nancy on the phone, and she was worried.

"Judy, you've got to get over here now, hurry, we can't talk on the phone."

I think Mom must have thought it was a serious fight or something between Nancy and Rod because she told me to keep an eye on Melanie and sit tight at home. Try to go back to bed if I could. Continue reading if I couldn't sleep. She promised to call if she wasn't back in an hour.

The only thing was, I could not sleep. No way. I could sense something was going down. I went back to bed and continued reading one of the Tarzan series books by Edgar Rice Burroughs I was deeply involved with at the time. I waited … and waited. No call. No surprise there. No worry either. I just held down the fort alone, standing guard until morning when Mom and Aunt Nancy arrived, covered in mud and dust and looking rather haggard and worn out from what was obviously a sleepless and arduous night. Mom made tea as I picked up the story of what had happened.

Mom had arrived at Nancy's to find her arguing with Rod, much as she expected. All Nancy would say at that point was "Judy, you talk some sense into him, will you? I give up."

Rod paced the kitchen floor like a madman. His dogs, sensing the mood of their master, paced the house on edge. The largest and meanest, Mondo, clung to his heels. Rod was hysterical and his voice boomed under the influence of another drug, an "upper," apparently. He should've smoked a joint, I thought. Rod needed stimulants like a submarine needed screen doors.

"I've seen the same brown car cruising our shit for over a week now, and too damn close!" Uncle Rod's eyes were bloodshot and his face twisted. "They're on to us! I feel it, yeah, and I trust the feeling too, baby. We're blown! We're blown!"

"It's only some fishermen looking for a hole," said Mom calmly.

"Bullshit, they're cops and I know it. They smell like cops!" Rod bellowed, blinking rapidly from whatever he was on.

"Then we sit tight. Everything's cool."

"Well CYA is what I say. Cover your ass! I'm gonna cover mine and yank the plants. We gotta do it now, in the dark. The shit's coming down tomorrow!"

And in the end, after hours of curses, threats, and promises, that was exactly what they did, that night, by flashlight. The trio yanked from the ground their entire crop of healthy robust marijuana plants and threw them in the Hassayampa River. What really made the whole fiasco worse was the timing. The plants were only a few weeks from harvest. Mom and Nancy cried while working, and cursed Rod whole-heartedly. They knew what they were doing was stupid. All they needed to do was stay calm. Cops weren't interested in three nobodies in the middle of nowhere. Everything had been whisper-smooth until this night of madness. All that work and to just to throw it away!

After Mom had a few days to think about everything that had happened, she sort of blamed herself. After all, she should have known not to get involved with Rod. It didn't require much insight or imagination to see he was unstable, the proverbial loose cannon ready to explode in any direction at any time and in any way. Maybe it wasn't even his fault. His recent Vietnam experience had surely impacted his life and colored his personality, but that didn't matter. Mom had to learn from this fiasco—take it to heart. It was dangerous to involve others, that much was clear. Nancy was another matter entirely. She was her closest sister, she was family, and that meant they would always be in it together.

I think the failed marijuana growing project marked the beginning of the end for our little family living in Arizona. Mom was clearly ready for a change. Like me, she was truly a gypsy at heart. And she was tired of, well … you name it.

"Brown, brown, I'm sick of all the brown. Rocks and tumbleweeds and dust and dirt and everything's brown," she lamented. I couldn't blame her.

Many things had been piling up in her life by that point. First, there was the divorce which had not gone smoothly to say the least. Mom and Dad had fought bitterly over everything they had accumulated during their seven-year marriage. But the worst battles had been over us kids. We were caught in the middle of a brutal war. Initially, Dad made a determined effort to stay in our lives and had repeatedly tried to get back together with Mom but he faced a deck that was increasingly stacked against him. While my grandparents had encouraged reconciliation, Mom's sisters, particularly my aunts Bonnie and Vicky, openly inserted themselves into the middle of the battle. In fact, the situation actually got so bad that on one particular day when Dad came to visit me and Melanie, Vicky and her boyfriend egged Dad as I watched help-lessly from a window. I can still see in my mind's eye him removing his glasses to wipe off the egg. The sight crushed me. It was a cowardly and cruel act, aimed at Dad, of course, but especially painful to me for I was only a little first-grader at the time. I wonder if Vicky even thought how it made me feel to see her humiliate my father like that. Understandably, Dad eventually gave up and I carried on without him, devastated. It was a real heartbreaker and I didn't get over it for a long time afterward. I just know that everything intended to punish Dad ended up punishing me the most. The icing on the cake? Not long after I saw Dad for what would turn out to be the last time for ten years, my little dachshund Rudi disappeared. I couldn't help but think a coyote got him. He had been my best friend and I cried myself to sleep that night and for many nights afterward.

As if the bitter conflict and all-around loss was not enough, it was followed by four months of Mom's hard work and desperate hopes only to end in abject failure. I don't know what would have happened next if fate had not stepped in.

My maternal great-grandparents were in their late 80s and destined for a nursing home if someone didn't come forward to intervene. German immigrants and fiercely independent their whole lives, they simply couldn't handle the everyday demands of living or keeping up with their 40-acre farm anymore. When Mom learned of their predicament, she immediately volunteered to care for them in their home and our whole family jumped at the opportunity. Great-grandpa Michael and great-grandma Mary knew and loved Mom and were absolutely horrified at the thought of winding up in a nursing home. Best of all, their farm was located just a few miles outside the small sleepy town of Live Oak, Florida. Mom was ecstatic. We packed our clothes in three suitcases and loaded our meager belongings in a few cardboard boxes scavenged from a dumpster and headed across country using money given to us by my grandparents. I didn't know it at the time, but it would be years before our family would cease living this sort of nomadic life. Dive house to dive house. I missed two full years of school by the time I was in sixth grade.

Aunt Nancy split up from Rod not too long after we headed for Florida. Irreconcilable differences, I guess, plus some legal trouble on his end. She took Amy and Allison and set herself up in the greater Phoenix metropolitan area.

Nancy had met a few key people during her time with Rod. Connections, I heard her call them. Important people who played the pot game for real. There was money to be made, they said. Loads of cash were up for grabs for anyone with the right combination of guts and the willingness to risk going to jail. These connections were experienced professionals compared to Mom, Nancy and Rod. They knew how to handle business—how to keep their cool.

I think Aunt Nancy knew, as did Mom, maybe without realizing it, that they had turned a corner in their thinking and there was no going back. What the pair lacked in know-how they made up for in youthful gumption. The lure of easy money was too tempting, their recent failure forgotten.

Kindergarten was over.

3

El Loco

God only knows how things might have turned out if El Loco had not entered the picture when he did, crashing headlong into our lives in his typical brash, straightforward, and unpolished style. His name was Frank Cory, but to my family he was affectionately known as "El Loco."

He had earned the nickname shortly after taking my grandfather up for a brief flight in a small airplane, a single-engine Cessna 182. Shortly after a masterful "pin-point" landing, "Baga"—that's what I'd called my grandfather from the time I could say three words—briskly exited the plane and exclaimed, "El Loco!" while staring back over his shoulder at Frank, who was grinning his lop-sided grin ear to ear. It must have been one hell of a ride to impress Baga, who himself had more than 40 years of flight experience both as a military and civilian aviator and didn't scare easily. Frank truly was a man who in the future would not only live up to his newly acquired moniker but surpass it with ease.

I'm not at all surprised that it was my Aunt "Blue" (another nickname of mine; her real name was Violet) who first introduced El Loco to our family. She appreciated people that broke the mold.

He had met Blue while they both attended Abraham Baldwin Agricultural College, aka ABAC, in the small south-central Georgia town of Tifton, which was El Loco's hometown. They hung out together both on and off campus and smoked a lot of weed and even managed to study a little. Blue was somewhat of a brain and studied quite a bit at home. She got consistently high grades in school. Although El Loco was naturally street-smart his book smarts were not far behind, though he wasn't one to flout it. He liked Blue in a romantic way and tried to get things going in that direction, but she just wanted to be friends.

It wasn't because El Loco was bad to look at, either. He was medium height with a powerful stocky build, short dark hair worn swept to the side, and his face usually wore an open, honest smile. I just think his raw intensity and over-the-top personality intimidated Blue. But that surely did not stop the incessant partying they both enjoyed. Partying was El Loco's lifeblood—what he lived for.

You see, partying was central to El Loco's business, as he supplied the party material. He specialized in high-quality smoke, nice green bud, and the ABAC students were good customers.

He sold about a pound of pot every other week, usually an ounce at a time. He got around town quite handily on a motorcycle, a Honda CB 275, with the marijuana bungeed on the rear of the bike. He'd smoke another ounce per week with friends and acquaintances at school parties. It was advertisement. Every decent businessman knew that, and El Loco was no exception. Nevertheless, he was somewhat an outsider around campus and slightly older than many of the other students. El Loco knew exactly what he wanted from life; he just wasn't sure how to get it. In the meantime, however, he was going to do his best to keep the party going and the herb flowing, making money, chasing girls, and flying. And let me say right here, El Loco was a natural-born pilot.

He was first bitten by the flying bug shortly after high school. He'd thought about flying earlier in life as a grade-school kid, but now he was out of school and bored, with no thoughts of college. Yet he had some decent spending money burning a hole in his pocket, cash he'd made from his fledgling pot dealing business. Besides, he had plenty of time on his hands and being a pilot had its advantages. Wasn't it a great way to pick up girls? He thought so, and the fateful decision was made. El Loco got serious.

Less than two months after starting part-time basic flight training at the tiny Tift County airport, he soloed after only eight hours of in-the-air instruction. After a perfect landing, his instructor, a few fellow flight-school students, and even a couple of his stoner friends greeted El Loco with well-deserved congratulations while making sure to tear out the back of the shirt he was wearing for the customary age-old first solo ceremony. Using a black marker, they inscribed it with his name, date, and the time of the solo, along with a few select humorous comments about the pilot.

BEWARE—FRANK THINKS HE'S ON A MOTORCYCLE!

FLYING HIGH … YES, INDEED!

And so forth. The shirt back would then take its place among the others that adorned the aviation clubhouse walls.

El Loco spoke often of his inaugural solo and you could see in his face the sheer enjoyment and freedom he must have felt that first time in the air, his very life in his own hands, all blue sky and clouds and sunlight with a toy-sized Earth below. And he never looked back. Within a year he'd logged almost 80 hours in the cockpit, which was nearly double the time required for a private pilot's license. All that was left to complete was a physical and the FAA exam which he passed with flying colors, pardon the pun. An endorsement to pilot multi-engine aircraft soon followed.

When it came to El Loco and flying, all that work studying was simply a labor of love. And who knows? Maybe it got his mental juices flowing because it was around this time he decided to return to school where he met Blue and eventually got the opportunity to really fly his ass off.

I could tell Mom had something on her mind the day she first met El Loco at Baga's lakefront house. He was introduced as "Blue's pilot friend from ABAC" and within five minutes the two were gabbing like long-lost friends. She smiled warmly as he spoke over lunch about an upcoming IFR exam which would certify him in instrument-only flying. He was open-minded, gutsy, and ready for anything—typical El Loco—and it must have showed. Mom continued to pick his brain.

After lunch, El Loco produced a joint from his shirt pocket as he, Blue, and Mom took a stroll down to the banks of the 127-acre Lake Alison which was situated practically in Baga's backyard. I tagged along as usual. I just loved hanging out by that lake. What 13-year-old boy wouldn't? Lots of great fishing and clean water for swimming. These were the kind of activities that could really cheer you up on a hot and muggy Florida day.

"Frank, you've got to come down some day soon and I'll take you fishing here. This lake's full of huge bass and catfish. The guy across the way there sells red wigglers and sand maggots," I said, pointing to a large farmhouse on the opposite shore. His eyes followed my gesture, and then turned on mine. He grinned in his zany way.

"I'll take you up on that. Thanks." He hesitated, thinking. "Michael David, right?"

"Close enough. Flip that. David Michael, actually." I smiled and we both chuckled and shook hands. I could tell he wanted to be friends and that made a strong first impression on me. There was nothing fake or insincere about him at all. He was the type of guy who always laid all his cards on the table. Mom also picked up on that in a hurry. Deep in thought, she passed the joint to Blue. They got high, silently staring across the lake for several peaceful minutes. Mom was the first to break the silence.

"Listen, Frank, I'd like you to meet my sister Nancy out in Arizona. I think you two could help each other out. She might be able to use a good pilot." Mom didn't elaborate and I don't think there was any need to. El Loco could put two and two together.

True to form he made a gut decision, and with a slight tilt of his head he instantly answered, "Why, hell yes! Let's go tomorrow—we can be there by Friday. I can probably rent us a 182." His pronounced south Georgia accent was noticeable.

We did not know it at the time, but El Loco was the type of person who had no problem whatsoever being utterly spontaneous. He would do nearly anything at the drop of a hat, much like a child. And when you started something with him you had better be ready and willing to follow through. Mom, of course, had no issues keeping up. She was a free spirit herself and loved adventure as much as he did.

"Great. That's perfect! I'll call her tonight and let her know we're coming. And be ready first thing in the morning."

I snickered at that. Mom whirled to face me with a mock half-angry, half-hurt look on her face. She knew I was teasing about her packing habits.

"Don't count on leaving too early tomorrow, Frank," I said. "I've seen safaris in *Tarzan* movies entering the deep of the African jungle with less baggage than Mom will bring."

It was the truth. Mom was a pack-rat at heart. Preparation advanced to an art form in her own mind. I sure hoped Frank knew how much weight the plane could carry.

"All right, we're off tomorrow." El Loco took one final hit of the joint and then flicked the roach into the lake where it sizzled out. He turned to Blue. "Wanna come along?"

I knew Blue was not fond of flying and could tell that this time would prove no different. Maybe she had a premonition or knew something we did not. Whatever the reason, she simply shook her head no.

But I had had a brief chance to think it over and thought it might be nice to see Arizona again after five years in Florida. I secretly hoped I might even get a chance to stop by and visit Dad. It was worth a try.

"I want to go," I blurted out, louder than intended.

"There's room," El Loco said to no one in particular as he began walking up the embankment that led back to the house above. Without a word, Mom looked over and nodded a silent yes. Yippee! I was on my way back to Arizona.

That evening was spent making calls, packing clothes and personal items and planning the impromptu trip. Little did I realize it at the time, but this "quick decision, quick execution" of a plan, any plan, no matter how complex, was sort of a model for the way Mom would handle things in the future. Personally, my main concern was what type of aircraft a "182" was, so I asked El Loco.

"It's a small single-engine Cessna I rent from a buddy of mine. He lets me have it super cheap. I learned to fly in it. Good on fuel."

"Oh."

"If you want, you can fly it some of the way out there."

"Sure!" Now he had me hooked on the trip and any doubts I might have had instantly disappeared.

Baga heard about the spur-of-the-moment cross-country trip and thought it was crazy, especially when he heard about the single-engine plane and El Loco's plan to fly straight through, non-stop, pausing only briefly for fuel as needed.

He tried to reason with Mom. His tone was one of disappointment.

"Judy, you're a fool, traveling cross-country at night in a single-engine plane." He shook his head slowly, deliberately. "You know better than that."

Baga was referring to a close-call he had had in his own plane years before and I knew the story well, having heard the tale numerous times around the family dinner table. He had experienced engine trouble in his single-engine Mooney and had to ditch in a farmer's pasture. Baga had always credited the safe emergency landing to calm nerves, military training, and the fact that it was daylight when the incident occurred. He was sure he could not have found a safe place to land in the dark.

Mom appeared to give in. "We'll stop at night, then, okay?"

That seemed to do the trick and Baga backed off, but the confrontation left me wondering if it really was that dangerous. Visibility was important, I knew, but engine trouble was, after all, extremely rare in a well-maintained aircraft. Besides, Mom had aviation experience herself and had come close to earning her private pilot's license back in her married days. I had even flown with her as she practiced touch-and-gos at the local airport. Surely, I felt, she and El Loco would be able to handle any problems that cropped up during the trip. Ignorant of reality, I relaxed. How little I knew what the next few days would bring.

We were up the next morning by five a.m., at the airport by seven, and had the fuel tanks topped off and the plane loaded and ready by eight. El Loco switched on the radio, asked for and received permission to take off, and a quarter after eight saw us a thousand feet above the Georgia countryside and climbing fast. Mom and I smiled at each other and enjoyed the view through the windows. I remember thinking, not for the first time, that flying would be perfect if only there was no engine noise. Minutes later, El Loco leveled the tiny plane at 7,500 feet and let me take the controls. What a blast!

Save for a brief stop for fuel somewhere in Alabama, the flight that day was magical as the terrain rolled steadily by, thousands of feet beneath us, and we ate sandwiches that Mom brought along in a small cooler with ice-cold sodas and a jug of iced tea to wash everything down. I thought to myself, "This small plane flying is pretty nifty! It sure beats flying commercially; I could get used to it. Maybe I'll be a pilot and fly people where they want to go in my own small plane." Lulled by the food and the drone of the engine, my thoughts began to drift. Gradually, daylight began to wane, but hey, that was no big deal, El Loco assured us. He said the weather was great, visibility excellent, and we would stop for the night at a convenient airport he had located on the charts. It was only 90 minutes away.

That sounded like an excellent plan to me. My long legs were cramped from the confines of the small plane and my body was vibrating all over. An hour later, I began to wonder if small plane travel was my thing after all. But if I had any doubts as to whether or not this type of travel was for me, they were soon reconciled by what happened when we arrived at that so-called "convenient" airport. It wasn't there!

Well, of course, that was not entirely accurate. It was there, charted public airports do not just vanish into thin air, but we sure as heck couldn't see it. The ground fog was so dense that only a few of the brightest lights below were barely visible. Landing in these conditions was clearly not an option.

"No problem, there's another one less than a half-hour south of here!" El Loco bellowed over the roar of the engine. "We've got enough fuel to make it, but it'll be close!"

Close? I did not like the sound of that one little bit, but El Loco didn't seem concerned in the least as he banked the Cessna sharply and throttled back up to cruising RPM. Mom studied the fuel gauges for a moment, and then leaned over to give me a reassuring glance.

"Don't worry, we're fine. There's more than enough fuel, I'm sure," she said, appearing very calm and serious and "in control." But her words at that point carried little weight with me. I knew that they were only a manifestation of Mom's positive thinking in action again. She would nearly always look on the bright side no matter what the odds or situation, and most of the time I felt it was a refreshing point of view. But occasionally it was irritating as hell and made it practically impossible to really understand her true feelings. This was precisely one of those moments.

"Yeah, okay," I muttered skeptically. By this time, the plane's vibration and noise were definitely wearing on me and my imagination took over. It seemed to me that the engine had now become a glutton for fuel, a Tasmanian devil, greedily consuming more than its share. For the first time in my life I began to think about the land and the sky as being eerily similar and comprised of threatening physical elements, each in their own way. Both were unforgiving and menacing to those who blundered into them unawares. Like us.

I sulked for 15 interminable minutes before finally giving up on the doom and destruction mindset. It was getting me nowhere, and besides, El Loco had informed us that we were almost there. Great! The sooner this night was over, the better. We could start fresh and rested with a full tank tomorrow.

"There it is!" El Loco hollered as he banked the plane and pointed to the airport's white rotating beacon below. Although none of us had voiced it, the past half-hour had been nerve-wracking hell. Now I could feel the tension begin to ease. Down below us it was still pretty foggy, but I was thankful the visibility appeared sufficient for landing. What a relief!

Minutes later, after one of El Loco's trademark whisper-smooth landings, we were on terra firma once more and I was thrilled. El Loco taxied to a small hangar next to a row of fuel pumps and killed the engine. The silence was instantly relaxing and soothed my jangled nerves.

"It looks to me like it's closed," I stated, really not having the slightest care whether it was open or closed or whatever. I was happy to be on solid ground, period. And hungry too, sort of like the plane seemed to be earlier. "Let's get something to eat."

The three of us tumbled out and stretched our cramped bodies. El Loco walked off in search of a payphone while I took a good look around. Except for the humidity in the air, the place reminded me of Buckeye. In a word, desolate. The night was pitch black as there were no city lights spoiling the total darkness; just the lone rotating white beacon was visible. I stared up at the night sky and the myriad stars which were shining with a seemingly supernatural glow. Mom lit a cigarette as El Loco returned and gave his report.

"Don't see a phone, and everything's closed. They don't open till eight tomorrow. Looks like we'll be sleeping in the plane if we don't move on."

"How can we go on without fuel?" Mom beat me to the $64,000 question. I listened with ears as big as Dumbo's.

"There's plenty of fuel in all those planes," El Loco answered, gesturing to several small private planes parked nearby. "Come on, I'll show you what I mean." Mom and I followed him over to the nearest plane where he demonstrated.

On the underside of each wing were small spring-loaded fuel valves. He showed us exactly where they were located on the various planes and how we could—by pressing a small button valve with our thumb—start a tiny trickle of fuel to dribble from the wing tanks. These particular valves gave pilots an easy way to check for water in the fuel, a dangerous condition for any plane, but only a small amount of fuel was necessary for that test. We needed gallons. That was the only way I would return to the skies aboard our fuel-thirsty plane. It did not seem feasible to me and I said so.

"What's the hurry?" I asked. "Let's wait for the airport to open."

Mom gave me a look that told me in no uncertain terms to shut up, but I was her son and that meant I had inherited a fair amount of stubbornness.

"Come on," I pleaded, "let's wait until morning; we can sleep in the plane."

My argument didn't cut it, and I cannot honestly say I was surprised when they overruled me and decided to go for the fuel in the planes. I felt like a fool with a death wish as I joined in to help.

For the next four hours we busied ourselves with the task at hand and it was not easy. For one thing, we had nothing to collect the fuel with other than a couple of empty soda cans that were left over from our lunch earlier that day. Their openings were so abysmally small and they held so little. We also had to laboriously strain the fuel through a T-shirt as it was poured into our tanks lest we contaminate them. After what seemed like ten thousand cans later, El Loco checked the gauges on our bird and decided we had added enough fuel to make it to a 24-hour airport. Before we left, I overheard Mom telling El Loco we should somehow pay for the fuel. Hearing that, I grabbed Mom's wallet from her purse and tucked $10 bills in the windows of each of the planes we had bled. I remember thinking that the plane's owners would be unlikely to even notice such a small loss of fuel from their tanks, only the mystery cash. I chuckled to myself at the thought.

Thankfully, at least as far as I was concerned, the remainder of the trip to Arizona passed without incident. Sure, we encountered a few dark and scary thunderstorms—El Loco dodged them for the most part—and severe turbulence quite often, but nothing as dangerous as that first foggy night. As we progressed westward the air became drier and fog rarer. We even caught a movie somewhere in the middle of Nowhere, Texas, when we were forced to land after first hearing excited radio chatter about a severe storm ahead of us and then seeing a black squall line materialize over the horizon. The movie was the original *Star Wars*. It had just been released and none of us had ever heard of it. It's funny, but the anti-empire rebels in the movie, much like us, had had their own fuel problems when it came to flying and they didn't seem to like them any more than I did. I thought then for the umpteenth time that maybe flying was simply not my thing and I promised myself then and there I'd find another mode of travel back home to Florida, possibly a bus, or even a boat. Now that would be an adventure! I pondered this as we landed in Phoenix on a typically hot and arid afternoon.

An hour after Mom found a payphone and announced our arrival in "the Valley of the Sun," Aunt Nancy appeared amid hugs, kisses, and smiles all around. She explained that she had recently moved into a ritzy bungalow nestled in the foothills of an exclusive Scottsdale neighborhood and I was glad she had moved up in the world, at least financially. I could tell she was excited to be reunited with her closest sister as well as to meet "Frank," as Mom introduced him. "He's a pilot." Nancy lavished her most charming smile upon him as she shook his hand. Mmmm. I could almost see the gears turning in her head as she studied him for a brief moment. The possibilities were enticing.

We quickly loaded the car with our baggage and everyone piled in, Mom and me in the back seat, Nancy and El Loco in the front. And that's when the unthinkable happened. The next thing I remember was a thunderously loud explosion, an ear-splitting boom, and an acrid plume of smoke coming from the front seat. Peering cautiously forward through the smoke, I felt sure El Loco had been shot. From the look on his face he was very likely mortally wounded, although I saw no blood.

He was devoid of all color, his face a shade of ashy gray, and his mouth hung open as if it held a golf ball or something similar in size. An unlit cigarette dangled precariously from his lower lip and his eyes bulged from their sockets. His body quivered gently, and by his right hand we were told, wordlessly, the whole story in an instant.

In El Loco's limp-fingered hand, loosely cradled and still pointing at the tip of the cigarette, was a small derringer-style double-barreled pistol. It was highly polished and had ornate engravings across both barrels, a golden finish, and a creamy mother-of-pearl grip. A multicolored cluster of jewel-like inlay on the butt completed its gaudiness. El Loco had mistaken a real gun for a novelty cigarette lighter. The cigarette finally fell from his lips. A .22 caliber bullet hole now existed in the driver's side door panel, inches in front of Nancy. All of us sat frozen stiff in shock-induced silence. The near disaster was just too crazy to comprehend, too close to contemplate.

Surprisingly, with the characteristic cool that would in the future become his trademark, El Loco was the first to recover his wits and retrieved the cigarette from his lap. He began stammering one apology and explanation after another, which of course everyone instantly and good-naturedly accepted without reservation. We were all so relieved. The shock was still palpable, my ears still buzzing as if they held flies. The gun really did resemble a toy, everyone agreed, and it had been sitting innocently out in the open in the between-seat storage compartment. Nancy locked it in the glovebox. It wouldn't be smart to tempt fate with another mix-up. As I relaxed, I began to chuckle and then laugh out loud. Everyone else soon joined in.

I guess it's safe to say that El Loco's adventure out west had really started with a bang!

4

South of the Border

If Aunt Nancy's suburban bungalow was any indication, she had moved up in the world considerably since she and Mom had parted ways. The house was a rental (she'd always favored renting over buying) but it was roomy and elegantly situated among mature palm and palo verde trees and had a pool with a Jacuzzi in the back. I was so happy for her and my cousins. If I had been forced to guess what she was doing to be able to afford her upgraded digs I might not have come up with many details, but I sure as heck knew she'd marched on boldly from the Buckeye debacle. Left it in the desert dust, in fact. Bravo, Nancy!

At the time, I didn't have a clue about much of what I was seeing as we entered the house. Was there a party going on? Everywhere I looked there was a sprawling assortment of humanity, something different happening in practically every room. In the living room, a huge bear of a guy was playing and singing The Doors classic "Light My Fire" on an acoustic guitar. I couldn't tell what was larger—his toothy grin or his beard. In the kitchen, a foul-mouthed guy with a faint but noticeable Boston accent bickered with my Aunt Bonnie. Other people lounged by the pool and the Jacuzzi brimmed with bobbing heads punctuated with bloodshot eyes. Floating above it all in a sort of haze was the sweet smell of marijuana smoke that permeated every nook and cranny of the place. Nancy, casually strolling ahead and smiling to those she passed, ushered us through the throng and back to our rooms.

Since the time Mom, Melanie and I had departed Arizona, Nancy had slowly and steadily built crucial connections with people who could either sell a few pounds of pot here or buy a few pounds of pot there. She was talented and smart and had become a sort of broker, trading a lucrative commodity. But above all else she was a people person and that was the key to her success. People liked her. They liked her gentle, straightforward, soft-spoken style. They liked her no-nonsense honesty. Most of all, I think they appreciated and recognized in her an innate kindness that extended itself almost effortlessly as an integral part of her marijuana dealing. It was just her style of doing business, yet along the way there had been a few bumps in the road that could have been disastrous.

Shortly after her divorce from Rod, he, along with his friend Wayne, a part-time drag racer, had attempted a hare-brained extortion-style bank robbery and were caught shortly afterward. Nancy wasn't involved, of course, but as she was Rod's recently divorced ex-wife she was investigated by the FBI which fortunately did not dig deep enough to uncover any current or past shenanigans. Fortunately, Mom, who had had a short-lived tumultuous fling with Wayne prior to us leaving for Florida, had come to her senses and dumped the violent and temperamental funny-car driver in time.

The much more serious incident—the one that had most likely shaped Nancy's, as well as Mom's, laid-back and low-key approach to pot dealing—had involved Mom and a guy she was dating at the time. Mom had dubbed him "Pretty Paul," exactly why I cannot say, as he was rather scruffy-looking in my opinion. He tended to follow Mom around like a puppy and was there the afternoon Nancy asked Mom to go make a buy from some new people. Paul volunteered to accompany Mom and off they went.

Mom and Paul arrived at the buy house—a cookie-cutter track home situated in a stereotypical middle-class Phoenix neighborhood—where they were greeted at the door by a smiling couple who invited them in and proceeded to light up and share a sample joint. As Mom recounted the fiasco, the mood was mellow and the deal was going nicely until a third guy "appeared from nowhere, marched boldly up to Paul, and without a word pointed a gun at his face." Paul had reacted instantly, lashing out with his right hand and slapping the revolver to the side. The move probably saved his life, as the gun fired upon contact. The small caliber slug entered Paul's left cheek and exited in front of his ear. He was a bloody mess, hurt but not incapacitated. Instinctively, he grabbed the gunman's arm—the one still holding the gun—and attempted to disarm him even as the previously peaceful couple entered the fight and tore into Paul with gusto. It was now three against one and things did not look good for Paul.

Mom was in shock, but sprang into action without hesitation. Barely 5'4" in shoes and slightly built, she quickly scanned the room for a weapon. Her eyes settled on a useful item, a fireplace poker just a step or two away. It would have to do. She practically leapt to snatch the makeshift weapon from its holder and entered the fray from behind the would-be killer and struck him over the head and shoulders with desperate abandon. Adrenaline and fear fueled each stroke until finally, mercifully, the gun clattered on the tile and the assailant staggered away. Apparently, the host couple had also lost their taste for the fight and wasted no time following him out. Mom, with Paul in tow clutching his bloody face, ran for the door and together they made good their escape.

Several blocks away, Mom pulled over and rendered first-aid by applying direct pressure to Paul's wounds. He was covered head to toe in blood, but close examination revealed the damage was not life-threatening as long as the bleeding was stopped. Mom drove back to Nancy's and patched him up and his face healed fine, but I never saw him without a beard after that. Too bad for Pretty Paul.

No one could say with any certainty whether the incident was a rip-off gone wrong or if the guy had intended to kill. Only one thing was clear: there was surely an element of danger whenever or wherever drugs or money were involved. It was a wake-up call in the predominantly peaceful pot trade. Occasionally, the risky business of dealing with relative strangers was necessary to keep the marijuana flowing. Being a middleman meant always buying from someone, and that someone might be a cop or, worse, a rip-off killer. Nancy, always a thinker and problem solver, had a plan in mind and already had crucial elements in place.

A few months before our arrival, Nancy had met a guy with connections in Mexico that could supply a steady source of commercial-grade marijuana at prices substantially lower than what she was paying stateside. The only catch was getting it across the border. Now that El Loco was in the picture the problem was history.

Her Mexican connection "O.B." was in fact a gringo who had spent time in Mexican jails on minor charges and had met locals inside (the best place, of course) with connections to pot growers and dealers in the Mexican state of Oaxaca. He didn't speak a word of Spanish before his incarceration, but spoke like a native after a few months inside. He was a big man, a straight-talker and an old-school biker looking for opportunity. Nancy soon arranged a meeting between all the potential players of the new operation at a seaside restaurant north of Los Angeles. As she made introductions, I stared intently at the motorcycle, a Harley chopper "rat bike" O.B. had just roared in on. He must have noticed the attention I lavished upon the bike because after everyone had stuffed themselves with spicy Mexican food and agreed to meet back at the hotel he made me an offer I couldn't refuse.

"Wanna ride?"

"Yeah!"

Minutes later, I found myself hanging on for dear life as we raced along the Pacific Coast Highway at 90 miles an hour. Back in the room, my nose was still numb from the wind as the adults planned and plotted how they would start what would shortly become Mom and Nancy's first foray into international marijuana smuggling.

The Mexican smuggling operation was at its very core rather simple and straightforward, and with all the requisite elements in place, it launched quickly. O.B. got the ball rolling in fine style when he was able to finagle a deal with the Mexicans to front a substantial portion of the first load which freed much-needed money for other necessities such as airplane rental and fuel. Even so, the operating budget was tight to say the least. It was agreed to by all that no one would get paid until the first load was sold. That was fine by everyone. For the moment, at least, egos were checked at the door.

I knew the first trip was a success when I woke up one morning and found multiple burlap-wrapped bales of marijuana stacked high in my bedroom. I hadn't heard a thing—I

Nancy during the Mexican smuggling operation, ca. 1977.

could sleep through anything when I was a teenager. During the night El Loco had decided that my room was the safest place to stash the load. He joked with me at breakfast, "Don't smoke it all up now, David Michael!"

Everyone at the table laughed hard at that since they knew that despite my long curly hair and rock 'n' roll attitude, I was really a straight-arrow kid that eschewed drinking and smoking altogether.

I soon heard how the trip had gone off without a hitch. After O.B. paved the way with the Mexicans with a few grand and the promise of a lot more to come, El Loco flew a rented Cessna to the private Mexican airstrip where a load was waiting. A gang of Mexicans loaded the pot while several others took care of the refueling. Minutes later, El Loco was airborne and heading back to the U.S. border and the most dangerous part of the flight.

There had been a lot of talk concerning the best location to cross the border when returning as that was where 99 percent of U.S. border patrol attention was focused. It seemed everyone had a different opinion. In the end, El Loco decided to focus less on where to cross and more on avoiding border radar in general and keeping hidden from visual identification as well. He accomplished this by timing his border crossings to always coincide with darkness and flying ultra-low, often using mountains as cover. Radio silence was his strictly-observed religion. Once across and back on home turf in Arizona it was easy as pie for catch men to get the plane unloaded and deliver the load to a safe house. From there, Nancy worked her magic and turned the water into wine. And boy, did everyone drink.

Everyone involved was well paid and a lot of money was frivolously squandered on restaurants and meaningless trinkets. Very little was spent on anything tangible such as real estate or education. Even those that didn't do anything were given money to blow, and this caused egos to flare. One particular tagger-on of this ilk was Aunt Bonnie's boyfriend Barry, who fancied himself a star musician. He'd saunter and strut around Nancy's home strumming guitar endlessly, ordering expensive take-out and doing his best to smoke as much pot as humanly possible. His lispy droning Boston-accented vocals didn't help his music either. I wonder to this day if he actually thought it was listenable. I only wish someone would have paid him to stay silent.

With all the money going around, it was a small wonder that everyone wasn't completely satisfied with what they were given. Bonnie, for one, always wanted more, despite doing little besides catering to the infantile Barry. That's not to say that Bonnie wasn't willing or able to do more. Nancy was just naturally inclined to protect her, and as the baby of the family Bonnie was the squeaky wheel that usually got the grease whether it was merited or not.

Also unsatisfied but deserving of her claim for a cut was Aunt Blue. As they did for most everyone, Mom and Nancy gave Blue a little cash here and there, but stopped short of giving her the traditional "connection" cut of the profits. Because she had introduced El Loco to Mom, Blue felt she deserved that share which amounted to around 3 percent of El Loco's take. When someone asked Baga, so often the mediator of Haas household disputes, he weighed in on Blue's side and insisted it was only fair to cut her in. Still, Mom and Nancy resisted, citing Blue's immaturity and youth. It was also an unfortunate reality that Blue's mental health over the years had deteriorated slowly and steadily into nothing less than clinical schizophrenia. Like many others with her condition, Blue had her good days and her bad days, and on one particularly bad day I saw her throw a single devastating punch that cold-cocked a show-off cop who had come to assist medical personnel who had come to take her to a mental ward. A true friend, none of this bothered El Loco. Ever the problem solver and fundamentally unselfish, he didn't allow bad feelings to fester long before paying Blue out of his own share. Money for its own sake did not interest him all that much. He was loaded and free and living for the moment and his nickname wasn't El Loco for nothing.

El Loco and I loved go-kart racing and he spent enough cash for us to become regulars at several local tracks. We got kicked out of others for aggressive and sometimes reckless driving. Because I was underage and didn't have a driver's license we used cabs to get around. El Loco had a driver's license but liked to drink and not worry about driving. As it turned out a DUI was indeed stalking him, but in an unusual manner.

El Loco was at Nancy's one afternoon when he decided he needed some beer and, wanting to avoid the hassle of calling a cab, jumped on a bicycle for a quick run to the nearby 7–Eleven. On the way there he was stopped by cops and arrested. Not for drugs or smuggling or anything else he was dabbling in. El Loco, as often careless as he was careful, was busted for DUI on my cousin's bicycle. Most of us were dumb-founded and had no idea that bicycle DUI was even possible!

El Loco bounced right out of that entanglement by paying a flurry of fines and emerged not much worse for the wear. He partied night and day, sampling everything life could offer, including hard drugs. Yet when it came down to business he never missed a beat. He and the plane were always ready and able. O.B.'s Oaxacan connection had proved so far to be a consistent source and the demand for marijuana was as strong as ever. The operation continued to roll smoothly and profitably—Mom and Nancy were a winning combination when each focused on their strengths. Nancy was the planner. Mom was the doer. For quite awhile it seemed that nothing could derail the train, and when the end came, so subtle and stealthy, no one even saw it coming.

What would become a fateful trip began as usual when Mom and O.B. flew down to Oaxaca with the buy money to inspect and pay for the load. But something was different this time. This time the load was crap. Well, it was decent commercial lower-grade Mexican marijuana compressed into one-kilo bricks, but it didn't compare with the earlier, fresher non-compressed bud. O.B. bitched and the Mexicans made several different excuses before they settled blame for the inferior load on bad timing. They promised they could deliver the usual quality in three weeks' time, and even offered a small discount. Mom and O.B. were disappointed, but what could they do? Their hands were tied. It was only a slight delay, no big deal. Mom considered a visit to Acapulco, then scrubbed it and decided to head home instead.

Ordinarily this would be no problem, but here again was a wrinkle. She had $29,000 buy money with her. Not much of an issue when traveling out of the country or within the borders, but clearing U.S. Customs with that much undeclared cash could be dicey. Also, it didn't help that the cash was primarily in twenties and therefore quite bulky. There were lots of options, but she was tired and made a bad decision. Mom ended up sealing the cash inside white envelopes which she then taped to her body and stashed in nearly every pocket of her outfit. Far from an elegant solution. The cash was now reasonably out of sight, but was it truly hidden? Cash-sniffing dogs were only one worry. A pat-down was another problem, another worry. She soon put all negative thoughts out of her mind. It was never Mom's style to worry for long about anything.

Baga, a former U.S. Border Patrol agent, once said that even humans have a tendency to "school" in cooperative movement in certain large-group settings and that a highly-trained and knowledgeable agent could discern a difference in the movement of a guilty person, or at least that's what he'd been told in training. Maybe it was just that simple. Maybe Mom was simply out of synch with the mass of humanity squeezing through LAX Customs that afternoon. Or maybe an agent noticed a suspicious bulge in her outfit or a dog silently sniffed her out. When I asked Mom what she felt led to her arrest, she mentioned Baga's observation but didn't really hazard a guess. I tend to think that maybe it was just bad luck.

Whatever the cause, she was unceremoniously pulled out of line and taken to an interrogation room by two seriously intent customs agents. Before it was all over, customs agents had confiscated all her money and Mom was arrested and charged with transporting more than $5,000 in undeclared cash into the United States, a federal felony. She bailed out of jail two days later and returned to Phoenix, tired and thankful to be home. The trip had been a real bummer to be sure, but it could have been worse. The charge did carry a possible prison sentence, however, most people charged with the crime received a fine and probation.

Mom hired an attorney and kept a positive attitude, but the momentum of the Mexican venture had reached a tipping point. The three-week wait for the pot wasn't such a big deal, though it didn't help either, because as far as I could tell unoccupied minds were especially susceptible to bouts of paranoia and Nancy's house became a hotbed of speculation.

Everybody wondered if people arrested for offenses such as Mom's would be placed on some sort of government watch list. Debate raged and the consensus was yes, Mom by now must be under some kind of scrutiny. Its exact nature was anyone's guess. Another big question was whether Mom was being, or would be in the future, investigated by federal authorities, possibly the DEA. At the time of her arrest, customs agents had questioned Mom at length about the when, where, and why regarding the cash. She had spun a tall tale regarding the purchase of a Mexican hacienda. The feds didn't necessarily buy her story, but they didn't press too hard either. Was she being investigated or were they simply waiting for her to screw up and bring it all down? These questions and others stressed Mom and Nancy to the core. Mercifully, Uncle Rod wasn't around to fan the flames of paranoia even higher.

The three-week hiatus initiated by the Mexicans morphed into six months as a sort of self-inflicted apathy set in and nobody did much of anything. Paranoia was the major issue, but it wasn't everything. Mom was in legal trouble, no doubt, and it was hard to tell what the outcome would be. Losing $29,000 cash was not to be taken lightly, yet thankfully it was an amount that could be tolerated and El Loco's bicycle DUI was fully in his rearview mirror. The future was wide open and it should have been all systems go, but that just didn't happen.

Mom and Nancy, with the laid-back attitude characteristic of true marijuana smokers, simply allowed everything to wind down. They neglected to return phone calls and didn't get out much. Occasionally, there was talk about getting a trip together, but the talk invariably was just that, talk. Everyone was high on their own supply and content to drift.

Then the day arrived when the other shoe dropped regarding Mom's LAX arrest. The first thing we learned was that she would not be going to jail, our main concern. However, she would be on probation for an indeterminate length of time. Knowing Mom, the mere thought of reporting to a probation officer monthly, along with written reports and possible drug tests, did not sound doable to me. She was a free spirit, a person who often didn't bother to keep track of the date and never wore a watch. I considered her chances of passing a drug test at that time commensurate with her becoming an astronaut. Fortunately, fate intervened and it never came to that.

I say fate because I just don't know what else to call it. It was also damned lucky. What else can you say when a person sort of just slips through the cracks?

Coincidentally, it was right about this time that Mom, Melanie, and I went to visit Bummy (my grandmother's nickname, also given by me) and Baga in north Florida. We had been away for awhile and enjoyed a warm welcome. Baga and I played a lot of chess. Additional extended family (including the parish priest) gathered at weekly after-dinner poker parties. Mom gradually unwound and saw the Florida greenery again as if for the first time. She started thinking again about growing marijuana herself. That was always her default position. It was not long before Mom found a cheap house for rent and voilà! Somehow, our Florida visit had turned into us moving back.

I never heard any talk of Mom's probation. It had disappeared. It was like she had ignored it away by not bothering to stay in contact. The court must have simply lost track of her after the move to Florida. I'm sure this would be very unlikely to happen in the Internet age, but Mom didn't hide or bother to change her name. Instead, she drew attention to herself when she opened a small sewing boutique and tried to meet every seamstress in the little town during her first week in business.

Surprisingly, despite the many thousands of dollars Mom had earned the past couple of years as a successful marijuana smuggler, she had saved none. We were essentially broke when we arrived back in Florida and only survived as a family because of the support given us by Bummy and Baga. Our home was a $60-a-month Florida "Cracker" house, with no A/C or heat other than an old wood stove. Needless to say, the family's circumstances were once again at a low ebb. Mom's boyfriend at the time, a real winner named Danny, actually stole our family cat named Panama (a seal point Siamese) and sold her to support his nefarious habits. Then, after weeks where I never let the theft go and bitterly protested on a daily basis, he brought back an imposter in a vain attempt to pacify me. Thankfully, Mom ditched him before he could do much more harm. For Christmas that year I remember getting a tiny plastic dinosaur filled with bubble bath as my only gift. But that's how we lived and at least we didn't starve, although I do remember eating a lot of beans and rice during that period. Our lives were basically a hand-to-mouth existence. Feast or famine, with moving in between. And we could never be sure about the way our day might go, since Mom was prone to impromptu decisions such as the one she made one afternoon after our electricity had been disconnected for non-payment. Melanie and I were moping around in a bum mood when Mom produced a jar of change from somewhere and proceeded to dump and count coins on the kitchen table.

"Let's get out of here. Okay?" she asked. Melanie and I perked up. "Would you like to go see a movie at the drive-in?" She now had our complete attention.

"Yeah!" we chorused, thrilled to be saved from hanging around in a dark house lit only by candles until bedtime.

"Come on." She waved us over. "Help me count this. I think it'll be enough."

We hustled over and dove into the jar. There ended up being just enough change to finance the night out at the drive-in. We were living in the moment.

Typical Mom.

5

Florida

Our return to Florida, though initially wrought with hardship, was a result of Mom's primal survival instinct as well as the first step of an unspoken decision. When things in Arizona had been clicking right along and everything was hunky-dory it had been easy to skim over life's little details as one day blurred into the next. After her arrest, the West seemed less hospitable and not as safe as before. Florida, so green and inviting to a gardener's soul, was more than merely distance away from Arizona, it was another world altogether. A place to regroup. Sanctuary.

And our situation did slowly improve. For one thing, Mom was focusing nearly all her effort on her new custom sewing and alteration business in Jasper. The little shop also stocked a couple dozen bolts of fabric as well as a basic selection of sewing notions. Violet's Alterations, named after my grandmother, wasn't setting the world on fire or anything, but the business was in the black and had quickly gained a loyal group of core customers who appreciated what Mom had to offer, for she truly was an extraordinary seamstress. Nevertheless, when her focus was on legitimate business she remained keen for any opportunity that might arise and constantly kept an eye out. Before long, one did, and Mom was the first to see it.

Rural Hamilton County in north Florida was not known for being a place that kept up with the times. It was nowhere near the cutting edge. One sign of this was that on Sundays there was a ban on the sale of beer, wine or alcohol of any type. Adjacent Suwanee County was the same—dry as the Sahara on Sundays. A third county, Columbia, shared a border with the other two at its northwest corner which also happened to be a convenient midpoint of the three. Somehow, Mom sniffed around enough and found a small run-down white stucco building for rent which was strategically poised in that exact area of Columbia County. The place was nothing special, but the rent was cheap and, most important of all, Columbia County was wet on Sundays.

Mom wasted no time and turned the building into a small bar in three weeks. It had a half-dozen tables, a jukebox in the corner, and a pool table. It was a no-frills bar for a no-town place, but it was the only bar for miles, especially on Sundays when competition in the area was nil. A beer and wine license was all she could afford, but business was good overall and on Sundays the carry-out sales were especially brisk. She named the place the Blue Sink after a local spring-fed swimming hole of the same name.

The Blue Sink's success caught everybody by surprise, including Mom. A couple months after opening, it was skipping along better than ever and still gaining steam. She had recognized an opportunity and seized the moment. From there it remained anyone's guess as to how far it might go, and all signs were positive. But the genie had escaped the bottle. The location was just too perfect, and once Mom revealed its potential it was only a matter of time before the owners decided to capitalize on what they had learned about their property. After owning the place for decades they suddenly wanted to own a bar.

They began their campaign to oust Mom by raising her rent. She paid it. They raised it some more. She paid that. When the rent raising tactic didn't work they decided to just go ahead and kick her out because she didn't have a lease, only a verbal agreement and a handshake. It was a raw deal for Mom and they knew it. She had fixed up the place and put it on the map and they rewarded her with a three-month notice to vacate. The greedy property's owners couldn't wait to take over and start lining their pockets.

The months passed all too swiftly and the Blue Sink's success continued unabated. I spent many afternoons there after school playing pool and listening to Rod Stewart, Freddy Fender, and The Eagles on the jukebox. Mom tried but could not find another location to move the bar. The Blue Sink's location was a one in a million. It was the golden ticket. The property's owners could hardly wait to kick Mom out.

Finally, Mom's last day as owner of the Blue Sink arrived. She had a few boxes of personal items and decorations that were going with her, but not much else. The coolers, jukebox, and even the pool table were leased and the "new" owners had signed their own contracts to keep them in place as is. It was sort of disappointing when I looked around the place as we were leaving and realized it was not going to look much different after we were gone. At the time, it did not seem fair to me that Mom should lose a business that way, especially to people who not only had not recognized the opportunity themselves, but had behaved shabbily toward her nearly every chance they got. As it turned out, a measure of poetic justice rendered my feelings moot on the subject.

A few weeks after the property owners took over the Blue Sink, a tiny one-room church decided to set up across the street, just a couple hundred feet from and caddy-corner to the bar. It's doubtful that many people noticed. Before long, the church's pastor began to focus on the bar and he rallied more than a few locals against the place. As luck would have it, a member of the congregation had a brother who was a lawyer and he quickly fired the first shot on behalf of the church, an injunction to close the Blue Sink citing its proximity to a place of worship. The battle between the bar and the church had begun.

The Blue Sink's new owners were spoiling for a fight. They had ultimately won the war with Mom over ownership of the bar but had lost many battles along the way and were still licking old wounds with little satisfaction. The Blue Sink was a winner and they weren't about to give it up without a fight. On the other hand, the church was a wily adversary headed by a motivated pastor with little incentive to negotiate as long as his pro-bono legal representation continued. The pastor knew his flock well. Nearly all of the congregation's members were elderly country folk with a lot of time on their hands. Many volunteered at church when their neighbors were at home drinking. Fighting the devil's drink was a time-tested cause they could wholeheartedly support and the church could always use good publicity.

It was an uneven battle from the outset. The bar was hopelessly outclassed by the church, which had plenty of experience rallying its members around a cause. Besides that, the church had also gotten off the first shot from which the bar never fully recovered. The church then followed up its strong opening by circulating a petition to rack up additional support. The pastor raved and ranted about the perils of alcohol every Sunday and Wednesday night and vowed not to quit his holy crusade until the bar was history.

The Blue Sink also suffered from built-in handicaps it could not avoid. The worst was that it was a bar, a drinking establishment, a place where people sometimes got *drunk*. And when a lowly bar is fighting a *church*—a holy place, a manifestation of God on Earth—it's an uphill battle all the way. And if that wasn't enough, the bar's biggest day of business was Sunday. Churchgoers regularly eyed the barflies from across the street and had picketed the Blue Sink on three prior occasions.

In court, the church cited the bar's relatively short tenure at its location as one of the reasons it should not be there. The Blue Sink's owners countered that since the church came after the bar it should be allowed to stay. That particular argument seemed to carry the day until the church pointed out that there had previously been a church at its current address, a church that pre-dated any bar. And once the court received proof of that information the ultimate decision came down to the basic fact that the bar and church were physically too close to satisfy the county ordinance that required a specified distance of separation. One of them had to go. The battle escalated.

Church supporters weren't shy about showing up at meetings and hearings ready to voice their opinion and be heard. They were organized and even carpooled to events. Conversely, there may have been legions of bar supporters in the county, but very few showed up at the crucial events that would decide the issue. They just did not seem to be very organized or motivated in their cause. Well, in this case the squeaky wheel got the grease and the church won. The judge ordered the Blue Sink closed just a few months after Mom had been forced out. For my family the whole experience had been just another ride on life's rollercoaster, a few more ups and downs. Mom had bar, Mom lost bar. Feast, then famine. Nothing unusual in that. But what was going on over at my grandparents' new house was anything but normal.

The Byrd estate, Baga and Bummy's new place, was actually not new at all. It was a pre–Civil War plantation house located in north Florida less than half a mile from the Georgia state line. The Byrd plantation was one of the few large homes in the area that had not been burned to the ground by the conquering Union Army during the Civil War. Locals said it had instead been used by the Yankees as their headquarters of operation and it was well suited as such. The sprawling main house had seven bedrooms, a spacious wrap-around porch, and a humungous separated kitchen. Additionally, there were two barns, a stable, a corral, and an icehouse. To top it all off, the entire park-like estate was situated on the banks of 220-acre Lake Alison. Bummy and Baga had a lease-option on this very special property and we all loved the place. Maybe that was because the house, much like our family, had been through enough to have a few secrets.

Put simply, the Byrd house was haunted. It was haunted in the classical sense with ghosts, poltergeists, and apparitions. When I look back on those days, I can't help but recall how the spirits revealed themselves incrementally, one small step at a time, seeming to very sensitively gauge exactly how much we humans could assimilate without going bonkers. A subtle indication of this was how Baga, the most skeptical member of our family, saw the first ghost.

He had just returned from town and was circling around to the back of the house to park when he noticed a woman. She had long, dark hair and was dressed in a full, old-fashioned dress. Strangely, she appeared to be sweeping the dirt around the base of the large ancient oak tree that spread dominantly over the backyard area. Baga figured the woman must be an eccentric friend of one of his girls or perhaps someone playing dress up.

As soon as he was inside, he asked Bummy (he called her Vi, short for Violet, her real name) about the woman.

"Vi, who's our visitor?" He motioned toward the back.

Bummy went to the window and peered out. "Who?" she asked. "I don't see anyone."

Baga went back outside and looked all around the house for the woman, but she had disappeared. Disturbed, he went back inside and very seriously explained what he had seen. We all thought it very strange and nobody volunteered an explanation. We also knew it was highly unlikely the woman could have been a lost stranger or an unannounced visitor as the Byrd house was set 150 yards off the main road and the property was completely fenced. The closest neighbor was more than a mile away. The funny thing was that not one of us ever once uttered the word "ghost."

A few weeks later, Baga had another mysterious encounter and told us in detail how he had just seen an unidentified something that he described as a "translucent two-foot diameter bluish sphere of light," moving slowly and silently around the front porch. This time there was a lot of talk about what Baga had seen. It was hard not to dwell on a supernatural explanation given the nature of what he'd seen. Something like this coming from a World War II veteran, pilot, and former U.S. Border Patrol agent had to be taken seriously. Without a doubt we truly accepted that something strange had occurred. I hadn't seen anything yet, however.

A month later El Loco visited. He was clearly happy to see everyone again and it was like old times when the poker game ran late into the night. Finally, well after three a.m. the game drew to a close and everyone said goodnight. Bummy put El Loco in an upstairs bedroom with the promise of a hearty Southern breakfast in the morning.

The house quickly became silent. All I could hear was the sound of summer June bugs buzzing in the trees. I was also in an upstairs bedroom, but in an opposite corner of the house and just starting to doze off when I heard a series of heavy footfalls somewhere upstairs near the center of the house: boom, Boom, BooM, BOOM, BOOM, and then, somewhere close, a door slammed shut with tremendous force, WHAM! I leapt from my bed like a jack-in-the-box and rushed out into the upstairs landing. As I switched on the light, El Loco stormed out of his room with a puzzled expression on his face. Mom appeared from down the hall. She seemed ready for anything.

"What in the hell was that?" As he asked the question EL Loco had a pained look on his face that I recognized. It was the look of a person that has just experienced something that blows their mind to such a degree that they must now seriously consider a paranormal reality. Maybe ghosts were real.

"That was awesome! Wow!" I gushed, a huge smile on my face. I had been prepared to accept the reality of a spirit world ever since going to church as a kid and making the choice everyone does. Either you believe in the possibility of the existence of other dimensions or you don't. To actually experience something paranormal was an exceptional treat to me. "It was so loud! Mom, you heard it too, right?" I looked into her eyes for confirmation.

"Oh yes," she answered, obviously stunned as she slowly wandered the landing, looking wide-eyed from floor to ceiling as if she were searching for something. "It was..." she trailed off with a whisper, lost in thought.

"Did you see anything?" I asked, looking at Mom and then El Loco. They both shook their heads.

"Neither did I."

By this time, Baga and Bummy had made their way up the main stairs from the first floor. Baga had an especially calm expression on his face as he glanced around the landing and at each of us in turn.

"The ghost?" He asked it like a question, but after what we had just heard we took it as a statement.

"Well, technically it's a poltergeist since we didn't see anything." I had read an article about the difference between the two. Ghosts were usually seen; poltergeists made noises but were generally not seen. So far, the Byrd house had presented us one example of each type. I was secretly hoping for more.

My heart was thumping, but not from fear. Far from it, I was thrilled with the contemplation of what I had just experienced. My mind reeled while trying to think of any logical explanation short of an elaborately well-planned and executed scheme. I did not believe either of my grandparents capable of doing anything like that. No way. The incident had woken the entire household, so I knew I didn't imagine anything as I was dozing off to sleep. Curiously, El Loco was probably the most affected, for his face still carried the expression of a shell-shocked soldier. A little forewarning had steeled the rest of us against the total shock and awe he experienced. The more I thought about it the more convinced I became that the "otherworldly" explanation held the most merit.

"I wonder if there was a blue light and we missed it." I was thinking of Baga's description and how it might fit in with what we heard. Somehow, the thought of the woman in the long dress holding a broom and stomping around slamming doors seemed less likely than a blue bundle of light and energy causing the ruckus. It just made more sense to me.

"There's definitely something going on in this house," Baga declared.

"Yeah, it's haunted!" I blurted out.

"You're damned right about that, David Michael!" El Loco bellowed through a big smile. He'd finally recovered from the initial surprise and was now enjoying the experience as much as I was.

"I'm scared," said a tentative voice from the hallway. Blue had quietly come out of her room and now gathered her robe closer around her as if she was cold. "It was creepy."

"It doesn't seem dangerous," Mom chimed in.

Blue very slowly shook her head from side to side and her eyes became wider. She was not satisfied. It looked as though we were headed for a genuine *Twilight Zone* moment when Bummy spoke up.

"Aw hell, we used to have ghosts in our house when I was a girl. Late at night we used to hear the sounds of a mother soothing her baby. We heard knocking and scratching at times. Music too. They never did us any harm."

Thankfully, Bummy's words had a calming effect on Blue and she turned around and went back to bed. The rest of us were way too hyped up for bed, so we took the rest of the ghostly conversation to the kitchen where the adults drank coffee as we discussed every conceivable angle of what could be going on. Everyone eventually agreed that the only rational explanation other than a hoax would have to be paranormal in origin. It was our firm consensus that Baga had seen, and we had heard, something supernatural.

Over the next two years, nearly everyone who ever spent much time at the Byrd estate experienced their own encounters with the variety of spirits that we believed inhabited the house and grounds. A visiting family friend, as well as one of my cousins, happened to see the sweeping woman on two separate occasions. El Loco and others saw the blue light spheres from time to time. Practically anyone who spent a week or two in the house could expect to hear strange noises: knocks, stomps, scratches, slams and a dozen other sounds with unidentifiable origins. Not nearly as common but sometimes accompanying these were physical manifestations. Doors and windows would open and close on their own. Enter a room with drawn curtains, open them, leave and return a few minutes later and the curtains would again be drawn. Drawers opened spontaneously. Lights and other electronics were also subject to otherworldly control as they randomly switched on and off. All of this took a little getting used to, but since the spirits' shenanigans were essentially harmless we grew to embrace the weirdness of the place. But there was always the possibility of the unknown lurking around the next corner. Besides the more common paranormal phenomena, I had only two other encounters with the spirits that added up to something extraordinary. I was with Bummy during an occurrence one night that I will never forget.

The entire house was still and quiet, and outside not a whisper of wind tickled the air. Bummy and I were in the downstairs great room at 1:15 a.m., each silently reading at opposite ends of the couch as we commonly did. We were totally engrossed in our books as a distant noise began to resonate in the silence, so low at first that it didn't merit attention. As the seconds passed, the noise slowly grew until it began to coalesce into something clearly recognizable. We went to the window and peered out in the direction from which the sound emanated but there was nothing visible.

What Bummy and I heard was what sounded like a stagecoach approaching at a good clip to round the corner of the house before rapidly fading into the distance. Clearly, I heard the jingle and squeak of the tack and the snorting horses' hooves hitting the earth with a sound so real I felt it. I heard the creaking of the coach and the rustling of the reins. The sound was loud and live, yet only my ears told me what my eyes did not see. They saw only an ancient stand of massive moss-covered live oaks mingling with a few statuesque virgin pines on a night whose darkness was pierced only by the porch lights we'd switched on. As the sound grew louder and came closer, we dropped our books and went out to stand on the front porch just a few yards away, staring in the direction from which it came. I can attest that it is an extremely peculiar feeling when your eyes and ears are at odds with each other. Incredulous, Bummy and I looked at each other and quietly laughed. This was something new and much more elaborate than a knock or a stomp. What can I say? The poltergeists had really outdone themselves.

What really helped Baga and Bummy (and everyone else, for that matter) come to terms and learn to live with the haunting was their education regarding the history of the Byrd estate. After being used in the Civil War as a local Union Army headquarters, it had become an active stagecoach stop which I found especially interesting considering what Bummy and I had heard. After taking some time to seriously consider everything, I thought it practically unnatural if a house of that age and pedigree should be without ghosts. If I didn't know any better I might have thought everyone at the Byrd house was stoned or drunk, as I'm sure some were from time to time, and this might have been a plausible explanation for the supposed haunting. The only thing I know for sure is that I wasn't stoned or drunk, never had been, and I had heard something very peculiar.

Instead of avoiding the place, I spent as much time with Bummy and Baga at the Byrd house as I possibly could. In truth, at this time in my life it was much more comfortable and normal to live with my grandparents than with Mom. This was mostly due to Mom's unrelenting habit of inviting people—some of them practically strangers—into our home. I think Mom had an aversion to being alone and wanted company, so she often invited people over. She felt sorry for anyone down on his or her luck and was quick to try and help. Men, women, sometimes families, it didn't matter. It was not unusual to come home and find new people hanging around, staying for lunch, then dinner, then overnight. Like stray cats, some stuck around longer.

To be fair, I have to say that Mom's open-door policy at home occasionally led to some interesting good times. Two or three times a month an impromptu party would form around a little food and drink and, of course, some pot. Men frequently brought instruments, mostly guitars, to the parties and the music and singing usually went on long into the night. The songs were mostly old country and folk numbers, but once in awhile someone would break out and play some Beatles or Stones. I had been playing guitar since age nine and had never had a lesson, so I was quick to seize any opportunity to learn and these musical parties gave me a chance to perform with others even though most of the time I was just a kid strumming guitar alone in the corner.

There is no doubt that the first few years our family spent back in Florida were crucial in deciding how things would go and where we would eventually wind up, as Mom continued her freewheeling "do anything, go anywhere" lifestyle. The sewing shop as a business was far from spectacular, but it generated a steady trickle of cash so she kept at it through all the ups and downs. The Battle for the Blue Sink Bar (as I liked to call it) had long since wound down to its anticlimactic end, and again our family was blowing in the wind and Mom was trolling for an answer, a path to something better even if she had no clue as to what that was. And like before, Mom gravitated to what she knew and loved: gardening. And Florida was still the perfect place, so the idea of having a magnificent marijuana garden was more tantalizing than ever.

But where to grow it?

Our house was definitely out of the question, with its revolving door and constant house guests. Nothing was sacred there and no real privacy existed. Ditto its property or the nearby woods. Just too much action. Mom considered renting a grow house because she knew she might be able to get Aunt Nancy to help with the considerable set-up expense. A grow house would allow precise control of the environment which would help nurture the crop like never before. It was an exciting idea, yet she let it go. There were simply too many things that could go wrong with that approach. One lucky cop or one suspicious neighbor could bring disaster. And besides, the power bill alone could be overwhelming and there would be no guarantee that Nancy could always help. Mom asked Baga and Bummy about using the Byrd house or grounds but they flatly refused.

With all the indoor options off the table, that left Mom considering an outdoor crop exclusively and there were numerous options in predominantly rural north Florida and south Georgia. The trick was to find a spot that was unlikely to have any foot traffic and was not near any obvious air routes. Nearby water was also a necessity, as rain could not be depended upon entirely. Concealment was also a major consideration. She needed an accessible place that had fairly dense cover but also received adequate sunshine throughout the majority of the day, as marijuana plants thrived in hot, sunny locations. Mom scoured the surrounding countryside and took back roads and alternate routes everywhere she could in hopes of stumbling on the right spot. The more she looked, the more elusive her dream became.

Then, as we were on our way to the Byrd house one day, a rather silly idea occurred to Mom. It was an idea inspired by her immediate surroundings. And as the idea grew in her mind the details fell into place and she felt it was not so silly after all.

6

The Problem
with Sunflowers

Sunflowers were everywhere, it seemed, from small wild varieties growing on the shoulder of the road to the much larger commercially-farmed varieties. The road we were traveling was flanked on both sides by sprawling commercial fields of adolescent sunflowers only a few inches high. I noticed that Mom was fixated on them as we neared the Byrd house. When I looked at the fields I saw the beginning of a farmer's cash crop and not much more. Mom looked at the fields and saw opportunity, for she'd had an idea. It was a daring and somewhat crazy idea, but that only made it more appealing in her eyes. Above all, she felt it just might work for someone with the guts to try.

Mom was just that person. She had the guts. And once she had a plan it would not be long before it went into action, as she had always been more of a doer than a planner. Even if problems arose later they would likely be ignored if that's what it took to keep the plan alive. And after her epiphany while driving down that dusty dirt road that day she could hardly wait to get started. The perfect outdoor grow spot had been right under her nose the whole time; she had decided to grow a crop of marijuana among the farmer's sunflower crop.

The plan had its merits. The sunflowers' summer growing season corresponded nicely with the needs of marijuana plants that preferred hot, sunny weather. Concealing the marijuana crop would be easy as sunflowers grew tall and had large heads which would provide excellent cover. Set-up time and labor would be minimal since the farmer had carefully prepared the soil for the sunflowers, making sure it was well-tilled, weed-free, and fertilized prior to planting. Best of all, the most difficult problem Mom faced with an outdoor grow operation was already taken care of as the sunflower fields had extensive irrigation systems already in place. It was only a matter of implementing a few details to get started.

The first job on Mom's agenda was to grow a sizable crop of marijuana seedlings, because she wanted to plant them instead of using seeds that might be eaten by birds and insects or simply fail to germinate altogether. She got right to work. Three weeks later she was ready with several hundred tiny quad-leaf pot plants happily growing in their little cardboard starter cups. She decided to begin the following night.

As far as Mom could tell, there was only one drawback to her plan. It required a ton of labor to implement. Fortunately she'd met a new boyfriend, Richard, at the beginning of the summer, and like most men in a new relationship he was eager to please, and Mom had no qualms about putting him to work.

The particular field she chose for her plants was less than half a mile from the Byrd house, so each night's work was staged from there. First, several hundred seedlings had to be transported to the sunflower field and carefully transplanted from their starter cups. This required not only carrying the seedlings themselves, but enough water to give the baby plants their first drink. To accomplish this, Mom and Richard used backpacks. That first week alone they made dozens of nocturnal trips to the different areas within the field where Mom chose to plant. It was grueling, back-breaking, and dirty work. Digging, planting, and watering on their hands and knees all night left them exhausted and filthy every morning. I could see that Richard, a self-proclaimed artist with soft hands and a prima-donna attitude, was becoming more and more disgruntled with the work when, a little more than two weeks into the scheme, they returned one morning and Mom declared the initial planting a success. If Richard thought that was the end of the hard work he was destined to be sorely disappointed.

In fact, it was only the beginning of much more work to come and Mom had stamina to spare. The crop was planted, but now the task of maintaining it was at hand. Practically every other night or so, Mom and Richard donned headlights and shouldered their backpacks and headed out to weed, spot water, fertilize, and otherwise care for the seedlings. The sunflowers were still young and short, so they used their flashlights as little as possible to avoid being seen. Yet, at the same time and no less important, they had to watch carefully for poisonous snakes, mostly rattlers, which were drawn to the fields by the numerous mice and rats that had come to eat any sunflower seeds that had failed to sprout. Breezy, moonlit nights provided the easiest working conditions. Rainy nights they took off.

As the weeks progressed the dual crops grew and flourished. The sunflowers' growth outpaced the marijuana's three to one which gave the pot much needed side-cover. Air cover was pretty much nil, but the pot plants were still small and didn't require any. And as Mom had predicted, since the time of their planting the sunflowers did not appear to have received any further attention from the farmer. This was as good as she had hoped. A farmer poking around his field would dramatically increase the chance of discovery. Sunflowers were known for being a low-maintenance crop; they just needed to keep growing to fulfill their role in Mom's plan.

The marijuana's care, however, was a completely different story. Even though it was a weed and a very hardy and tenacious one at that, Mom lavished it with every ounce of tender loving care she could muster. To her, each plant was a baby worthy of the utmost attention and love required to bring it to adult perfection. Mom's green thumb came in handy and enabled her to "read" the plants. She could easily tell when one was under stress from insect attack or needed additional watering or its soil aerated. When an errant weed popped up it was promptly pulled. If a plant was injured it was doctored and propped up. Parasitic insects were immediately destroyed. And the crop responded accordingly to all the benevolent attention. Only a few weeks into the plan and the plants were looking great. Mom's spirits soared. Richard hung in there.

The primary worry at this stage was the accidental or intentional discovery of the marijuana. As far as cops intentionally finding it, Mom wasn't terribly worried. It was common knowledge that cops occasionally snooped around in helicopters, hovering over backyards and small clearings within wooded areas looking for marijuana plants, but the thought of them searching in the middle of one specific sunflower field seemed farfetched. There was just so much agriculture in the area. The surrounding countryside was loaded with fields of corn, soybeans, watermelon, and tobacco. No, cops weren't going to be a problem. Accidental discovery from anyone other than the farmer who cared for the sunflower field was also unlikely. After all, who would have a reason to go traipsing through a sunflower field miles from town and far from any hiking trails or an established hunting area?

The farmer himself was another matter. So far, Mom hadn't seen any sign at all that he had returned to the field since its planting. The automatic irrigation system was obviously on a timer and had been working perfectly. As the days passed it appeared more and more likely that the sunflowers would be left alone until harvest as long as nothing malfunctioned or broke down. Mom kept her fingers crossed and continued to think positive. Being a grower was hard work, but it was a downright genteel occupation considering the news she'd recently heard through the grapevine about a smuggling trip gone bad.

El Loco had recounted the story he'd heard from a friend of Nancy's who had been involved with a Florida marijuana dealer that had attempted to start a smuggling operation out of Colombia. What really hit home with me was the fact that I had previously met the two pilots involved at Nancy's house a year previously when I had accidentally walked in on them while they were frolicking (his face buried in her crotch) on my bed in the room I was using during my stay. Later that evening (after laundering my sheets) I got to know them a little better. Tim was tall, blue-eyed and blond-haired. He liked horses and flying. Stephanie was an athletic brunette, pretty and petite. She liked guns and Tim. They were a cute young couple and I hated to think of anything bad happening to them. The tale I heard was a stark reminder of the many risks involved in international drug smuggling.

According to El Loco, the smuggling trip at the center of the story should have been a resounding success. All the pieces were in place, including enough financing to ensure that multiple trips could be made in a very short time period. This was important because Colombia's rainy season was fast approaching and it was imperative to move the marijuana out of the country before it could begin to mildew in the storehouse. Thousands of pounds of prime Colombian pot were waiting. Two young and relatively inexperienced pilots left Florida in a twin-engine Cessna to go and get it, but they never arrived.

Tim, the pilot, along with his co-pilot girlfriend Stephanie, was on his first smuggling trip. He held a lower-level pilot's license and had logged only a few dozen hours since receiving his twin-engine rating. He was not instrument rated. Stephanie also held a basic pilot's license upon which the ink was not yet dry. For the last leg of the trip, they chose the most direct route to Colombia, which involved quite a bit of over-water flight and exposed them to weather variables that could make the journey even more challenging and unforgiving to amateurs. In light of this, it would not have been too surprising to hear that the ill-fated couple had fallen victim to bad weather or a technical problem they couldn't handle. Instead, they succumbed to a fate much more cruel.

The couple had made it as far as the Colombian border without incident, but that was where their luck ended. A Colombian version of the Civil Air Patrol picked up the southbound Cessna on radar shortly after it ventured into Colombian airspace and attempted to hail the plane on VHF radio. Unfortunately, neither Tim nor Stephanie spoke more than a few words of Spanish, so they ignored the communication attempt. (At this point of the story, El Loco volunteered that if he had been similarly discovered while flying into a foreign country on a smuggling trip he would have instantly turned around and headed back into safe airspace.) Instead, Tim maintained his course, speed, and radio silence, probably hoping to be left alone. That naive decision only escalated the imminent danger of the situation and substantially diminished their chances for survival. The point then arrived at which events took an exceedingly bad turn.

The dispatcher immediately notified the Colombian air force, which scrambled two fighter jets to intercept the trespassing private plane. Within minutes, they were on scene, each jet flanking the much-slower Cessna. Colombian authorities insisted that it was their policy to first challenge intruders and then order them to submit to being escorted to the nearest base where they would probably be arrested and their plane impounded. No one knows for sure the exact details of what transpired next between the fighters and the would-be smugglers, but at this juncture Tim and Stephanie must have clearly seen the fighters and known the danger they represented. Those that knew them best insist they must have complied with any orders they were given that night, especially knowing that their lives were on the line and escape was impossible, and many fear that the language problem prevented them from complying and that's what led to their demise. Whatever the case, it was a sad fact that Tim and Stephanie, both in their 20s, lost their lives when one or both of the fighter jets opened fire with machine guns and shot the Cessna down. After I learned what had happened to Tim and Stephanie, I was doubly glad that Mom was no longer involved with smuggling. Being a marijuana grower was surely a dangerous occupation from a legal perspective as anyone caught was likely to serve substantial jail time, but it wasn't fatal.

I also couldn't help but notice that it was during this period of time that Mom appeared happier and more relaxed than ever. She really enjoyed growing pot. It suited her well. That's not to say there weren't temptations. From time to time, we would be visited by Nancy, O.B., and others who approached Mom and proposed various escapades that usually revolved around some sort of marijuana dealing or smuggling, but she didn't budge. Growing was her thing. She was dedicated and had a purpose with an attainable goal in sight. Not all of her former smuggling friends were as fortunate, however.

El Loco, for one, was not faring so well. He, unlike Mom, had saved much of the money he had earned and it was burning a hole in his pocket. He rented planes and traveled aimlessly between Arizona, Florida, and Georgia, where he briefly returned home only to leave again after he felt "suffocated" by the small town. He crashed his new sports car in a ditch and just walked away, only to buy another a month later. His life was in a downward spiral.

Drugs were at the heart of it. Back when he was "on call" as a smuggling pilot, he drank and did all sorts of drugs but never let himself go completely. But now things had changed. He did any drug he could get his hands on: pot, coke, ecstasy, acid, and even heroin, which he bought from the call girls he'd begun seeing. If not for his tremendous physical and mental constitution he might have died at this time of his life. As it was, he became ever more dedicated to following the party wherever he whimsically thought to find it. That was his motivation the day he arrived at the Byrd house, high as a kite, and declared that a séance was needed so "our ghosts" could be shown the proper respect they deserved. Coincidentally, I had finished my Eagle Scout project the week before and was at Bummy and Baga's decompressing from all my work. The séance sounded like fun to me, so I decided to help.

Neither of us knew much about the ritual, so El Loco and I drove to the library and did a little research. Regrettably we did not find much helpful information, so we instead relied on what we both could remember having seen in movies. The first full moon was only two days away so we scrambled to prepare.

The Byrd house's main dining room was chosen as the ideal spot, as it had a huge table and had been the epicenter of more than a few strange happenings. Bummy spread out a dark tablecloth as El Loco and I scoured the house for candles. We drew the curtains to block any outside distractions. Pretty soon we felt as prepared as we could possibly be, yet something was still missing.

During our research, we had read that a séance would be enhanced by the presence of a relic suitable to the occasion. The book mentioned, for instance, that if one were trying to contact a deceased relative it would be desirable to have a personal possession of that person present at the séance. The relic would serve as a sort of homing beacon for the ghost to use as a guide between the spirit world and ours. Given that we had decided to go all-out with the séance I made it my mission to think of something appropriate. I brainstormed much of the following day until the perfect item came to me.

Opportunely, I had been in possession of the relic for quite some time. A short length of old rusty chain, it was an item inextricably linked to the Byrd estate in ways I could only begin to guess. I had found it one day as I was scouting the grounds of the estate, shooting arrows and imagining myself back in time as an Indian hunter or something of the sort. After one particular shot I missed my target and, not wanting to lose the arrow, began searching for it. The ground I was scouring was covered with a thick blanket of dead oak leaves and pine straw and I used my feet to shuffle and scrape the fodder away in hope of catching a glimpse of the arrow. I was on the verge of giving up when my foot hit something very hard and very heavy, so hard and heavy, in fact, that I stubbed my toe in the process. At first I thought it must be a root, but when I looked down I saw instead a circular iron plate about three feet in diameter.

The plate was quite rusty and nearly two inches thick. There were indications that something, perhaps a handle, had been attached to the top but had long since rusted off. Because it appeared to be a lid of some type my first inclination was to move it aside to see what was underneath. I tried with all my might but it wouldn't budge. My lost arrow was forgotten with the advent of this new mystery.

Later, I returned with a homemade rope leverage sling (I had taught myself the art of marlinspike seamanship while becoming an Eagle Scout) which I used to remove the plate. It turned out that it was situated on the upper rim of a fairly large underground pit. The pit was shaped like a brandy snifter and completely lined with red bricks. I shined a flashlight into the pit toward its bottom some 15 feet down but there was nothing to see but a dirt floor. Lacking anything further to explore, I decided to flip the lid over. Underneath it had four short lengths of badly rusted chain attached to a stout ring and I easily removed one of them with bolt-cutters.

The pit became the subject of much family discussion and speculation in the weeks following its discovery. It seemed everyone had an opinion. Baga and Bummy thought it had probably been used to store some kind of farm crop or commodity. Mom agreed. The storage explanation was reasonable, but I had issues with questions that remained unexplained. Why the ultra-heavy and extra-stout lid? Why did the pit have such a peculiar shape? And most of all, what were the chains used for?

I gave these questions and others a lot of consideration before I came to the opinion that what I had discovered was in fact an old pre–Civil War slave pit. It was the only explanation I could find that covered all the facts. And because slaves would reasonably have been leading anguished lives (especially any of those unfortunate enough to be thrown into such a horrid pit) and ghosts are often thought of as being discontented souls at death, I considered it was likely our haunting may involve former slaves. At the very least, I figured that the fragment of chain I'd recovered was a stark link between the present and an element of the Byrd estate's unsavory historical past. It would serve as a catalyst and become the relic for our séance.

Finally, the night of the full moon arrived. I had read that 3:15 a.m., the "witching hour," would be the most auspicious time to conduct a séance, but Baga and others complained about that late hour and threatened not to participate, so we settled on midnight. El Loco was the designated leader and I was his assistant. Besides the two of us, Baga, Blue, Mom, Richard, and a very tipsy Bummy were in attendance. We each lit a candle and placed them in front of us on the table. The chain fragment was laid at the center of the candles and the mood was suitably spooky as El Loco, who was sky high on something strong, began the séance by asking the spirits to reveal themselves.

Nothing happened.

He asked a second time. And again there was no response of any kind. A third, more impassioned plea was also met with silence. Frankly, up until the last query we had all been stone-faced serious and more than half-expectant that some disembodied voice or apparition would manifest itself. But as the candles fluttered and the silence around the table deepened, I looked around and noticed smiles growing on all our faces. Two seconds later, the room exploded with pent-up laughter that didn't abate for a solid minute. As the laughter subsided El Loco pushed his chair back and stood up.

"Now, who wants a beer?" he tentatively asked.

The laughs erupted all over again.

Whether or not the spirits of the Byrd house appreciated our attempt at a séance I cannot say, but it was a lot of fun nonetheless. We ended up playing poker till the wee hours of the morning and El Loco turned out to be the big winner. Baga continually teased me and El Loco for years afterward, calling us "Ghostbusters" years before the movie of the same name came out.

El Loco stayed on at the Byrd house several weeks that summer as he didn't have much else to do. He and I, along with Baga, went fishing nearly every day. Practically every other night or so family and friends gathered for dinner as well as the inevitable dessert, a grand game of poker. Mom, busy with her own "garden" and pleased with the way it was going, offered to give El Loco a guided tour one night. He accepted.

El Loco, dressed in dark clothing and similarly equipped with a headlight and backpack, left the next evening with Mom and Richard. As usual, they left clean and rested and returned filthy and exhausted. I had not seen Mom's crop, but judging from El Loco's enthusiastic return I could tell it must be impressive. He rambled on and on about the sheer number of marijuana plants he saw as well as their size and quality. It was obvious to me that he felt Mom was really on to something that was going to be a big success. Mom was as proud of her crop as a new mother would be of her baby.

By that time the sunflowers had reached their maximum height of around seven feet. Mom's marijuana plants were less than half that height but they were very bushy and dense. She had expertly pruned and man-icured them with the utmost care to ensure they would produce the greatest quantity of high-quality buds. When I heard El Loco ask her how many pot plants she had, she lifted her shoulders with an "I don't know" shrug, but they had to number at least a few hundred. Mom promised to save him a nice bag to sample.

Before long, the summer days began to grow shorter as autumn approached. Mom and Richard tirelessly continued the hard labor they'd begun months before. They had been in and out of the field so many times that Mom began to worry that trails were forming along their well traveled routes so she altered them to avoid possible detection. Occasionally, small planes would fly near the field and cause her to worry before they buzzed off into the horizon. On two or three occasions she saw a pickup briefly stop at the field's pump-house, the farmer probably checking on the irrigation system, but it soon moved on. She constantly kept an eye out for any other sign that the farmer had been back to tend his crop in any way that required going into the heart of the field but found none. As the days passed, Mom became ever more optimistic about her eventual success and even started thinking about the next crop and what possibilities it might bring.

"You could move here and we could grow two or three times more," I heard her tell Nancy on the phone one day. "Come down and see Momma and Daddy and I'll show you everything. You'll love it!"

Well, I'm sure Aunt Nancy would love the pot Mom was growing, but I wasn't so sure she was cut out to be a grower. For one thing, Nancy was more of a city girl than a country bumpkin. She just wasn't the outdoorsy type. Also, the small talk many country people appreciated was not something she would be able to tolerate for long. Privacy was the cornerstone of her life as a dealer. She would have stuck out like a sore thumb in the sticks of north Florida. No, I felt sure she would not be coming to join the growing operation, but she would be there to help sell the marijuana that Mom assured her was coming soon.

Spurred by the shortening daylight, the marijuana plants were producing gorgeous buds. From time to time Mom clipped a small bud as a sample and found it more than satisfactory. Like a virtuoso musician who had just written a hit song, she knew she had knocked the ball out of the park. It was an exciting time, for the harvest was close. Sweet success was only a few weeks away. Mom and Richard were on cloud nine with anticipation.

Then, one night as they arrived to work on their crop, Mom noticed something new, and not in a good way. The first plants she encountered appeared a little limp and had lost a few of their leaves as well. This in itself was not catastrophic as she knew there were multiple things that could cause such symptoms, but when more plants exhibited the same issues her worry grew. However, plenty of others appeared fine and her worry dissipated. They finished work late that night and collapsed in bed, utterly spent.

The next evening was a nightmare. Mom could hardly believe her eyes. There was clearly something horribly wrong with her precious crop. More than three-quarters of the plants were dead or dying, the primary symptom being the loss of their leaves and fledgling buds. More ominously, the sunflowers were suffering far worse than the marijuana. Most had lost all their foliage, leaving nothing but the stalk with a large flower head perched atop. Mom diligently searched for an answer to the problem. Frustrated, she checked soil pH and looked for signs of insect infestation but found no indications of anything amiss. She and Richard returned to the Byrd house that night deeply troubled. For the second time in her life she had lost a beautiful marijuana crop. It was disheartening to think of all the hard work that had been invested only to be met with failure so close to the ultimate victory.

It was clear just by viewing the field from the road the following morning that the once fabulous marijuana crop had now become a total loss. Richard shook his head and raged against nothing in particular. Mom bowed her head and silently wept. Their relationship couldn't weather the failure and they broke up soon after.

The mystery of the crop's demise was solved by Baga only a few days later. After talking with a local farming couple he learned that sunflowers were commonly aerially sprayed with the defoliant Parquat a few weeks before harvest to make the flower heads more accessible to the harvester combines. Knowing what had occurred did not make it any easier for Mom to accept the horrendous outcome. I felt very sorry for her.

One thing I knew: the loss signaled a change was coming, I was sure of it. Mom was not the type to accept defeat. And when Aunt Nancy heard what had happened, she insisted that Mom make a reconnaissance trip to a little Caribbean island she had heard good things about. She even offered to pay. Never one to say no to an opportunity, Mom, with me and Melanie in tow, left for parts unknown before there was even much time to think about it.

Adventure had called. And as usual, for better or worse, we answered.

7

Jammin' in Jamaica

Mom loved Jamaica from the first time she ever laid eyes on it. For one thing, Jamaica was green, deep green, and warm. Those were two attributes that mattered the most. I think that Mom always measured a place by how well she felt she could grow a garden there. By a "garden," I of course am talking about a marijuana garden. But we had just arrived in Jamaica and that meant there was no need for Mom to grow her own. There were plenty of marijuana plantations in Jamaica already in full swing, especially in the Blue Mountain region.

The flight from Miami International to Montego Bay was mercifully uneventful given the collective flying experience of Mom and me. My sister Melanie was, as usual, relaxed about air travel. The landing approach into Montego Bay required the Boeing 737 to execute a steep bank prior to descending low over the bay to touch down only yards from the water. Minutes later as I was strolling and stretching my flight-stiff legs I met my first Jamaican. He was a young smiling guy in his 20s, dressed American-style in jeans and tennis shoes.

"Hey, mon," he greeted me, approaching fast, as my long legs were eating up the ground and I would have blown by him in seconds, "I like your boots, how much." His voice carried a hint of an English accent mixed with characteristic Jamaican patois. He glanced down at my boots, then directly up into my eyes. "I'm Wayne," he declared, holding out his right hand.

"David Michael." I extended my hand and we shook. He looked down at my boots again, this time with obvious admiration. They weren't anything special, typical Frye cowboy-style boots, plain brown, not too old or badly worn, but far from new. I looked down as if I were seeing them for the first time.

"Oh, these? They're not for sale. Only pair I have." I smiled my

Mom in Jamaica, ca. 1979.

widest 15-year-old grin, wondering why anyone would be interested in my rather scruffy boots.

Wayne immediately sensed that I was off balance and went in for the kill.

"Ya like horses, mon?" he asked. "Yeah, I sure do!" I replied. And I knew he had me then. I loved everything about horses and I'm sure my eyes gave it away.

"I have many horses, very nice horses. For your boots, ya can ride any of my horses as long as ya like for as long as ya here. Okay?" He was clearly trying to make a deal and intently serious. I wasn't crazy about the idea of trading my boots, but the idea of unlimited horseback riding was appealing. I wasn't sure how long I would be in Jamaica, but suddenly a trade seemed like the right decision.

"Okay. You got a deal!" I stepped over to the nearest bench and whipped off my boots in five seconds flat. Wayne swiftly sat down, tore off his sneakers, and slipped my boots on. He was on cloud nine and couldn't take his eyes off his new boots. And he must have had a good eye, because they were a close fit from what I could tell.

Three minutes later, after another parting handshake and a zillion "thanks" from Wayne, I found myself standing in my socks holding a scrap of paper that contained the address of Wayne's stable. His family's stable, actually. For a brief instant I wondered if I'd been swindled, but pushed the thought out of my mind. I had been warned that certain goods were not readily available in Jamaica and I figured boots must be hard to come by, so the trade was mutually beneficial. Besides, I felt I had made a friend.

I donned the sneakers I had packed as backup and they felt just fine as the filthy little taxi we had hired at the airport queue sped along a narrow potholed road at breakneck speed, heading toward a location

I only heard referred to as "Mockingbird Hill." The driver made small talk and barely kept his eyes on the road, preferring to ogle Mom's cleavage instead. Traveling like the English on the left side of the road was a bit disconcerting, but what seemed worse was the apparent lack of road signs or traffic signals. Montego Bay was like a ramshackle circus crossed with a smelly, overcrowded flea market. Yet when we finally cleared the city limits and crossed the American River on an ancient-looking rusted trestle bridge, the best parts of Jamaica were revealed.

Dense tropical foliage grew up the mountainside on our left as lesser scrub sloped down to the edge of the bay on our right. The road itself seemed just a thin ribbon of crumbly pavement clinging to the mountainside. The air that had felt warm and thick at the airport now enveloped me like an invisible fleece sweater. I was dripping, but didn't have long to contemplate Jamaican weather before our driver downshifted abruptly and whipped his little death-trap of a car in a sharp turn down a jungle-shrouded driveway I hadn't even seen from the main road.

"Mockingbird Hill," he announced with so much glee it was like he owned the place.

I still did not see anything but jungle as we steadily wound our way up a corkscrew driveway, climbing gradually for about half a mile until we neared the top of a large hill, then rounded another hairpin turn and entered a large clearing which flanked an even larger courtyard that was the central feature of an expansive hilltop ranch-style estate. It was magnificent, with views of the mountains as well as Montego Bay and the open Caribbean Sea beyond.

We creaked to a stop near the double front doors of the largest building and were instantly and warmly greeted upon exiting the cab by the estate's live-in staff, which was headed by a 40-something husband-and-wife team. Roy, with a kind face, craggly teeth and open smile, functioned as butler, chauffeur, and all-around gofer. Geneva, corpulent and giggly, was the estate's food-shopper and cook. Everyone shook hands and introductions were made against the background cacophony of birdsong and insect buzz I was just beginning to notice now that the car was silenced. It took me all of five seconds to decide I liked both of them. Geneva stepped over to help Mom with her bags while Roy helped Melanie with hers and proceeded to show us to our rooms.

The estate was fit for a king, and that was not much of a surprise considering that it was originally owned by a partner of the Jack Daniels Whiskey Company. Mom had rented it (rather cheaply too) for the duration of our stay in Jamaica. My bedroom, complete with an expansive adjoining private bathroom, was large and airy with immaculately white cool marble floors and quadruple French doors that opened onto a private veranda overlooking a manicured garden as foreground to the bay. After I took a refreshing shower it was dinnertime, and before long there was a knock at my door. Roy showed me the way to the dining room.

The dining room's walls were nearly all glass panels, floor to ceiling, which allowed a diner, no matter where he or she was seated, practically unobstructed views of the grounds, mountains, and bay. A massive mango tree shaded and dominated one view. Mountains interposed with the sea, another. On the table was a smorgasbord of Jamaican fare. There was jerk chicken and curried beef, fried breadfruit and plantains and small fried fish complete with their heads intact and staring eyeballs. There were so many unknown vegetable dishes I simply didn't know where to begin, so I used my fork to spear a sample of the nearest dish and, holding it up for display, asked Roy what it was.

"Ackee," he stated matter-of-factly.

The fruit, ackee, which bore a strong resemblance in looks and taste to scrambled eggs, was just one of the many exotic foods that I would encounter during my stay in Jamaica. It grew wild in pod-like clusters on medium-size trees throughout the country and was a favorite staple of most Jamaicans. Oddly, it was poisonous to humans until its pods opened naturally when they became ripe and the large, shiny ebony seed at the end of each pod was removed. Ackee was almost always served sautéed with onions and tomatoes and soon became one of my favorite dishes. Still, strange foods were just the beginning, for as usual it was not long before Mom started mingling with the locals and began inviting them up to Mockingbird Hill.

The most crucial of her new friends was a young, slightly-built Rastafarian called Desi. Desi had a perpetual smile and laughed easily. I can't remember ever seeing him down about anything. Like most Rastas, he covered his dreadlocks with a colorful stocking cap. He had approached Mom in town one afternoon as she was shopping and offered to sell her a small bag of "ganja" (marijuana) which she quickly accepted. Its quality was excellent by anyone's standards, and Mom's standards for pot were quite high. She asked Desi if he could get more and he immediately said yes, probably thinking she wanted another small bag like most tourists, but she asked, "How much more?"

Mom's question evidently didn't give Desi as much pause as it would have given someone in another country such as the United States at that time, with strict anti-marijuana laws and severe penalties for even relatively small violations. Although the possession and sale of marijuana was illegal in Jamaica, law enforcement correctly considered it endemic to the country and embedded within its culture. Possession of marijuana was most commonly dismissed with an "on-the-spot" bribe, and even larger violations were often dealt with through payoffs to authorities. Desi was indeed just a small-time street dealer, but he knew bigger fish. One of the biggest of these was a man he referred to only as "Rock." Desi wasted little time before bringing him up the "Hill" to meet Mom.

Rock's real name, never used in all the time I knew him, was Cleveland Roger. He was a tall, bearded, 40-something Rastafarian who was made even taller by the towering mass of dreadlocks he kept piled under a multi-colored green-black-gold stocking cap atop his head. When he spoke, his eyes unfailingly focused directly on his subject, regardless of the situation or any superfluous distractions. He exuded an undeniable charisma when he spoke, but I think that was due to the quality and tone of his voice more than the actual words he used, for his voice was extraordinarily deep and resonant. It reminded me a lot of the voice of actor James Earl Jones.

The first thing he did after being escorted into the great room at Mockingbird Hill was to produce a small bag of ganja and roll the most massive marijuana cigarette I had ever seen. It was in the shape of a club, large and blunt on one end and tapered to a point on the other. I did not smoke—in fact had never so much as tried a single puff of pot— but I had seen tons of the stuff by then, and plenty of joints. But this monstrosity was on an entirely new scale altogether. Rock called his creation a "spliff," which he pronounced more like "spleef."

While Mom, Rock, and Desi smoked the humungous spliff, I put some music on the record player. The estate had a decent collection of albums which included an artist I had not heard much before, Bob Marley, and his band, the Wailers. I thought reggae music was great and it really seemed to gel with the laid-back Jamaican lifestyle. As was my habit by this time, I continued to hang around the adults, listening to the conversation and keeping quiet for the most part. And their talk mostly consisted of—what else?—Mom's favorite subject, marijuana.

They quickly got around to the fact that Rock, a well-connected and trusted senior Rasta with his own posse, could supply just about all the marijuana Mom could ever want. He explained that the pot was primarily grown in eastern Jamaica's Blue Mountains, an area of some 350 square miles centered between Jamaica's capital, Kingston, to the southwest, and Port Antonio on the country's northeast coast. This was a rugged and remote area, lawless by default. Most importantly, the soil and climate were perfect for growing high-grade marijuana. Rock promised to take Mom there soon and show her around.

Before the month was out, Mom and Rock had made several trips to the Blue Mountains, where she had joyfully sampled various strains of marijuana, seen multiple grow sites and made a few more friends. One amiable fellow, whose handle was "Shorty," was particularly proud of his farm and for good reason. An expert grower, he had been farming pot for years and many of his plants were generations upon generations old and produced a superior grade of marijuana the Rastas called "Lamb's Bread." Time after time I heard people who tried it gush with enthusiastic praise because of its smooth taste, sweet aroma, and mind-blowing euphoric high. More about this later.

Mom saw the possibilities and, in her typical style, she focused on the positives and pretty much ignored the negatives. Here was a plentiful supply of high-quality weed that could be bought cheaply. In fact, Mom found that the Jamaicans were willing to front a significant portion of the first planeload of ganja for just a token amount of up-front cash. A few thousand U.S. dollars spread out among a handful of Rastas went a long way in securing the source for Mom. What sealed the deal for good was when Mom arranged, with Nancy's help in Florida, to buy an elaborate, state-of-the-art hi-fi stereo system for Rock. They agreed that a large portion of his initial payment would be covered by that single trade. Beyond a doubt, it was a spectacular high-end system worthy of a professional audiophile with dual turntables, graphic equalizers and amplifiers, and a half-dozen massive three-way speakers with sub-woofers. My musical background and live sound reinforcement experience came in handy as I helped with the setup. Rock had wanted one for years but they were simply unavailable at the time in Jamaica for any price.

One of the hurdles Mom made light of was the actual transport of the marijuana out of Jamaica. It was a given that she would utilize small planes as the Arizona–Mexico operation had, since their smaller radar signatures and flight economy would be more crucial when facing ever-increasing law enforcement challenges, but now there was a much greater distance to overcome and much of the flight path would be over water. Florida was the obvious destination of choice, but the trip would not be as short as it appeared. Sure, the mainland coast of Florida was only about 500 miles from the coast of Jamaica as the crow flies, but taking into account the extra distance that must be flown inland to the actual airstrips added a minimum of a few hundred more miles. Adding even more distance to the trip was the absolute necessity of flying around, and not over, Cuba. Unauthorized aircraft in Cuban airspace could be shot down. Longer distances meant more fuel would be required.

Besides the fuel issue, adequate Jamaican airstrips were an issue, and again, this factor proved to be more problematic than its counterpart in the Arizona–Mexico operation. Unlike the topography in southern Arizona and northern Mexico, which offered many remote areas of level open land ideal for landing planes, Jamaica was riddled with hills, streams, and large vegetation, especially in the mountainous region close to the grow sites. A suitable glade or clearing would need to be found and many of these valuable tracts were already being utilized by farmers for agricultural purposes. Maybe some cash would grease the wheels?

Mom, never one to delegate tasks, did however realize the need to bring help to deal with some of the logistics. While El Loco, as Mom's chief pilot, worked on certain problems from the Florida end, a real character, invited by Mom, showed up at Mockingbird Hill one stormy afternoon and I never saw him coming.

He and Mom had met months before when they had been introduced by a mutual friend they both trusted. His name was Greg Kiljoy. Tall, strawberry-blond, blue-eyed, big-boned and kind of brash, Greg presented a smiling, swashbuckling braggadocio that at first take masqueraded as extreme confidence but later seemed to me to be the defense mechanism of someone a bit insecure. Seconds after Roy ushered him through the front door, Greg was hugging Mom, pumping my hand in an energetic handshake, and telling a joke. And he was funny! He had a witty, sarcastic way about him that was charming as well as disarming.

Initially, I couldn't really tell much of the time whether he was serious about what he was saying or just kidding. Mom later that night told me he was a pilot and was in Jamaica to help. That may have been the case, but it was easy for me to see that Mom was infatuated with Greg and they already had an intimate relationship well underway.

Over the ensuing days and weeks, as Mom and Greg spent most of their time like a couple on vacation, I got to know Greg better and really came to like him. He was smart, quick to laugh, and often self-effacing. However, his skill as a pilot remained unclear.

He and Mom, guided by Rock, concentrated on scouting a suitable landing strip, preferably two, in case a backup was needed. They eventually located a remote site that had been shown to Rock by a fellow Rasta. Nestled in an elevated secluded valley in the foothills of the Blue Mountains was a natural clearing that only required some rock removal and a fair amount of smallish scrub to be cut and burned. It was nearly perfect; its only drawback was the fact it was somewhat on the short side. There was always give and take regarding airplanes and their operating logistics, and takeoff distance versus payload capacity was a biggie. Larger planes had more capacity for fuel and cargo but needed a longer runway. Smaller planes could squeeze onto shorter strips but lacked the necessary range for this operation. Still, a strip had been secured. It must be made to work. Again, Mom marched on boldly and didn't dwell on negative details. Greg tagged along.

Meanwhile, El Loco, with Baga's valuable assistance, sorted out the range issue over the kitchen table at Baga's house. They devised a plan that would extend the flying range of Mom's twin-engine Aztec to enable it to fly its clandestine route to and from Jamaica, fully-loaded, and equipped with a survival liferaft to boot. Together, they drew up an impromptu diagram that also listed particular design and performance requirements the missions would require, such as making sure any new switches and monitoring gauges be located in the cockpit close enough for a solo pilot to operate. For quite awhile it seemed they were contemplating doing all the work themselves, but when Mom heard about it she insisted the job be done professionally. She thought it would arouse no undue suspicion if they could manufacture a believable cover story for the modifications. Together they came up with one. El Loco was satisfied.

"It'll work, no problem." He stated this emphatically, with confidence.

Baga glared down at the crude diagram. "Bubble gum and bailing wire."

Baga didn't care for what he termed "eyeball engineering"—determining something worked based on its appearance. El Loco operated on guts. If it felt right, it was right. Two different styles, but they complimented each other. El Loco respected Baga. And Baga had learned, little by little and step by step, to respect El Loco. After all, El Loco had guts and proven flying skill. A potent combination.

"It's your life." Baga snapped the folder shut for emphasis. EL Loco stood impassive. He smiled.

"I'll take it nice and easy, like a walk in the park." El Loco was methodical and had faith in his preparations. He would oversee the fabrication of the entire long-range fueling apparatus himself. Other than that it was just a matter of self-confidence.

Meanwhile, down in Jamaica, Mom and Greg were still partying and occasionally discussing a few of the critical details. Mom as usual was the eternal optimist.

They calculated that the plane, a twin-engine Aztec, could transport two thousand pounds of pot per trip, with due consideration to all the variables, namely fuel, weather, and distance. Rock assured her he would be ready with the two grades of marijuana that would comprise each load. Around 1,500 to 1,700 pounds would be decent quality "commercial grade" Jamaican ganja. By United States standards as compared with much of the marijuana that was coming into the country via Mexico, Central America, and Colombia, this was some very nice marijuana indeed. I can't attest to this personally, but I distinctly remember the smiles on the faces of everyone I saw smoking

Mom and El Loco during the Jamaican smuggling operation, ca. 1980.

it. The other variety—"Lamb's Bread"—was on an entirely different level altogether. Mom and the others had tried some when they met Shorty, but didn't get the whole story. I will explain.

Lamb's Bread was the premier quality Rastafarian marijuana. This was the ganja that assumed an almost quasi-religious status and was smoked by headmen exclusively and others on special celebratory occasions only. Translucent green shot with golden-reddish hues and no seeds, the buds infused a room with a heady, sweet and pungent aroma even before a spliff was lit. Was it strong? Well, I remember seeing several experienced pot smokers sharing a single joint of this marijuana and not finishing half of it. After convincing Shorty to relinquish some of his prized stock, Rock agreed to supply Mom with around 200 pounds of Lamb's Bread per trip. This was a major coup for Mom. The supply was now in place. Meanwhile, life continued Jamaican-style, back on the Hill.

I was strumming my favorite guitar and jamming with Mockingbird Hill's live-in gardener, Mitchell, when Rock showed up in his VW van one afternoon not long after the first components of his stereo system had begun to arrive. Mitchell, 64 years old with the physique of a 30-year-old athlete, was showing me how to play a Jamaican favorite, "Yellow Bird." Great fun! Mitchell was a natural guitar player and singer and his style was open and unassuming. The strings on his guitar looked about a thousand years old—musical accessories were another rare item in Jamaica. I had a few extra sets with me and gave him one. I imagine he still has them.

"Sounding good, mon," Rock rumbled in his rich bass tone as he stomped a few steps of an impromptu dance. Mitchell and I hit the chorus of the song with gusto. *Yellow bird, high up in banana tree…. Yellow bird, high up in banana tree.*

Rock's gaze caught my eye. "David Michael, would you like to see Rose Hall?" I immediately stopped playing. "I'm going by today, if you want to come."

I jumped at the opportunity, for I had heard that, much like Bummy and Baga's Byrd house, Rose Hall, a magnificent 18th-century plantation estate just outside Montego Bay on Jamaica's northern coast, was haunted. The legend centered on a woman named Annie Palmer, born to English-Irish parents, who was raised in Haiti and taught voodoo by her childhood nanny. After the death of her parents she later moved to

Jamaica and married the owner of Rose Hall, John Palmer. Years later, she murdered John and two more husbands before finally being murdered herself by one of her slaves. Jamaican folklore dubbed her the "White Witch of Rose Hall." Legend has it that she haunts the home and grounds of Rose Hall to this day.

Riding along in the passenger seat of Rock's van on the way to Rose Hall, I decided it was time for some tunes to accompany our little trip. Rock had a small collection of 8-track tapes he kept in a shoebox between the seats and I soon found what I was looking for. Bob Marley and the Wailers, cranked to the max, began to work their magic with "Jammin."

Rock fired up his ever-present spliff as we swayed to the beat, gazing over the expansive view of shimmering Montego Bay. Life was good and I had made some new friends. Excitement was in the air. I was truly jammin' in Jamaica.

8

"We jammin', yah?"

Rock ceremoniously flipped the last switch in the row. The entire rack, consisting of nearly six vertical feet of dials, switches, and sliders, lit up like some futuristic Christmas tree. His eyes expanded in wonder.

"Okay," I said, pointing to the sliders. "Now, slowly turn the volume up a third."

Rock was beaming ear-to-ear as he reached for the console and steadily raised the volume to three. The music was loud, crisp, and defined. Trebles had bite and the bass thundered and I could not hear even a hint of distortion. Rock, his fingers still on the slider, began to sway a little to the music. I rubbed my hands together in anticipation. "All right, let's see what it can do. Bring it slowly up to nine."

Rock steadily pushed the slider up. As he did, the music morphed from something I merely heard into something I felt resonating deep inside my chest. Rock obviously felt it too, as he abandoned the console and began a slow shuffling victory dance around his living room, head thrown back and both arms raised high, delirious with joy. Despite the unbelievable sound pressure, the music remained clear and undistorted and sounded like we were at a live concert. The only thing missing was the crowd.

Rock and I had just finished the final tweaking of his new hi-fi stereo system and I was giving him a little advice on its overall operation since he had never even seen such an extravagant rig in person, much less operated one. Today was the culmination of much planning and a lot of detailed effort. It had taken several weeks for all the different pieces to arrive in Jamaica and clear customs, then a couple more days to set up and integrate all the various components. Looking back, I'm sure Rock's rig had to be one of the best personal stereo systems in all of Jamaica, or "Jamrock," as many Jamaicans called their country at the time.

As I started to hedge my way over to where Rock was celebrating, his wife and a couple giggling kids entered the room and started dancing. The high fidelity music seemed to have a life of its own and held everyone who heard it in a thrall, including me. When I finally reached Rock he bent down to bellow something in my ear but I couldn't catch what he said over the loud music. He cupped his hands together and tried again, this time giving it all he had.

"We jammin', yah?"

Nodding, I smiled broadly and held two thumbs up, then slapped his waiting hand a high five. Rock wasn't a musician, but he really loved music and often expressed himself in musical terms. I got it. He was jammin', and in more ways than one. The pure music blossoming from the speakers was an undeniable force, but even more significantly, the first trip had been completed successfully the previous week and Rock was super stoked about the future, although that's not to say there weren't some hairy situations that had to be dealt with along the way.

To get the operation up and running required a team effort. There had been a multitude of details to work out and for awhile it seemed doubtful that anything would be ready by the tentative date that had been set. Thankfully, Mom resisted the urge to try to accomplish everything herself and delegated most of the work. El Loco, with Baga's and Greg's help, made sure the plane was ready and began studying weather patterns between Jamaica and Florida and

Boy Scout David Michael at the height of the Jamaican smuggling operation, ca. 1979.

meticulously planned the route and timed each leg to coincide with the most favorable times of transit. Stateside, O.B. brought his younger brother Gary onboard as the lead catchman and, along with a trusted friend, Herman, located primary and secondary catch sites, after which they remained on-call and ready. For her part, Mom, at Rock's suggestion, decided to inspect the first load to make sure everything was perfect. So, with nearly everything in place, Mom made her way to the Blue Mountain grow site where the first load was waiting.

They started the trek early, for the route to the clandestine Rastafarian enclave was a narrow and tortuous trail that twisted through the Jamaican bush for miles as it climbed steeply towards its destination. Anyone unfamiliar with the area would have had little chance of not becoming hopelessly lost in short order, as the trail had numerous twists and turns and occasionally forked, offering a false trail that led to nowhere but a dead end. Her guide, an ancient and shriveled little Rastaman everyone called the "Donkey Man" because of his scraggly, big-eared mount, hummed a tune to himself as he unerringly led her and two other Rastas on the exhausting three-hour trek to the sacred Lamb's Bread plots.

It was a particularly beautiful morning as they set out on the journey; the air was crisp and still, the scenery breathtaking. Mom could hardly believe the flora and fauna that surrounded her. Everywhere she gazed was evidence that here was a place that nurtured and glorified life in a million forms. Exotic birds with unusual plumage and strange voices fluttered here and there, oblivious to the trespassers. The bush was so dense it seemed to rise up from the side of the trail to form a kind of tunnel that restricted a traveler's line of site to just a few yards. This might have been confining if it weren't for the natural clearings they encountered from time to time along the way. And after rounding a particularly sharp bend in the path Mom stumbled upon one and was treated to a sight she would never forget.

The remote clearing was bathed in early morning sunshine that reflected off the dewy grass. But what was most remarkable were the thousands upon thousands of tiny spider webs that clung to the grass, each strand of which was beaded with silvery dewdrops that danced in the light like living beings. The sight caused Mom to freeze in her tracks, mesmerized. After what seemed like forever, but must have been only a minute, she took a deep breath and hurried on to catch up with her companions. She was glad Donkey Man was on island time and therefore in no hurry.

Donkey Man spoke little and kept to himself for the most part, apparently content to hum and mutter a word or two of encouragement to his donkey, usually when it paused to nibble on tender grasses at the trail's edge. As the strange little party had already passed several seemingly suitable growing locations that were obviously much closer and therefore more conveniently located than where they were now headed, Mom couldn't help but wonder why they were not being used, so she decided to ask. The elder of the two Rastas told her the Lamb's Bread had to be grown apart from other plants.

Mom, an accomplished marijuana grower herself, knew what they meant. The grow site where she was being taken was one where Shorty and his men cultivated the special Lamb's Bread ganja. These sites were kept isolated and separated from the other marijuana for the express purpose of preventing cross pollination, for if female plants were pollinated they would develop seeds and no longer be sinsemilla (without seeds). It was an essential precaution. The vastness of the bush she'd been traversing the past few hours did not seem to be overcrowded with marijuana farms, but it was hard for Mom to tell and the Rastas obviously had inside information. She continued to absorb her surroundings like a sponge as they pressed on toward their destination.

They arrived at the grow site around noon and Mom was offered an indigenous stew of homemade dumplings for lunch and then shared a joint with Shorty and his headman as she was shown generations-old marijuana plants that towered above even the tallest man. Many appeared stout enough to climb. There were drying racks with ganja buds a foot long hanging from them as well as other pot already baled and waiting for delivery. It was by far the most magnificent marijuana she had ever seen or smoked. With high hopes and her ever-present can-do attitude, she made the final arrangements for the load that afternoon. Later that evening Shorty threw an impromptu party at his place to celebrate. Mom spent the night there, staying up late with Shorty and his wife talking about the success they all envisioned.

The date of the first trip had been chosen to coincide with a favorable weather window that was fast approaching and that was only one of many variables to consider. There were just so many things that could go wrong. In light of that, Mom felt that she should be on-site when El

Loco arrived to pick up the load the following morning, so, with that goal in mind, she had just enough time to return to town, make a few calls, and pick up a change of clothes before heading to the strip which entailed a journey almost as arduous as the one she had endured with Donkey Man the day before. Yet Mom was dedicated to see it through and arrived at the small clearing adjacent to the strip just before nightfall. She was fairly surprised to find that there was not much there besides a rough runway, a few fuel barrels, and a sizeable stack of baled marijuana waiting to be loaded. Since there were no other accommodations and she wanted to avoid sleeping on the ground because of snakes or other vermin, she pulled her blouse close around her shoulders and slept on the bales of pot. She was so excited that sleep was nearly impossible.

When Mom woke the next morning before sunrise the jungle air was saturated with moisture and her clothing clung to her uncomfortably. A Rasta offered her some excellent coffee (the region was famous for its coffee) and she smoked a cigarette as she became fully awake. Then, as the dark sky began to gradually lighten with the impending sunrise, she noticed that a thick fog bank covered the entire area. How high it reached was anybody's guess. Right away she knew the entire trip was in serious danger, for fog could prevent El Loco from being able to find the airstrip and make landing exceedingly dangerous, if not impossible. She also knew that it was likely the plane did not have enough fuel to fly on to an alternate landing site. It was a do or die situation. Even as she pondered the problem and said a silent prayer she began to hear the sound of a small plane approaching. Her worry grew as the buzz of the plane grew louder and more distinct. El Loco had arrived! But could he find the tiny airstrip in the dense fog? She hoped so.

Five minutes later it was clear to her that the fog had prevented El Loco from finding the strip, for she could hear the plane circling overhead in a vain attempt to catch at least a glimpse of the strip. Making matters worse, she knew that there was not enough fuel to circle much longer and any attempt to land blind would be a disaster. Something had to be done, but what? Mom, near full-panic mode, clutched the crucifix she wore around her neck and prayed aloud for an answer, and then, mercifully, one came.

Heedless of the several burly Rastas that were standing by to help refuel and load the plane, Mom boldly whipped off her blouse (the only thing she could think of that was both flammable and dry) and used her cigarette lighter to set it on fire. Once it was burning, she carefully set it on the ground and gently began to fan the flames higher. Despite all her efforts the fire remained stubbornly small, but because of the cotton-polyester blend of the fabric it was quite smoky and fortunately that was what mattered. As Mom stared skyward, jumping and waving with her breasts threatening to burst out of the skimpy bra, a lone tendril of smoke snaked skyward through the fog. For the third time that morning, she muttered a hurried prayer and hoped for the best.

Meanwhile, El Loco, circling overhead in a plane running on fumes, had said more than a few prayers of his own. And to his credit he had stoically maintained his aerial vigil even as he knew the situation was probably hopeless. He knew damn well that time was running out and told himself that he would continue circling for another five minutes (the maximum time he felt he had to gamble with) before descending lower to attempt a landing while he still had running engines to do so. Maybe the fog would clear closer to ground level and allow him to quickly locate the strip before he crashed. It was the best he could hope for and he had resigned himself to that course of action when he noticed a tiny smidgen of blue-black smoke rising from the fog below. Was it meant for him? He swiftly decided he had no choice but to go for it and find out.

El Loco throttled back, lowered his flaps and descended blindly into the fog where he thought he had seen the smoke, not knowing if he was flying straight into a mountainside or not. If there was trouble below he would have little time to avoid it. For the better part of an interminable minute he flew utterly blind, descending fast. Then, miraculously, he broke through the lower level of the fog bank to see the strip not far below. He banked sharply and brought the Aztec in for one of his picture perfect landings.

A much relieved El Loco taxied to a stop and killed the engines. The experience he had just endured had taken a heavy toll and he paused in the cockpit for a moment to collect his wits. When he swung open the hatch and jumped to the ground the first thing he saw was Mom, half-naked and running toward him with her arms open. She was giddy with relief as they hugged and laughed like children arriving at Disneyland.

"Thanks for the smoke!" El Loco exclaimed, shifting from foot to foot with nervous energy. "Couldn't see a thing from up there. I was on my last leg."

Mom laughed some more as she led him by the hand over to where her blouse still smoldered. She pointed down.

"My blouse," she said through a few more chuckles of relief.

"A new one's on me," El Loco replied between laughs.

The Rastas had cautiously approached the pair during their mini-reunion and that brought Mom back down to Earth. She gave them the go-ahead to get the plane loaded and refueled which they accomplished with a few words of direction from El Loco. He was eager to get airborne as soon as they finished, but decided to wait a few extra minutes as the rising sun burned off the fog. At last he declared it was clear enough to depart and with handshakes for the Rastas and a big hug and a "Be careful and God bless!" from Mom he climbed back aboard the plane and was off once again. The powerful engines revved high and Mom said yet another prayer as the now heavily-laden plane barely cleared the trees at the end of the runway and climbed out of sight. She knew she had given everything her best shot and it was all out of her hands now. What a relief! Hours later back at Mockingbird Hill she received a call telling her that the load was secure at the safe house in north Florida. The inaugural trip from Jamaica was a success! Now it was just a matter of getting the load sold.

Nancy was slated to broker the sale of the majority of the load and considering its quality she felt that should not be too much of a problem. The balance of the load, some 300 pounds of commercial and 100 pounds of Lamb's Bread, was going to be handled through a new and experienced connection from the New Jersey area, Jeannie Tumulty. Jeannie was ten years older than Mom, heavyset with short bleach-blonde hair, and reputedly had ties to the Italian mafia. Her subordinate business partner and sometime lover, John Parella, often accompanied her and was present when the three first met in Florida not long after the arrival of the initial load. Mom and Jeannie hit it off okay and that was all there was to it. They were both strong-minded women struggling to make it in a business heavily dominated by men and their male egos. John was introduced, but other than that didn't have much to say. At the time, Mom had the impression that John was Jeannie's "muscle," a glorified gofer and not much else. There was talk that John himself was

Jeannie's mafia connection and he certainly fit the bill, but it was anybody's guess.

When I met Jeannie, she was friendly and had an easygoing attitude that reminded me of someone's grandmother. She just didn't seem to fit the role she played. However, John was another story. With his salt and pepper hair and a Fu-Manchu mustache, he had a disconcerting way of avoiding direct eye contact for any meaningful length of time. That, coupled with his verbal reticence, led many people he met to avoid his company. Mom's catch man Gary was an exception.

Even though Jeannie and John rarely interacted with anyone in Mom's organization, Gary hung around with John every chance he got. The times I saw them together their relationship struck me as that of one between a master and his pupil, John being the master and Gary his ever-eager-to-please pupil. Their relationship seemed strange to me, but it was none of my business and I did my best to keep it that way.

One notable hiccup in those first early days of Mom's Jamaican operation revealed how relatively inexperienced the Jamaicans were in the marijuana trade at the time. When buyers first laid eyes on the Lamb's Bread (all wrapped up in smiley face paper) they were decidedly unimpressed and unwilling to pay anywhere near top dollar for the premium weed. This was because the Rastas had neglected to manicure their ganja to the standards most U.S. marijuana dealers expected of high-grade pot. The buds were minimally trimmed and sloppily packaged and quite a bit of that first load was sold at near giveaway prices as a consequence. More than a few deals were made where this ultra-primo ganja sold for just a few hundred dollars a pound! Thankfully, once buyers and their customers actually smoked the mediocre-appearing marijuana they were absolutely blown away by its quality and couldn't wait to get more.

With the first trip now a bona-fide success, Mom really got down to business and let the momentum build. Rock and his Rastas were gung-ho and ready. Nancy and Jeannie had customers lined up and waiting. El Loco was a new man now that he was flying with a purpose again and swore he'd be able to undertake as many trips as needed and as often as necessary. Bonnie was on hand to transport cash to wherever it was needed. Gary and Herman were geared up and playing cards at the safe house in anticipation of getting a call to catch a load. And Baga was standing by stateside to keep an eye on things and see to it that no one ran astray and nothing went amiss. Mom saw the green light and stepped on the gas.

Several trips were summarily planned and executed in quick succession and once again Mom was riding high on a wave of success. Money poured in so fast there was no way to spend even a fraction of it, and let me tell you, she definitely tried. And when spending money for its own sake became boring, Mom tended to give it away. This often happened in the form of bonuses to her associates, which Baga thought was foolish in light of the crazy amounts of money everyone was earning.

"Why does he need an extra $10,000?" he asked in exasperation one morning after he saw Mom give Herman a bonus the prior evening.

Rock in Jamaica preparing a classic Rastafarian ganja remedy, ca. 1979.

"Oh Daddy, he deserves it," she replied with a smile. Then came the line I heard Baga repeat over the years to his daughters, though to no one more than Mom.

"A fool and her money are soon parted."

I'd heard the proverb many times before and considered it wise and probably quite true. Mom had surely squandered a small fortune already and had bought countless useless trinkets for no good reason whatsoever, but I saw Mom part with money in other ways I thought were particularly generous and kindhearted.

For example, one afternoon Melanie accidentally ran over and killed a small pig while practicing driving on the long private driveway that led up to Mockingbird Hill. I saw that it was not her fault, as the pig ran out in front of her without warning and shouldn't have been on the road in the first place. Later that evening two impoverished and scraggly-looking Jamaicans hiked up the Hill, examined the pig, and then claimed it as their own, after which they brought its rather spare corpse to our door and asked to be compensated for the loss. Mom took one look at the poor farmers and handed them a $100 bill, more than ten times the ten dollars they had asked for and the actual value of the pig. Their faces were gleeful as they turned to go, leaving the dead pig behind.

"Hey guys," I blurted out after them, "you're forgetting your pig!"

They whipped around. "No mon, it yours, you buy it." They turned back around to leave again.

"You can have it if you want it," Mom piped up.

They could hardly believe their good luck. "Tanks! Tanks!" they stammered through huge smiles as one grabbed the pig and hoisted it over his skinny shoulder. I watched them as they left, glancing back from time to time as if Mom might change her mind. I later heard that the farmers had a pig roast that night and I'm sure Mom was pleased. She liked to see people fed and she hated to see kids without shoes. It was a pet project kind of thing with her.

Rock arrived at the Hill one morning after yet another load was on its way to the U.S. and asked Mom, "Violet, what's with the shoes?"

Rock, like everyone else in Jamaica, knew Mom only as "Violet," Bummy's given name. The shoes he was asking about had arrived on the plane with El Loco that morning. Mom had bought hundreds of pairs of brand new children's sneakers to be distributed among the many poor shoeless Jamaican children she saw nearly every time she traveled the streets of Kingston or Montego Bay.

"They're for the kids. Pass them out as you see fit, would you, please?"

"Irie…. Irie," he replied, nodding. *All right…. All right.* Rock was already a highly respected headman and giving away free shoes would only enhance his prestige in the community. Whatever Mom wanted to give away was fine with him. For her part, she was just happy to see some kids get new shoes. And after all, Mom could afford to be generous for she had just begun a lucrative period in her life that would result in her becoming one of biggest marijuana smugglers in the world.

9

A Parallel Universe

Mom's marijuana smuggling organization, as successful as it was and would become, was in reality only a small part of an already multi-billion-dollar worldwide industry, and although she only had contact with a minuscule portion of the many other dealers and smugglers who operated during the same general period, there was one particular marijuana smuggler extraordinaire that warrants closer scrutiny as his story is a fascinating one. While she never met him during the time they both functioned as the heads of their respective international marijuana smuggling organizations, Aunt Nancy and Jeannie knew him well and valued him as a reliable connection as both a buyer and a seller of top-quality marijuana. Everyone has heard the saying that it's a small world and I believe it, because Mom eventually met this smuggling colleague years after she quit the business and came to know him well and they remain good friends to this very day. His story is a compelling study of the similarities and differences of two parallel pot smuggling operations, one East Coast and the other West Coast. This smuggler has been dubbed the "King of Pot," but Mom and I know him as Bruce Perlowin.

To call Bruce an interesting character would be a gross understatement. Born in Philadelphia in the early 1950s, Bruce exhibited entrepreneurial tendencies from a tender age and was a natural-born salesman if there ever was one. He first demonstrated his aptitude for business as a child selling various items door to door, and from there he never stopped or even slowed down. Driven by a multitude of varied interests and possessing many talents, Bruce nonetheless was particularly drawn to looking at the world from a holistic point of view which led him to lifelong interests in ecology, conservation, and natural foods and medicines, among other topics. It's no wonder that, much like Mom,

Bruce was powerfully attracted by marijuana's multi-faceted nature that transcended its being just another drug intended for the sole purposes of producing a high. And after I met Bruce and got to know him a little bit, it was easy for me to suspect that these beliefs, coupled with an innate passion for sales, were possibly the catalysts that propelled him to become what many considered the largest pot smuggler in U.S. West Coast history.

Much like his contemporaries the world over, Bruce started small, but in stark contrast to most of them (including Mom), he always had a plan and a goal. Reflective of this mindset, in the mid–1970s when his highly successful marijuana-dealing business in south Florida not only earned him an arrest warrant but also became negatively impacted by the violent "cocaine cowboys" of the era, Bruce solved both problems with a single bold stroke. He packed up his operation and headed west to California. It would prove to be a momentous decision destined to catapult him to the apex of the marijuana smuggling world.

Bruce's California pot smuggling organization was called simply "The Company," and for good reason. Unlike many marijuana dealers and smugglers both then and now, Bruce exercised his considerable business acumen and applied it directly to his operation in a variety of innovative ways. He formulated a business plan, lined up investors, and organized his employees in a manner more comparable to a Fortune 500 company than a drug enterprise. And when it came down to making decisions Bruce had an unusual style compared to most other smugglers. Where Mom would be likely to just "wing it" and go with an impulse or a feeling, Bruce would patiently and methodically gather information wherever and however he could. For example, before he decided where to bring ashore his illicit loads of marijuana he hired a research firm to analyze past smuggling busts as well as the strength and proximity of U.S. federal resources, including the Coast Guard, at various U.S. West Coast ports. The firm's report named the Port of San Francisco as the weakest, so Bruce chose that location to be the center of his operations.

Bruce's smuggling operation substantially differed from Mom's in other ways as well. For starters, he smuggled Colombian pot. When I asked him why, he explained, "I wanted good quality marijuana and the Colombians had it—more buds, fewer seeds, and less shake. I also needed more quantity than other places could provide. The Colombians could supply tons of pot, and that's what I needed."

Bruce wasn't kidding. During roughly a four-year period The Company used relatively small commercial fishing vessels (most less than 100 feet long) to smuggle a reputed 250 tons of Colombian "Punta Roja" worth millions of dollars into the United States. The method was straightforward in that he hired former and current commercial fishermen to undertake month-long round-trip voyages to Colombia and back. Simply leave with an empty boat and come back loaded without getting caught. On the surface it seemed simple enough, but in keeping with his businesslike style Bruce left as little to chance as possible by implementing a few unique safeguards.

In order to provide captains with valuable and timely information that could possibly make or break a trip, The Company commissioned the creation of a specialized recreational vehicle that was equipped with a variety of communication and surveillance equipment designed to monitor the whereabouts and activities of the San Francisco area Coast Guard and other law

Bruce Perlowin, "The King of Pot."

enforcement entities. Because the RV was mobile, it could be positioned strategically at precisely the moment it was needed, do its job, and then disappear. It wasn't cheap, but it was an investment that made good business sense and gave the smugglers a crucial edge. In much the same fashion and at no small expense The Company acquired its own

1,000-foot pier which allowed its vessels to dock and unload tons of marijuana in relative privacy and security. These innovations and others allowed The Company and its founder to amass a fortune law enforcement declared was in excess of $100 million.

At the height of his pot smuggling success Bruce was 30 years old and living in a $3 million mansion with gold-plated plumbing and a tennis court, surrounded by lavish pools and gardens, and was arguably one of the most successful pot smugglers in the world. And although Bruce's methods differed from Mom's in many ways, they were very much alike in one significant way. Both he and Mom had taken their smuggling enterprises all the way to the top. But much like a ship on the sea, a smuggler's life is a series of ups and downs, on a crest one moment and down in a trough the next. And of course, Bruce's story would today be unknown if he hadn't been caught, and I am sorry to say that the reason for his demise, unlike nearly everything else about the man, was typical. What else? Snitches, lots of them.

Bruce's organization was definitely larger than Mom's in terms of personnel. Where Mom maintained a central core of a just a few key people (most of them family), two or three pilots, and had Aunt Nancy handle much of her distribution, Bruce's company employed as many as 200 people in various positions: accountants, distributors, salesmen, computer and radio operators, and attorneys handling a variety of issues including money laundering and investments. And then there were the boat crews and captains, three men per boat per trip. All these employees added up to serious risk in the event that any of them were busted and decided to snitch to save their own skins. Unfortunately it only takes one and in Bruce's case there were several, all pointing their fingers straight at him—the man with the plan. But the feds couldn't care less about the details. They were interested in taking down the top dog because in the war on drugs that is where the money is. In March of 1983 Bruce was arrested by the FBI on multiple federal charges stemming from his smuggling operation.

When I asked Bruce who the first person in the company to "roll over" on him was, he wasn't quite sure and was in fact very magnanimous in his recollection of the snitches both as former associates and human beings. "Oh, they're great guys, really good people. And who knows what anyone will do when they're in those shoes?" Well, Bruce was definitely forgiving of those who snitched on him, but when he had his chance to spill the beans to the feds and become a snitch himself, he declined. Bruce's decision not to snitch on any of his former employees surely prevented many of them from going to prison, but it cost him dearly at his sentencing, where he received 15 years in prison. Much of that time was spent in the federal penitentiary at Pleasanton, California, where he would, years later, meet another big-time former marijuana smuggler named Judy.

10

High Times

There I was, once again heading out to dig for buried treasure. By no means the leader and really only tagging along, I nevertheless had a distinct sense of déjà vu as I grabbed a shovel, a backpack, and an axe and clomped down the back porch's wooden stairs heading for the nearby woods that surrounded the Byrd estate. What would be found this time? Whatever it might be it was sure to be interesting, and that's why I was reminded of an earlier outing with a similar goal.

Years before, Mom and Nancy, with me and Melanie in tow, had spent several days scrabbling and searching to find buried treasure consisting of a small fortune in U.S. $20 gold coins. Mom had often spoken of how my great-grandfather Michael Haas swore on his deathbed that years earlier he had filled a one-pound coffee can with the gold, then placed that can inside a larger can and buried the treasure between two forked roots at the foot of a particular cedar tree, the location of which he also provided detailed directions to. Mom and Nancy had bought a metal detector and scoured acres upon acres of farmland, first concentrating on cedar trees that seemed to match Grandpa's instructions, then moving on to any tree that they considered a possibility. I must have dug ten holes myself. Mom and Nancy dug many more. Eventually, it was a bust and we gave up. Mom concluded that the cedar tree we were looking for might have been cut down or had died and the gold was therefore lost forever. Nancy felt that Grandpa Michael had played Mom for a fool and there never was any gold. I believe Grandpa was telling the truth as far as he could remember, but by the time he told Mom about the treasure he was 89 years old and near death. It seemed logical to me that he could have gotten a few facts mixed up regarding the location of the coins. Maybe it had been buried on a different property or maybe our metal detector was crap. Whatever the truth, Grandpa's $20 gold pieces, if they ever existed at all, are still safe and sound and waiting to be discovered.

But now, Bummy and I were on the hunt and the prize would be an unknown amount of cash that had been securely stashed, then buried in watertight Tupperware containers. She had pushed for our present course of action after Baga had dug up a small duct-taped Tupperware container several days before and found that the supposedly watertight container had leaked and the cash inside, about $60,000, was wet. Even though it had been buried only months before, the unmistakable smell of mold and mildew had filled the room when it was opened. The water itself was not a problem as everyone knew paper money dries, but mold and mildew could quickly ruin cash, so there were huge concerns about the rest of the buried money. Baga had faith in the integrity of the rest of the containers and repeatedly expressed his thought that the failure of the one container was a fluke and the rest of the money was safe and dry. Bummy felt otherwise, citing that the Tupperware was brand new and had been carefully burped, sealed, and then taped as an extra precaution yet had still leaked for some unknown reason. Baga and Bummy were champion adversaries even when Bummy was sober, so they dusted

Bummy and Baga, ca. 1980s.

off their gloves and bickered over what to do for quite some time. When I suggested the compromise that we begin by digging up just one more container and only dig up others if it had leaked, Baga caved in and brought out the handdrawn maps outlining where the rest of the cash was buried. "Let me know if the next one's wet," he reminded us before heading into the great room to watch a football game. I assured him we would and then proceeded to study the maps. I sort of felt like a pirate.

In the early days of the operation when seriously large amounts of money had begun to arrive, Mom, Nancy and Baga had used several tactics to deal with the duffle bags of cash that were regularly delivered. They rented large safe-deposit boxes at several local and out-of-town banks and crammed them full of high denomination bills to make the most efficient use of the space. Other cash was used to buy expensive gold and jewelry from private parties that would not report the cash sale of the items. Still more cash was laundered through more conventional means such as legal businesses, but there was always more coming in, so, like pirates of old with bootie to hide, burying the cash was always the ultimate fallback and it eventually became the family favorite. It was relatively easy and everyone considered it a safe option, at least until the discovery of the leak.

As they had handled most of the other financial moves, Mom and Baga had done most of the money burying and they had done a good job. They had packed the cash carefully and buried it deep. Bummy and I decided to go for a mid-sized container first, and we also picked one that was not buried in the vicinity of the one that had leaked. Within an hour we'd recovered our prize and laid it on the kitchen table to open.

The container was a filthy mess, so we took the time to clean it as we cut and peeled several layers of duct tape that had been carefully applied to the seams as added protection against the elements. It was like we were performing surgery. Then it was time to open the box and settle the argument once and for all. When I raised the lid I really expected the contents to be dry, but surprisingly that was not the case. The money, upwards of $150,000 when we finally counted it, was soaking wet! Somehow the sealed container had leaked. Bummy's intuition had been right on target. There was now no doubt that an untold amount of money was in jeopardy and all the containers had to be dug up and examined. It was going to be a big job, but since I was hanging out with my grandparents for the summer I volunteered to help. Bummy, Baga, and I began early the next day.

Right off the bat we agreed to excavate and open the containers one at a time. That way we could halt the digging at any time and save a lot of hassle if we found no more leakers, for Baga still thought the two previous containers were flukes and expected further digging to be short-lived. But I had my doubts. It seemed to me the leakers were simply not up to the rigors imposed by direct burial, no matter how tough and secure they appeared. We would find out. This time Baga zeroed in on a large one about the size of a medium suitcase. Forty-five minutes later found us breathing heavy as we tossed the muddy container on the kitchen table where yet another opening ritual was performed. To Baga's profound dismay this container had also leaked.

Now it was clear we faced a problem that had only one solution, and so without dissent, Baga started digging in earnest and continued the rest of the day. We had quite a stack of containers by dusk so we quit for fear of stepping on a snake. The next morning Baga was so sore from his efforts I took over on the shovel and he pulled and stacked. We labored on well into the afternoon until Baga declared, "The next one is the last one!"

I don't remember exactly how many containers we'd unearthed, but I was very glad to finally be done with what I thought at the time was going to be the hardest part of the job. How little I knew!

We saved a lot of time that go-round by rinsing off the containers with a hose before bringing them inside, reasoning that if the cash was already wet it would do it no harm, and if dry, the container was watertight and impervious to the rinsing. Opening each container was a pain because of all the layered duct tape and it was well into the early morning hours of the next day before the last one was opened and examined. Like most of the others, it had leaked.

The three of us just sat there quietly for awhile with several mountainous piles of soaking wet and partially mildewed cash stacked strategically around the kitchen. We were all tired, but Baga was the first to rise and head for the door.

"Goodnight. I'm done here." He rubbed his eyes as he looked questioningly in my direction. I, too, was beat, and got up to make my exit.

"Wait!" Bummy hopped up out of her chair with more energy than I'd thought possible. "We can't leave it wet like this. The mold and mildew will ruin it. It's already starting to stick together."

She was right, of course. The individual bills were becoming stickier as they dried. And judging by the smell, the mold and mildew already had a good head start. Baga threw up his hands in disgust.

"What can we do?"

"Let's put it in the dryer," suggested Bummy.

While they each gathered heaping handfuls of cash and headed for the laundry room I started brainstorming for other ideas. The only thing I could think of that might be useful besides the clothes dryer would be the oven, so I began an experiment.

Using four large baking sheets at a time, I painstakingly peeled $100 bills from their $10,000 bundles and dealt them out evenly on the sheets like cookies. Then it was into the preheated oven. Since I had no prior experience with anything even remotely similar, I singed a lot of money before trial and error taught me the correct temperature and "cook time." Before long, I had a system going and had even set a timer that paced the interval between each batch. I already had a respectable stack of dried cash started when Baga and Bummy returned.

"How did it go?" I asked.

"Not good," Baga answered, handing me a small wad of bills to examine.

I saw what he meant. The bills were dry, but stiff and badly wrinkled. They would not lie or stack flat either. I'm sure they would spend okay, but it was clear they had been through something. I pointed to my stack on the table. Baga picked it up and liked what he saw and felt, Bummy too.

"How did…?" He began, but before I could answer the oven's timer signaled another batch was done. "Beep, beep, beep, beep, beep."

"Hungry, anyone?" I joked as I slipped on oven mitts and casually sauntered over to the oven and removed the cookie sheets. Baga and Bummy started laughing as they inspected the bills, which were perfectly dry and in nice condition.

"And this won't ruin my dryer with a lot of mold and mildew," Bummy observed.

So … that was that. Joking and generally having fun, the three of us fed a vast amount of cash into that oven like an assembly line long into the night, and we continued the next day, and even the next, pausing only to eat, shower, and sleep. We removed the last tray from the oven with deep sighs of relief. I wondered how much was there. A million?

Several million? I'll never know for sure, but I'll never forget seeing the tightly bundled cash, most of it $20, $50, and $100 notes, stacked ten inches deep and completely covering a large dining room table. It was ample evidence that Mom and crew were riding high indeed.

We'd returned from Jamaica the year prior after spending 15 months "in country" and leaving had been bittersweet. I had felt almost like a real "Yardie" (Jamaican), as Desi sometimes teased me. I had mastered driving on the left-hand side of the road and had even gotten a Jamaican learner's permit. My ear had become attuned to Patois, and though I could not speak it I understood the dialect just fine. And the icing on the cake was the literally free rein I had had at Wayne's stables. I rode my favorite horse, a feisty Appaloosa mare named Lucy Grey, several times a week as I explored the bush and played cowboy. Mitchell the gardener and I continued to jam and my repertoire of island music grew and Roy the butler had proven to be a solid friend from whom I'd learned a lot about Jamaica and had many a laugh as well. Why we'd made the move back to the United States at that particular time was an open question, but it might have had something to do with a run-in Mom had had with the local Montego Bay police.

Somehow, Mom had been arrested one afternoon in Montego Bay for possession of a single marijuana roach. How she accomplished this amazing feat is a mystery that remains unanswered to this day. Busted for a minuscule amount of ganja, in Jamaica of all places. Who would have thought it possible? Believe me, it's possible.

Desi, as fun-loving as always, was at the wheel when he and Mom were stopped by a couple of scruffy local traffic cops in sweaty khaki shirts with oversized pistols at their sides. Mom hadn't been alarmed in the least, but lo and behold, the next thing she knew, one cop was frisking Desi and the other was rummaging through her purse. I would imagine the odds of finding anything specific in Mom's purse to be on par with finding a 1943 copper penny (in other words, very long), but somehow the cop managed to maintain enough motivation to find the roach among the chaos of her purse.

"Aha!" he exclaimed, holding up the roach as if he was about to light it himself. His partner turned from Desi to the roach as a mischievous smile slowly crept across his face. There was a look in his eyes that Mom later said reminded her of a bird of prey. Choosing action over indecision, Mom was about to ask for the wallet inside her purse to honor the local custom and grease the wheels of justice with a little cash when the other cop grabbed her wrists, pushed her against the car, and slapped on handcuffs.

"You are under arrest for possession of marijuana!" he loudly and proudly exclaimed. This caught Mom totally by surprise as she had never given much thought to the legality of possessing a small amount of ganja in Jamaica. Pot smoking was rampant in Jamaica and, like most visitors, she had assumed it was legal, it was such an integral part of the culture. As Mom took a deep breath and gathered her composure Desi was also cuffed. They spoke sparingly on the way to Montego Bay's downtown police headquarters.

Once there, both were thrown into the general population holding cell—a large foul cage set atop a concrete slab with cubicles at its perimeter. Mom asked to make a phone call and was ignored. Frustrated, she and Desi found a clear spot and sat down to wait it out. Within an hour, Desi's name was called at the door and after he agreed to pay a $60 fine he was released. But before he left he assured Mom, "I'll get Rock."

Mom waited until after sunset before she began to wonder if she would be spending the night in jail for having just one little roach! It was practically unbelievable! This was Jamaica, after all! She asked again for a phone call and was ignored a second time. What was going on? Then, as if in answer to the unspoken question, she heard the first tentative cries, quiet at first, then rising in volume and intensity as more and more inmates joined in the chant.

"Rock, Rock, Rock, ROCK, ROCK, ROCK! ROCK!"

Like a prizefighter stalking his way toward the ring before a championship fight, Rock confidently strode down the main hall that ran adjacent to one side of the holding cell. Two or three times he raised his hands and nodded in muted greeting as the chanting continued. It seemed like everyone knew him, and most probably did, for as I have said, he was a much respected headman with a reputation for generosity. When he entered the office at the end of the hall the chanting died down and what passed for normal in the cage resumed. Mom waited patiently, and only 20 minutes after his arrival she was footloose and fancy free, smoking one of Rock's humongous spliffs in the passenger side of his tricked-out Bronco and heading for Mockingbird Hill. Characteristically, she appreciated her good fortune to be free, but had to ask, "What just happened?"

"Violet," Rock answered simply and directly with a voice as rich and thick as Memphis barbeque sauce, "it's all money, my dear."

Rock later explained in detail how he had first bargained for, and then paid, a fine of U.S. $2,000 cash for Mom's release. He knew it was a bribe and the Montego Bay police department knew it was a bribe, nevertheless bribery was alive and well in Jamaica and the cops had just had a banner day. As far as Mom was concerned, two grand and a few hours in jail hadn't been all that bad, but she was a gypsy at heart and had developed the habit of moving to avoid conflict ever since her contentious divorce so many years before. So, the next thing I knew, I was saying my goodbyes with tears in my eyes and feeding Lucy Grey the last carrot she would ever receive from my hand. The trade for my boots had been so worth it! At that moment I felt I could have gone barefoot the rest of my life just to have taken her with me.

It was sort of a strange feeling the day I returned to the United States after the short flight back, for within the span of two hours it seemed as though I had traveled decades forward in time. What I had previously failed to see was now crystal clear. Ours was a country of riches. Many things that Americans took for granted were rare luxuries in Jamaica and I vowed to try to remember and be thankful. It was all a bit humbling and I actually experienced no small measure of culture shock on the cab ride home from the airport.

"Home" at the time was actually a rental Mom had arranged shortly before our return. It was a large, comfortable, three-level pool home located smack-dab on the beach in southeast Florida. Acting on instinct and hoping for maximum privacy, I chose a smaller room far from the center of the house and I was glad I did because it was not long before a new crop of questionable houseguests sprang up like weeds after a spring rain. I did my best to avoid them, but for the most part it was impossible. They roamed the house at all hours and it seemed that no place was off-limits. If I decided on a late night snack, a trip to the kitchen might involve running into some sketchy character, high on his or her drug of choice and spouting inane religious rhetoric or some other idiotic gobbledygook. An innocent visit to the bathroom might involve encountering a naked stranger in the tub or yield a nasty surprise in an unflushed toilet. And I cannot even count the times I came home to find some unfamiliar person sleeping in my bed or poking around my room. It was all kind of surreal, and I did not doubt for a second that the circus atmosphere was fueled by Mom's money. Craziness was normal, and when Aunt Nancy came for an extended visit the place rose to new highs, and lows.

Many evenings followed a similar pattern. First, the Newbies would show up. These would be people who'd never been over before but might have an acquaintance that had been at our home previously. Sometimes, a Newbie would be invited. Those Newbies would then quickly join in and by the next day become a Standby, which tended to hang around the house all day, dividing their time between grazing in the kitchen, sleeping, or scrounging drugs (most commonly pot and booze), using any method at their disposal. The combined Newbies and Standbys then sequestered themselves strategically around the house and waited for the inevitable night out at a restaurant or a shopping trip at the very least. Typically, either alternative resulted in a small motorcade headed out for an evening of excess. Mom and Aunt Nancy blew a small fortune that year on pretty much nothing more than some fancy overpriced food and Dom Perignon champagne. Out of boredom I often tagged along on these soirées and occasionally they were great fun, but as the same pattern repeated itself I increasingly found the decadent lifestyle distasteful, primarily due to the idiotic and often pointless rambling that masqueraded as conversation at many of the dinners. One particular nutcase and tagger-on, a chronic Standby named Larry, was a prime example.

Larry had first ingratiated himself with Mom after being introduced as a pilot. I can't say much about his piloting skills, which were dubious at best, but since Mom and Greg's on-again, off-again relationship was at the moment off, Larry's magnificent wrestler's physique captivated Mom sufficiently to keep him hanging around. His brain was another matter entirely. He often spoke of invisible malevolent thread-like entities that descended from the sky to sink into your skin and contaminate your body, and I was immediately convinced that this specific paranoia of his was merely a drug-induced hallucination, but it was creepy all the same. He might have remained on the scene longer but for a close call he and Mom had while flying from Florida to the Turks and Caicos Islands. Larry, acting as pilot, had neglected to properly adjust the fuel mixture to the engines, a simple but potentially dangerous oversight. They lost the first engine on final approach and nearly lost the other before making a frenzied and nerve-wracking emergency landing. Their relationship had cooled appreciably by the time they returned to Florida.

The high times continued on other fronts. Aunt Bonnie and her new husband, a marijuana and cocaine merchant who had dealings on his own as well as peripheral involvement with Mom's business as a connection, bought an extravagant 80-foot-plus motor yacht named the *Pearl Necklace*, complete with a hired captain to run it. They lived it up and partied like there was no tomorrow. When I met Bonnie's new husband and got to know him I found that I liked him a lot and was happy that she had finally met somebody smart with a personality. El Loco raised his game as well. He added exponentially to his car and motorcycle collection and constantly sought the eternal party he knew existed somewhere; it would be his Shangri-La, he only had to find it. Herman and Gary roared around on new Harleys and tried to keep up with the old pro, El Loco. And Mom and Aunt Nancy traveled and spent money like there was no end in sight. Baga, conservative to the core, scolded Mom the day she bought nearly every plant at a nursery and had them delivered in a huge semi-truck. The only thing that mitigated his ultimate anger was the fact that Mom had at least taken the plunge and bought the house they were intended for. I for one did my best to keep to myself and spent a lot of time camping, fishing, and hunting with my cousin Robert, who was like a brother to me. One time Robert and I, along with our entire Boy Scout troop, were snowed in by an extremely rare south Georgia snowstorm in March. Those were good times!

Meanwhile, Mom's Jamaican enterprise kept chugging along fast and furious, so much so, in fact, that it was around this time she brought another pilot onboard. His name was Frank Maars. He was an extremely experienced, commercially-licensed former Eastern Airline pilot with thousands of flight hours logged. And he brought other benefits to the operation as

El Loco at the Byrd estate, 1977.

well, for besides being a competent professional pilot he had access to a private airstrip strategically located outside Sebring, Florida. The strip eased logistics when it came to storing and maintaining Mom's smuggling planes, which now consisted of an Aztec, a Cessna Citation, and a Queen-Aire.

Frank was a family man, a clean-cut, all-around good guy that exuded trust and I liked him from the moment I met him. Together, he and El Loco streamlined flight operations and made improvements that had been ignored or avoided up until that point. One of these upgrades, wholly endorsed and financed by Mom, was the purchase of an automatic life raft that she insisted was to be standard equipment on all flights. And this turned out to be a truly life-and-death decision because only a few trips after it was added the complicated fuel extension system on the plane El Loco was flying went haywire and he had to ditch at sea. Luckily, the seas were calm and he managed a smooth glide landing. Even better, it turned out he was only 25 miles from land and a favorable current swept his raft in the right direction. But that's not to say his little side trip wasn't an adventure. Sharks had circled his raft on several occasions and he'd had no drinking water for the 40 hours he had drifted toward the mainland. And once ashore, he'd had quite a trek to the nearest phone and mosquitoes had nearly eaten him alive, but all things considered it could have been much worse.

Greg, the acting co-pilot on many of both El Loco's and Frank's trips, was lucky he was not on that trip. He wasn't on that trip because he and Mom had just switched gears back to an "on-again" relationship. How long it would remain so would depend on so many variables it was not worth consideration, but Greg's drinking had to be a major factor. For the moment he was content with a steady intake of beer which he handled without complications, especially since his chief activities for weeks on end had been cooking various elaborate dishes (Southern cuisine was his favorite, because he liked to make jokes about the food) and keeping Mom company.

Greg was really fun to be around as long as he and Mom were getting along, but apparently a nearly inexhaustible amount of money is not a guarantee that a relationship will thrive and that was the case with Greg and Mom. Their romance was always rocky at best and continually on the brink of either breakup or reconciliation. Maybe that's the dynamic they wanted, but it sure was crazy at times. They would have a thunderous, knock-down-drag-out argument and then 15 minutes later Mom would pour a glass of wine and put on an album while Greg would strut to the kitchen and ask in a faux–Southern drawl, "Now who wants some chitlins and black-eyed peas?"

It came as no surprise to me when one day Greg was gone again. As I said before, he would come and go without warning so it was no big deal when he did either, and since he was only a co-pilot his absence was not a serious problem. El Loco and Frank would often team up and make a trip together. What was a problem, however, was when Frank Maars went missing right after Christmas. Everyone asked around but he'd just disappeared. And because he'd previously run off on a binge a time or two, most everybody assumed that was what had happened. But then Mom had gotten a call from her corporate attorney, Ed Sawyer. I can still remember how surprised everyone was when we heard Frank was dead, but when we heard he'd been murdered it was so shocking a development I was left speechless. Mom, Nancy, and Bummy wept openly.

Frank's brutal murder was awful and it was a setback to the Jamaican operation, but like a raging river the momentum of what Mom had started kept going just as the stream of ganja kept flowing and everybody involved became richer and richer. I found it hard to think about Frank and what had happened and preferred instead to remember him as he was the day I had met him and he'd loaned me, a long-haired 16-year-old with a new driver's license, his brand new sports car. "The tank's full," he'd said with a smile as he threw me the keys. "Have fun and drive safe." I drove that car to my high school's out-of-town football game that weekend and got my first speeding ticket on that trip. Frank was a good man and didn't deserve the fate that befell him and I still think about him from time to time. They're only memories now—memories both good and bad. Thank God for the good ones.

On that note, it was around that time that Mom pulled a doozy. Over breakfast she announced to Melanie and me that she was expecting a baby and Greg was the father. Naturally, I asked the due date and oddly enough the due date was the same day as my birthday! The pregnancy was still quite new so Mom had no idea if the baby was a boy or, as Melanie openly asked for, a girl. Wow! A new baby was good news as far as I was concerned and was very exciting. Then, almost like it was an afterthought, Mom capped off the noteworthy morning with a question.

"Are you guys ready to move?"

I surely was, because I knew exactly where we were going. Our new home was actually an 1800s-era Victorian in White Springs, Florida. Mom had bought the house a few months earlier and had begun extensive renovations that were not yet complete but she figured the house was large enough to live around the work as it was being done. Filling the house was a veritable jungle of houseplants she'd imported from the nursery and a monumental buying spree at some local furniture stores and antique shops furnished the rest of the house which consisted of eight bedrooms, five bathrooms, and two kitchens. It was a great house and the best thing about it was its proximity to my grandparents.

We made the move with ease as the furniture in the beach rental stayed with the house. It was my secret hope that the move might also shake some of Mom's chronic Standbys loose along the way—there was precedent, it had happened before. Maybe the pregnancy had something to do with it or maybe it was just my wishful hoping, but life did seem to become a wee bit simpler after we arrived in White Springs. There were far fewer houseguests in general and many of the Standbys had indeed fallen by the wayside. I was thinking about the positive turn of events when I first stepped into the backyard of our new place and was met with a pleasant surprise. There was a 35-foot cabin cruiser in the backyard!

Now, I have always loved boats, so I couldn't wait to get closer to check this one out in detail, and as I did, an old, gray-haired man with twinkling eyes and a wispy beard popped out of the main salon with a pipe between his teeth and a paintbrush in his hand.

"Howdy, young fella," he said around the pipe as he gave me a little wave with his free hand.

"Howdy," I repeated.

"I'm Theron Gaulding." He took off an old wide-brimmed, paint-stained straw hat and set his brush down. As he moved over to the boat's gunwale he wiped his right hand on his paint-spattered striped overalls before offering it to me.

I reached up and shook his hand. "I'm David Michael. Nice to meet you." His hand was that of a working man, heavily calloused. "Is this your boat?"

"Yep," he said with a whimsical smile playing across his face.

It was his boat, all right. And not only that, it was his creation, his baby, a labor of love. In fact, he'd been building the boat from scratch for the previous seven years. Its hull was built of oak and marine plywood with a fiberglass overlay and its interior was resplendent with highly-polished natural wood cabinetry and bronze hardware. It was breathtakingly beautiful, a work of art. And it did not come as a surprise to me when I learned that Mr. Gaulding was an artist, a talented painter with several notable pieces to his credit. He was also a perfectionist, a jack-of-all-trades, and a quirky, down-to-Earth, old-fashioned Southern gentleman who it seemed to me could have easily sprung from the pages of a Mark Twain novel. Although his activity level belied it, Mr. Gaulding was 80 years old. When I saw Mom later that day, I asked her to allow Mr. Gaulding to finish building his boat where it sat and she agreed.

Over the next two years, I helped Mr. Gaulding with many boat projects, both large and small, and he taught me more than I could ever remember. He would tell me old forgotten stories of the nearby Suwanee River and the surrounding area as well as tidbits regarding the famous songwriter Stephen Foster, whose memorial was in town. When I asked his intentions regarding the boat he spoke of a plan to sail up and down the Suwannee, painting river scenes as he lived aboard his floating art studio. It sounded like a grand idea to me. My lifelong romance with boats had begun! I had met a kindred spirit in Mr. Gaulding and we became great friends despite our age difference.

One morning as Mr. Gaulding homed in on the culmination of his grand project he called me over to the stern of the boat and gestured toward an overturned five-gallon paint bucket. "Just sit right there," he said.

I sat and waited as he opened a large wooden box I hadn't seen before. It contained his art tools, brushes, and specialty paints. He selected a couple different size brushes and a small vial of royal blue paint. "Today, she gets a name. It's about time, don't you think?" he asked.

I merely nodded and looked on with excitement as the boat's name slowly took shape under Mr. Gaulding's talented hands. When he finished, I had to ask, "Isn't a boat supposed to have a female name?"

Mr. Gaulding's sense of humor, always sharp and often unexpected, emerged with a chuckle, "Now, David Michael, you know a young lady at my age would bring me nothing but trouble, don't you?"

"I suppose so, Mr. Gaulding," I laughed.

And I had to admit, the name he chose made a lot of sense, especially when he explained it to me in terms of the lifestyle he intended to lead once his boat was launched and he was living on the Suwanee as an itinerant artist.

He had named his boat *Refuge*, and the more I thought about it the more I liked it. A refuge was a place of safety, a place where one could take shelter and be safe from pursuit, danger, or trouble. Little did I know at the time, my family would soon be in dire need of just such a refuge. Unfortunately for us, such a place did not exist.

11

Loose Lips Sink Ships

Cash, cash, and more cash. There could be no doubt that high-quality marijuana was a hot commodity because Mom could not even import enough to satisfy the demand created by her own connections. Even so, as each planeload of green ganja was exchanged for green paper, her fortune increased. How much was it? Well, Mom was never one to keep close track of anything and even less likely to take notes, but it would be safe to say that it was like she had discovered a modern-day version of the Lost Dutchman's Gold Mine when she began her Jamaican operation. A green gold mine. To say that business was fabulous would be a gross understatement. So, what does a successful marijuana smuggler do after she's done it all? She quits, that's what. At least that's what I felt Mom should do, and I pressed hard for just that one morning not long after the birth of my new baby sister Morgana (named after the Arthurian legend, at my suggestion).

"Just quit, Mom. You don't need to go on anymore. Let it go," I begged in my most pleading voice.

"But I can't just walk away."

"Oh yes, you can!"

"I just can't. I've got the planes," she protested.

"Let Greg have them, you don't need 'em," I said, not nearly ready to give up. Then I played the most powerful card in the deck.

"Mom, think about Morgana. She needs a mother. She can't lose you. What if you get caught and go to jail? What then? You've got to be smart and quit while you're ahead." Morgana, only a few weeks old, wrapped tight in a swaddling blanket, sitting in her bouncy seat and quiet until that moment, gazed up and let out a little gurgle like she had recognized her name.

"I'll think about it," Mom replied flatly with a tone of finality.

I knew I had made the best argument possible so I let the matter rest. What I had said made perfect sense. Mom could retire if she would just eschew greed and muster up the gumption to do what few people dared. Just say, "To hell with everything," and walk away from it all. If I had honestly asked myself at that moment I would've placed the odds of Mom quitting at less than one in ten considering the pressure I knew she must have been under to continue at all costs through thick and thin and never stop no matter what. Yet Mom was nothing if not unpredictable and—wouldn't you know it?—she somehow made the decision, pulled the trigger, and quit cold turkey. She did it so quietly that few outside her closest circle even noticed. Very low-key. I was extremely proud of her and her decision and have to admit that although I had pushed for just such an action I was still rather surprised.

Everything was accomplished with little fuss and even less fanfare. Mom merely made a few phone calls and paid a visit to Baga who handled the rest of the details which didn't amount to much because at the heart of it she really did just walk away. She didn't fret over the disposition of the planes, the stash houses, or much of anything else, for that matter. The only thing that remained unfinished was approximately $270,000 she was owed by one of her connections for some pot she had supplied on a front, but from what I saw she lost little sleep over the debt. Mercifully, her exit was also surprisingly swift. There was simply no other way to do it where the break would be clean. In for a penny, in for a pound, as the saying goes. Well, she was out. Completely.

I rejoiced. Mom was done as a smuggler and I could not help but feel relieved. In all the years since Mom and Dad's divorce and all the ups and downs of her businesses, both legal and illegal, my life had been such a roller coaster ride that I never felt settled and always remained on guard. I suppose my defensive posture resulted from never knowing if or when Mom might finally be busted for something serious and sent away to prison for many years, maybe permanently. In hindsight, I guess it was premature for me to think the coast was clear just because Mom had quit, because that only meant the end of her involvement, not the end of the Jamaican smuggling operation. Like the leviathan it truly was, it would not die easily or quietly.

Understandably, Mom's decision to quit had indeed caught everyone by surprise, but since she had merely walked away and not shut anything down per se, a space was left that begged to be filled and into this void stepped Greg. After all, he knew most of the key players personally and if there was anything he didn't know already he was prepared to learn or simply ad lib. Mom had done it so he could too. Undoubtedly some new blood would have to be brought in to fill the obvious gaps in the operation, for in addition to Mom, Baga was out of the picture, as well as Nancy and Bonnie, but this did not deter Greg. Within the span of just a few weeks he surreptitiously met with Jeannie and El Loco and the rest of the gang and found that they were raring to go and a visit to Jamaica confirmed all was ready on that end. The internal momentum of what Mom had started appeared unstoppable. So, without so much as a hiccup or two in the overall scheme of things, the operation was back on track once again. In hindsight there is little doubt in my mind that it would have been far better for Mom and our family if she had taken overt measures to disband the operation and "scuttle the ship" when she left in order to cover her tracks and minimize risk. Certainly it would have been better to leave nothing behind and nothing ongoing for authorities to discover; that way there would have been far fewer opportunities for disaster to strike. But everyone knows that hindsight often brings revelations that are not quite apparent at the moment and at that time our family was focused on the future, not the past. And the one person who appeared to be most squarely in the center of the rearview mirror at that time was Greg.

Greg had always been someone who came and went, seemingly at random, to and from our house ever since I first met him and as Mom's due date approached he was around less frequently than ever. After Morgana's birth, I never saw him. I'm sure he was busier than he had ever been and he and Mom were not on the best of terms by then, but it went deeper than that, I'm sure. Even as a carefree teenager I could appreciate the fact that the responsibility of a baby could be intimidating, however Greg needn't have worried about his freedom. It wasn't that he was a bad person or a kid hater or anything like that at all. In fact, he and I had spent many cheerful fun-filled days together camping with my Boy Scout troop and he came from a large, loving family himself. He just wasn't father material at that point in his life. So whether he knew it or not Mom was not of a mind to expect anything from him and for that I was grateful. It just wouldn't have worked out anyway.

The year and a half that followed Morgana's birth was a joyful time for our little family. It was a new and delightful experience having a baby in the house, made all the better because Morgana was generally a very happy baby and not prone to crying or fussiness. I spent much of my time swimming down at the old White Springs 19th-century springhouse on the Suwanee River only 100 yards from home and playing my guitar and singing. Mr. Gaulding finished his boat and our house remodel finally ended as well. Mom went shopping all the time, grew a magnificent backyard vegetable garden, and sewed new draperies for the house. For the first time in my life we were all together as a family, the bills were paid, and something that resembled a normal life began to emerge. And best of all, though Mom still carried the vestiges of an entourage that visited from time to time, there were far fewer strangers in our home than ever before. I only wish it could have stayed that way. I see now that it was naive of me not to realize that it would not be so easy to escape the past when the past was nipping so closely at our heels. Those idyllic days were merely the calm before the storm.

There are numerous ways I've imagined over the years how things in our family went from great to horrible, but I know the seeds of the eventual catastrophe were sown when Greg first took up the reins and continued the Jamaican smuggling operation after Mom's departure. I believe it goes without saying that the odds of getting caught at something increase as it is repeated over and over again, and Greg had continually rolled the dice time and time again. To his credit he had kept the basic operation much the same, but there were crucial differences in style and substance between the two. For instance, Mom had given gratuitous bonuses, glossed over setbacks or simply ignored them, and had prayed for luck and that's pretty much what she received. On the other hand, Greg did not believe in bonuses (El Loco told me as much) and sometimes rubbed people the wrong way, especially when he was drinking as was often the case in those days. And in a business that depends on the loyalty of those involved, one weak link or loose tongue could be enough to get the DEA or FBI snooping around or even starting a full-blown investigation. Over the years I've heard several stories, some outlandish and some reasonable, regarding the precise reason why and how the feds initially focused on Greg and the Jamaican operation. But it's a moot point because once they did it was the beginning of the end. All over but the crying. He was busted.

Even then, in a world where a stand-up man accepts responsibility for his own actions and acts accordingly, things may not have gone so bad for Mom and the others who'd quit when she did. But just like it's usually depicted on TV and in the movies the cops' basic modus operandi when questioning a suspect is to seek out the "big fish," the person in charge, el jefe, the "head honcho." Nothing less will suffice, and even if they have the true boss right there in front of them their instinct is to always shoot for more. And who can blame them? But rather than allow the buck to stop with him and just keep his mouth shut, Greg started talking. Big time.

Right out of the gate he gave up Mom as the current head of what the authorities eventually dubbed the "Haas Organization" once they learned, again via Greg, that several of Mom's close relatives (all with the Haas surname) were involved. It obviously did not matter to Greg that Mom had been out of the organization for over a year, nor did it matter that she was the mother of his only child, a baby who would be sure to suffer if her mother was imprisoned. I wonder if he even stopped to think about it. Greg knew so many names, dates, places and facts regarding the operation that his interrogators were mesmerized by all the details, and when a few of the agents expressed some skepticism that an attractive and rather harmless looking mother of three was indeed the mastermind and present leader of a multi-million-dollar international drug smuggling organization, Greg doubled down. Unbelievably, in his effort to convince the feds of his assertions, he claimed that he was afraid for his life should he testify against Mom and asked to be placed in the federal Witness Protection Program. That did it. The feds bought his story—hook, line, and sinker. Mom was going down. It was just a matter of how and when.

12

Take Down

The bomb dropped without warning on an otherwise extremely pleasant spring morning in March. And much like the atomic bomb that had fallen on Hiroshima some 38 years before, its effect was devastating. Where there was once a family—a mother, two teenage kids, and a toddler—nothing remained but a broken shell. My sister Melanie sobbed uncontrollably on the porch steps and my baby sister Morgana screamed bloody murder in my arms after being unceremoniously torn from Mom's breast.

It all began rather innocently with a knock on the front door of our house in White Springs. An insistent knock, heavy handed. To this day I can't help wondering why the feds chose to knock on our front door when they came to arrest Mom. She was, after all, suspected of being capable of extreme violence if Greg was to be believed. Why not bring in the SWAT team to take her down? Why not bust down the door? Greg was slated for witness protection because he said he was afraid of Mom. Did they believe him or not? It defies logic.

It was early and Mom was in bed nursing Morgana and it took more than a minute for her to answer the door. When she did, a cluster of aggressive agents barged in and grabbed Mom, threw her down, and cuffed her. And like angry fire ants whose nest had been disturbed, they kept coming and proceeded to swarm the quiet house. There were so many it seemed like every lawman within 100 miles had been invited to the shindig. Representatives of the GBI (Georgia Bureau of Investigation), FBI, and the United States Federal Marshals were all there in addition to a few local county cops along for the fun.

Our house was a large two-story Victorian so I did not hear anything in my upstairs bedroom and had no clue what was happening until some of the invaders entered Mom's bedroom and woke baby Morgana. The sight of strange men in suits and uniforms, many bristling with equipment and crackling radios, must have scared her witless as she let out a blood-curdling wail that chilled me to the bone. I immediately ran to the stairs and started down and was met halfway by a phalanx of unsmiling agents, a few with guns drawn and the rest with their hands settled on semi-automatic pistols. Frozen stiff, with Morgana's shrill screaming serving as a pitiful soundtrack to the horrific scene, I mentally struggled for a moment while I took it all in. Mom, standing with her hands behind her back and flanked by suited agents, looked up my way with a brave but worried half-smile. My heart pounded hard, even as my shoulders slumped with the realization that one of my worst fears had finally come true.

"Come on down, son, and take your little sister," a short, pudgy, white-haired agent called, not unkindly, from the foot of the stairs. He waved me down and over to where I saw, once the clustered feds moved aside, a female cop holding Morgana in a vain attempt to comfort her.

Without a word I took Morgana in my arms and tried to do my best to soothe her but it wasn't easy. It was as if she sensed that I was in emotional turmoil myself and I had no doubt by that time that the only person capable of calming her was now being led out the door to a waiting car. But Mom gave it a try anyway.

"She's still nursing!" Mom pleaded, glancing from agent to agent as if hoping to find a sympathetic ear. "Can I please just nurse my baby for a few minutes to calm her down? She doesn't know what's happening. She's scared!" I could hear the mounting anguish in her voice.

"Can't do it, Judy," said the white-haired agent, who seemed to me to be the one in charge. His face was cold, unsmiling, and grim as he spoke the words, despite his familiar tone and colloquial speech.

Surprised to hear him use Mom's given name as if he knew her, I refocused my attention and gave him a closer look. A small man, he looked to be in his early 50s with a white mustache that matched his hair, and a belly protruding over his belt so far that I could barely see the badge underneath. Big gun in shoulder-holster ... bigger gun than all the other agents. Smug, pugnacious expression on his face. Okay, I thought, here is a man who takes delight in the suffering of others and maybe has a bit of a Napoleonic complex to boot if the oversized gun is any indication. Dangerous. I later learned that he was a U.S. federal marshal out of the Valdosta, Georgia, field office and Mom would have the misfortune to be under his thumb for the foreseeable future. His name was Al Pitzing. Once I got to know him, I nicknamed him "The Pitz," as in "the bottom" or the pits of hell. Poor Mom. Poor Morgana. She never nursed again.

But the trouble wasn't over after Mom was whisked away. Feds searched the house, probably looking for money more than anything else. They didn't find anything other than a small amount of marijuana, Mom's personal stash. There was less than an ounce. There was no money to be found either unless they were ready to dig, which they were obviously unprepared for. Eventually I was told that Mom had been taken to the Valdosta city jail where she would be held until further notice. I was happy to see them go when they finally left.

Even though Melanie was a mess, she had settled into a sort of numb shock and my attention was still completely focused on Morgana. She had never stopped crying since her brutal separation from Mom. And it was brutal in every sense of the word. Needless to say, Morgana was very much attached to Mom, but the situation was made all the more traumatic because she was a breast-fed baby. I scrounged up a bottle but it was a poor substitute for the living connection that real flesh and natural milk provided and she refused it. I was devastated by losing Mom, yet I was a hundred times more devastated witnessing the suffering of my baby sister. It truly tore my heart to shreds. I decided that I needed help so I called my grandparents but got no answer. Strange.

Not to be deterred, I swiftly packed a bag and headed for Bummy and Baga's house in Valdosta, Georgia, which was less than an hour away. But little did I realize the extent of the bomb that had dropped upon our family that day, for atom bombs produce a massive explosion that's felt far and wide and this one was no exception. As soon as Bummy opened her front door I read the sad truth written on her tearful face.

"Oh David Michael, they got him. They came early this morning and took him away." Her eyes shifted to Morgana simpering quietly in my arms from sheer exhaustion. "Oh poor baby!" She reached out and I passed Morgana into her waiting arms.

"Mom too." I stepped forward and embraced both her and Morgana together in my arms. When I stepped back Melanie moved in and did the same. She had hardly said a word on the drive up and by the time she had disengaged from the hug fresh tears were starting to flow again. I felt very sorry for her and didn't know where to begin trying to comfort her because I had no answers. Only questions. What was going to happen next? Can Mom and Baga be bailed out of jail? And most important of all, what were we going to do about Morgana? Even though I had worried many times before about the dark day that had finally come, I really hadn't come to grips with all the dire consequences. My mind had always shied away at the threshold of the worst thoughts, much like a bad dream in which I was falling but managed to wake up at the last moment before I hit the hard ground. But this was no bad dream. It was bitter reality. I was not going to wake up from this. I wondered, not for the last time, how Mom was holding up, but quickly pushed the thought aside. She would have to fend for herself for the time being. Baby Morgana was right there in front of me, hurting. Another wave of despair washed over and through me as I fought an almost overwhelming urge to just flop down on Bummy's sofa and cry myself to sleep.

"She hasn't taken a drop of anything for hours. I'm worried," I said as Bummy and I locked eyes. "What should we do?"

"Don't worry, honey, she'll be all right. We just have to stay calm. Let's try a bottle."

All I know is that it was a tremendous relief to have Bummy by my side during those first few hours as together we tackled what problems we could (primarily taking care of and comforting Morgana) and ignored those beyond our abilities. Fortunately, as Bummy had predicted, the natural drive of a healthy baby kicked in and Morgana began accepting a bottle once she became hungry enough, although she frequently cried and was much fussier than normal. I'm sure she missed Mom terribly, even though at her tender age she had no way to rationalize the punishment that had befallen her. I wish I could say that the worst was behind us and things were on their way to getting better, but that was not to be. The next day we learned, from lawyers as well as newspapers, the true scope of trouble our family now faced.

For starters, we learned that Aunt Bonnie had also been arrested the same morning as Mom and Baga but had been released late that same evening after posting a $25,000 bond. That was good news for sure. She was at least free to be with her family and conduct her defense from outside of a jail cell. I was very happy for her. And there was more good news as well. Aunt Nancy called and reported that not only had she not been arrested, but El Loco and Gary had also escaped the dragnet and there were no outstanding warrants for their arrest either.

Bummy and I found that strange, but we weren't about to "look a gift horse in the mouth," as the old proverb says. The good news ended there.

Mom and Baga had been indicted by a federal grand jury in Macon, Georgia, on numerous federal charges including the importation into the United States of more than 5,600 pounds of marijuana, racketeering, conspiracy, possession of marijuana with the intent to distribute, transporting more than $5,000 cash out of the U.S. without filing a report with U.S. Customs, and federal income tax evasion, to name just a few. There were 17 total counts on the indictment and Mom's name was beside every one. Baga's bail was set at $200,000, Mom's at $500,000.

Besides them, Jeanne and John Parella had both been arrested in New Jersey, Herman (the kind catch man who had taught me wonderful card tricks) was arrested in Dallas, and Mom's Miami lawyer Ed Sawyer in south Florida. Conspicuously absent from the indictment was Greg.

In subsequent days we learned that the feds were also attempting to confiscate two remaining airplanes, Mom's Cadillac, our home in White Springs, and, oddly, a Rolex watch which I don't remember Mom ever owning. In fact, the only person I do distinctly remember owning a Rolex was Greg. Hmmm. Did he accidentally leave it at Mom's and want the feds to retrieve it for him? I think so.

The day of his arrest, Baga had hired a local Valdosta attorney named Converse Bright to represent him and Mom and Bonnie. If I had to describe Mr. Bright today, I'd say his appearance was remarkably similar to Mitt Romney. Eager to learn anything, Bummy and I went to meet him straightaway. What an impressive name for a lawyer, I thought to myself as we drove to his office. Surely he'll be able to work a bit of legal magic and at the very minimum get Mom and Baga released on bond. After all, what's the big deal about a mere $700,000? What was the money sitting in the ground for if not to buy freedom? I thought Baga and Mom's release would be a slam dunk. Boy, was I wrong!

Alas, as it turned out, although Mr. Bright's name impressed me mightily, his performance did not. Not long after our meeting he began offering statements to the press where he seemed to be making more of a case for the prosecution than the defense. For instance, when he was asked about the charge of taking more than $5,000 to Jamaica, rather than offering an innocent explanation, such as the money might have been earmarked for real-estate or another legitimate business venture (or just keeping his big mouth shut), Bright responded, "Obviously, the inference they [the cops] are making is that they [his clients, Baga, Mom, and Aunt Bonnie] took that money to Jamaica to buy marijuana." Even to a teenager like me, with zero legal knowledge or training, Mr. Bright's comments appeared unprofessional and incompetent. But when he began speaking about the potential of a bond (a subject very dear to my heart as I was desperately clinging to the hope that Mom would get out of jail soon) I was downright shocked. "We're working like a beaver to get them out on bond," Bright said, "but I'm sure Judy will not raise bond."

Was he serious? I just couldn't believe what I was reading! The story of Mom's arrest had already been plastered across the front pages of several major newspapers and the feds had often gleefully proclaimed hers was a $250 million-a-year operation. How could someone like that be unable to post a measly half-million-dollar bond? It did not make sense to me and I was sure something weird was going on, only I just didn't know exactly what. In retrospect I now realize my ignorance was because I was an innocent kid and not even close to thinking on a criminal level. I did not stop to think about the consequences of Mom producing a huge chunk of cash out of the blue. Because she only owned one house, and therefore had little real estate bond collateral, that's exactly what she would have to do. That single act would have proven a significant part of the feds' case against her, so Mom was effectively painted into a corner with no way out.

Bummy and I visited Mom and Baga often, baby Morgana in tow, and it was heartrending every time. Ironically, the worst visit was when Mom somehow convinced a guard to allow her to hold Morgana. When she did, poor Morgana immediately began searching for Mom's breast and tried to latch on to nurse, but it was too late. Mom's milk had already begun to dry up after she'd finally been given an injection after days of suffering with swollen breasts and no baby to nurse. It was bittersweet to see the pair briefly reunited, baby Morgana plaintively looking up into Mom's tearful tragic eyes. All too soon, the kindhearted guard came to take Mom back to her cell and they were forced to separate once again, leaving only trauma and heartbreak behind. It was almost too much to bear.

Baga, for his part, stoically suffered in silence and provided a strong shoulder for Mom during those tough first few days, for they were in adjacent cells. They even managed to play cards, invisible to each other except for their hands, around a partition that separated the cells. I'm sure Mom was greatly comforted by Baga's presence, but it did not last long. Surprisingly, Mr. Bright had managed to work a small miracle and had arranged for Baga to be bonded out. Mom was now on her own. The future was wide open. Anything could happen.

In her efforts to figure out a suitable path for her defense and possibly even a bond of her own, Mom met with Mr. Bright on several occasions, and on their very first meeting two odd occurrences transpired. Because Mom was a federal prisoner she was required to be directly supervised by Federal Marshal Pitzing, aka "The Pitz," whenever she was released from her cell. A notable exception was when she met with her attorney. To facilitate this attorney-client privilege and ensure privacy their meetings were held in a small, windowless room, devoid of anything but a single steel desk and two chairs. On the day in question, the Pitz led her into this room and pointed to a chair. "I'll be right outside," he deadpanned as he left the room, digging for keys under his overhanging belly. They rattled against the steel door as he turned the lock. Mom sat and waited for Mr. Bright, glad for the change of scenery.

When Mr. Bright hadn't appeared after some time, Mom stood to relieve the tension. Worried about Morgana, worried about her case, she tried to focus on better days as she paced in a small circle around the desk. Looking down, she noticed a drawer and opened it. Inside was an unused legal pad. Too bad there was nothing to write with, but it could come in handy later so she decided to keep it. A few minutes later, more clanking keys announced the arrival of Mr. Bright, fashionably late.

"Judy? Converse Bright," he declared as he extended a manicured hand in front of his broad smile. "It's very good to finally meet you in person." Although his grin was a world-class politician's, it lacked sincerity. Mom took his hand.

"Nice to meet you."

"Now, first we need to—" he began, but Mom interrupted.

"Mr. Bright, what's the penalty for escape?" she asked. Years later, as Mom recounted this event to me, I asked her what in the world had prompted her to ask such a question, especially to a new lawyer she had just met. She told me it must have been on her mind and just "spilled out." When I asked her Bright's response she couldn't remember. But according to her there was one thing she would never forget about that meeting: Marshal Pitzing's first words to her after Mr. Bright left.

"Now, Judy, don't you dare ever try to escape," he said as his beady black eyes bored straight through hers. Mom stood mute.

Mom thought about the Pitz's words long after the event and came to an inescapable conclusion that she swears by to this very day. The room was bugged. Illegally, no doubt, yet bugged all the same. And I have no reason to think the Pitz was above listening in on a privileged attorney-client conversation because I soon endured my own singular encounters with law enforcement that I feel crossed the line between right and wrong.

Agents of the FBI and the GBI were the first that hauled me in for questioning. And when I say they "hauled me in" I'm being nice. They in fact arrested me with what I can only call unnecessary force. The harassment began with a traffic stop in an unmarked car, a single blue light on the dash, flashing ominously. I immediately pulled over and stopped, hands on the steering wheel and questions in my head. What was going on now? Well, I didn't have long to wait for an answer. Multiple agents in suits and ties swiftly surrounded my Land Cruiser, opened the door, snatched me out of the driver's seat and threw me up on the hood, much like a rancher grabbing a bale of hay and loading it on a wagon. Yet, unlike a bale of hay, the wind was knocked out of me and my nose surely did not appreciate the agents' attempt to relocate its position on my face, as they violently pressed my head on the hood. I tried to catch my breath as cuffs bit into my wrists, hands slapped over my body in a rapid frisk, and my arms were hoisted behind my back as I was led to their car. Once inside, I asked if I was arrested, and if so, what the charge was. My questions fell on deaf ears so I gave up.

It was a short ride to the nondescript office-type building with the windowless room where they took me. To this day I still don't know where it was or exactly how long I was there. It could have been 20 hours or two days, maybe more. I wasn't wearing a watch and I did not get a phone call. Time lost meaning. The men did identify themselves as U.S. federal agents of multiple varieties but I was not read my rights. I was not offered a lawyer even though I continually asked for a phone call. What I chiefly remember was a never-ending parade of agents in suits and polished shoes, asking a million questions and making a thousand threats, sometimes delivered in a normal tone of voice, often barked harshly.

It did not take long for me to realize that most of their questions were focused on Aunt Nancy. Not Mom, not Baga, not El Loco, and, curiously, not Greg either. They probably should have mixed a lot more of the good cop into their good-cop, bad-cop routine, because although I had been thoroughly intimidated at the outset and was more than a little scared, I was also deeply offended and insulted. More important, I felt I had done nothing wrong and was therefore untouchable in the long run. Bottom line? I gave them nothing.

Toward the end of my kidnapping, for that's what I've come to think it was, a "good" cop offered me a soda and asked me to take a polygraph (lie detector) test. I had never had one before and without giving it a second thought I gave the agent a big smile and said I'd be glad to take one. He could not conceal his surprise and scurried from the room. More waiting ensued and I fervently wished I had a book … anything to pass the time. A couple hours later an agent with the machine arrived and hooked me up like a modern-day Frankenstein. The examiner agent asked many of the same questions I was asked before. I gave the same answers. Finally, he announced the test was over and even though he was behind me and I could not see his face or the machine I could hear the disappointment in his voice as he packed up and said goodbye. Soon after, "bad" cops came to inform me that I had failed the test and should therefore cooperate or I was going to jail, but my gut knew better and they released me not long afterward. No charges, nothing.

I didn't know it at the time but I later learned that the way I was handled by the agents was actually not illegal because they had special powers as U.S. federal agents that surpassed those of regular city, county, or state cops. Were the feds that picked me up a little overzealous in their duties and treatment of me? I think so, especially considering that I was an Eagle Scout and student, well known in the community and church and had no criminal record. But I have to honestly say that I don't bear any ill will toward the vast majority of cops whom I consider to be good people doing a tough and often unrewarding job.

Among the myriad emotions I experienced following that first nasty experience with authority was the undeniable feeling that I was vulnerable. I was vulnerable to those in a position of power and willing to use it to advance an agenda. And what was the 1980s "war on drugs"? What was its agenda? There are many opinions out there but I know that the feds weren't just looking to keep Mom in jail and give Aunt

Nancy an adjoining cell; they were looking to confiscate wealth—cash and property both. Greg had given them plenty of information to get the ball rolling and make some arrests but ultimately it was the money that mattered. Another question loomed large in my mind. Where was Greg when the world was turning upside down and his baby girl cried herself to sleep practically every night? El Loco had obviously pondered that same question and voiced his opinion over dinner one night not long after Baga bonded out.

"I think Greg's a rat," he spat out the words like there was something unpleasant or poisonous in his mouth. Baga and I nodded our heads in agreement. Bummy's eyes widened as she turned to him.

"Why do you think that?" she asked matter-of-factly, like a judge equally weighing an argument before deciding which way to go.

"Well, nobody's heard from him since way before y'all were busted," he said, glancing Baga's way, "and nobody's seen him neither. I've tried to call him a dozen times. It's like he just disappeared."

"I've tried calling him too. Nothing." Baga spoke with conviction. "And how in the hell did he not get popped?"

No one at the table had an answer to that. At least not one that was innocent. It really seemed like Greg must be involved somehow. We surmised that if he had been named in the indictment and then disappeared he might just be on the lam and laying low. That made sense. But the thought of him betraying his friends, his lover and the mother of his baby (as well as his baby daughter herself) was hard for me to swallow, especially since he chose to carry on with the smuggling after Mom had quit. I tried to put myself in his shoes. I tried to conjure up a rational scenario that would explain the facts we had at that time. Bummy and I brainstormed late into the night much like we did when we were discussing a new book and came up empty. The chickens all came back to roost in one place. Greg. He had to be a snitch. Once again, and not for the last time, I reminisced about the venomous snakes, scorpions, and black widow spiders of my desert childhood and I realized I must have grown up quite a bit since then, for the vermin I knew of now were far worse.

Meanwhile, as each day melted into the next, it became more and more apparent that Converse Bright's words were true. Mom wasn't going to get out of jail. Bummy, Baga, Melanie, Morgana and I visited her so much that we knew the routine by heart. The Pitz remained consistent with my initial opinion of him and would throw curve balls that made our life, and Mom's, much harder than it had to be. His behavior was heartless and vindictive for no reason. He'd switch visitation hours and days at the last minute. He'd allow us to bring Mom certain luxuries (a particular food item or book, for example) then confiscate them as soon as we left. It was capricious and unnecessary cruelty. Being a prisoner with a baby was tough enough as it was. Mom kept a stiff upper lip and tried her best under the circumstances to minimize her predicament and look on the bright side, but for me Mom being locked up was every bit as bad as I'd feared it would be, maybe worse. What a fool I'd been to think that her quitting the "business" would keep her safe. It was only a childish illusion, I realized. Maybe that was why so few, if any, criminals quit. Maybe they knew it was no use and the past was something that could not be left behind or outrun. It was not something one could change like a new suit of clothes. Many times on my way home from a visitation with Mom thoughts like these churned in my brain and I felt like just a stupid kid. I had a hard time with it all and tortured myself constantly.

If Mom had any bright ideas, other than hiring a good lawyer (which she did) and mounting an exuberant defense, I was unaware of it. Our conversations were stifled by the jail environment. Because she and I were very close and knew each other well, I could sense her mounting desperation. Both of us knew she was guilty of being a marijuana smuggler and both of us knew the consequences. It was common knowledge that even low-level dealers were often sentenced to decades in prison. What would the punishment be for a marijuana smuggling "queenpin"? Yes, it was only pot, but it was the early 1980s and Reagan's almighty war on drugs was in full swing. Some heads were gonna roll, many of them from my family, and Mom's head was the one most squarely under the guillotine.

Yes, they were desperate times. And desperate times often called for desperate measures.

13

Escape

For months, it seemed that anyone and everyone with even the slightest whim to do so had visited Mom in the Valdosta city jail. And not just family either. Friends and acquaintances that had not been in touch for years made attempts—some successful, some not—to visit her. I'm sure their motivations ran the gamut, but curiosity had to be a major one. Like King Kong in his cage, here was the malevolent drug-smuggling criminal. Behold! She looks just like us, but she's not!

The Valdosta police department continued to bask in the attention their infamous prisoner provided and was proud its facility was sanctioned to temporarily incarcerate federal prisoners. As days turned to weeks, and weeks to months, Mom's notoriety increased. Newspapers, without benefit of interviews since the Valdosta police department wouldn't allow them, went wild with speculation and the handful of authentic facts leaked through law enforcement sources. The size and extent of the Haas organization was anybody's guess, so that's just what they did. Marshal Pitzing continued to strut around like Wyatt Earp. A cop named Captain White (in charge of Valdosta jail policies) enacted tougher, increasingly arcane visitation rules. Visiting Mom remained a bittersweet event.

I was stressed out, to say the least. Mom being locked up was bad; Morgana was still only a toddler and losing her mother at that age was no joke. Morgana and Bummy had developed a routine by this point and they were as close as could be expected, but there was simply no explanation I could provide that was suitable for a two-year-old. I sure as heck didn't have the answers. Then came the day that changed everything and shook my universe. And it came on like a tidal wave … a tidal wave of cops.

It's no understatement to say that it was a shock when Mom was initially arrested, but somewhere deep in my mind I must have previously considered the possibility and was therefore able to reconcile all the emotions. I "dealt with it," as the saying goes, and it wasn't easy. However, the day the cop tsunami hit, it was a total knockout—totally unexpected 100 percent chaos.

The White Springs house had become a band house and was just beginning to stir with life in the early morning hours after a late night rehearsal. Of course, as young musicians, we were not that hip on rising at the crack of dawn anyway and the sound of multiple vehicles tearing down the street and screeching to a halt in the front yard was the first indication that the shit was hitting the fan. Car doors slamming, leather accessory belts creaking, boots pounding, and hardware jingling—all this was bad enough—but the obvious sound of cocking guns and chambering rounds was ominous and unnerving. Were the cops coming for the band?

To my surprise they actually knocked on the front door. I'm sure it would have been kicked in seconds later, but I immediately threw it wide open and braced myself for the inevitable onslaught. What would it be this time? How long would I be held?

Not for the last time, I felt sorry for my band. They were guilty of nothing more than a little underage drinking. We were only teenagers playing rock music in the home of an accused smuggler, yet here again were cops at the door. And this time there was a distinct edginess to their actions, an energy that was previously missing. This time they were clearly and utterly pissed off.

The whole gang had showed up for the fun this time, with a grimacing Marshal Pitzing at the head of the column of cops bowling me over at the door. In seconds flat I was thrown to the floor and cuffed. Cops swarmed the house like angry bees and soon had the rest of the band trussed up as well. I did not bother asking about a warrant, but I did wonder why this particular shitstorm involved so many cops.

"What's this all about? What did we do?" I blurted out, directing my questions specifically to the Pitz.

He glared at me and did not answer and that's when I saw the depth of his anger. What had I done? Based upon his prior treatment of Mom I knew he disliked and probably hated her. Now his enmity included me.

"What's going on?" I repeated. I was worried now. I knew I had not committed any crime but I thought one might be trumped up against me anyway. A lot of my family had already been charged. Did they really want me now? Was I next?

The Pitz himself hustled me to his unmarked car and I had barely enough time to manage a quick glance toward my bandmates Jud and Chris on my way out the door. I hoped they knew how sorry I was that by simply being near me and being my friends they were being harassed and possibly arrested. What a bummer.

On the 45-minute drive back to Valdosta, the Pitz broke his silence. And after thinking about the event later with a clear head I'm sure he had planned it that way. He probably thought I was just a longhaired kid and easy picking.

"Your mom's escaped," he said through clenched teeth in a tone of voice evenly mixed with anger and disgust. "But you already know that, don't ya?"

At first I thought I must be hearing things and was stunned into silence. I could not believe it! Mom escaped? No way! But the Pitz remained silent, staring at me in the rearview mirror through the steel lattice. I felt his anger swell and the feeling convinced me I had not misunderstood. My mind was suddenly flooded with questions. How? When? Where is she now? Will I ever see her again? I'm sure the cops, Pitzing foremost among them, had many of the same questions running through their heads. The only trouble was that the Pitz obviously thought I had at least some of the answers.

"So, where is she, son?" His tone was moderated a little toward the nicer side, but not much. Coming from him, being called son just sounded wearily patronizing. Right then and there, uncomfortably cuffed in his backseat, already tired and with no end of the ordeal yet in sight, I nonetheless felt a surge of joy at the thought that Mom had escaped and decided that I would never tell him Mom's whereabouts, even if I came to know them later. But the simple truth was I could not answer him even if I had wanted to. I had not been involved in her escape in any way and her location was a complete mystery to me. I just hoped she was okay.

"I have no idea. When did she escape?"

"I'm asking the questions here, understand?" He practically spit the words at me. The bad cop was back.

I nodded. We rode on in silence for a minute or two.

"So, when did you last see her?"

"I saw her Friday or Saturday, I think."

"Which one, Friday or Saturday?"

"Friday, I think. It's on the visitation log, isn't it?"

I was answering his questions easily as I did not have anything to hide. He must have felt otherwise or maybe he just did not have any other leads to go on. The interrogation went on and on. Lots of the same questions repeated over and over. We were just a few minutes from his office when the good cop in him tried to make a small comeback.

"You know, son, what the penalty is for aiding and abetting the escape of a federal prisoner? Five years in the federal penitentiary." Our eyes met in the rearview mirror. "If you tell me all about it you won't go to jail."

"There's nothing to tell," I said, sticking to the truth. "I don't know where she is." But the Pitz did not want to hear it. Since he was the federal marshal in charge of Mom's custody he was responsible for her escape. If he could somehow manage to re-capture her he would at least be partly vindicated. If he couldn't, his name was mud in the law enforcement community. Even though his desperation was somewhat pathetic and begged a sort of sympathy, I could not feel sorry for the man. He had been too cruel to Mom during the long months she had been under his thumb. Baby Morgana had suffered more than necessary because of his inflexible visitation rules. I felt as though Mom had merely turned the tables on the little man with the Napoleon complex.

Finally, back at the Pitz's office I was hounded with hours of questions and threats by more law enforcement officers than I care to remember and they all seemed to have one thing in common. They were angry and humiliated. How could this little woman have done this? In their opinion only a well-planned and well-executed escape could have succeeded and she must have had outside help. Their egos would allow no other explanation. They were hell-bent on getting to the bottom of things.

Valdosta city detectives tag-teamed with the Pitz in an attempt to bully me into admitting something that I did not know in the first place. When they tired of the sport, the GBI tried the same tactic with the FBI as partners. Of course, this did not work either as I was telling the truth and was far too strong to ever allow myself to be bullied or tricked into incriminating myself. Yet I can understand how some people can, and do, falsely admit to crimes they did not commit. These cops were no fun, for sure, and dealing with them was hard labor, but I was kind of battle-hardened from my first go-round with some of the same characters and I eventually outlasted them. They released me later that night and Bummy came down to pick me up. I went back to her house and slept like a log.

It was almost three years later that I heard, from Mom herself, the details of the events that transpired before, during, and after her escape.

Oddly enough, it had begun with the planning and execution of another inmate's escape. A fellow prisoner, a middle-aged Georgia country boy jailed for a relatively minor offense, had spent a solitary, furiously busy night in his cell sawing noisily away at a single bar. Mom was astonished that his sawing had been so loud and yet had still gone unnoticed the entire night. The next morning his escape was discovered, an alarm was raised, and searches conducted, but the prisoner—Mom never learned his name—remained at large.

Something else had also occurred that night that no one ever noticed.

The night of his jailbreak Country Boy had passed by her cell on the way out and, noticing Mom was awake and aware of what was transpiring, looked her straight in the eye and asked, "Got any money?"

Mom calmly went over to her cot, retrieved a plastic bag that held a few dollars of change, and passed it through the bars to the escapee. He promptly took the money and gave Mom the hacksaw blade he had used to cut through the bar to enable his own escape. She accepted it with a silent nod of thanks. Mom retreated with the treasure, and after some thought, stashed it inside a bottle of hair conditioner.

The next morning when Country Boy's escape was discovered the jail erupted in a frenzy of sporadic and haphazard searches and shakedowns. Captain White went ballistic. The Pitz kept his composure, as Country Boy wasn't a federal prisoner and therefore not under his charge. To Mom's astonished disbelief, nothing came of the entire ruckus and life in the Valdosta city jail returned to normal.

Mom conferred with Jeannie (who had recently been transferred to the Valdosta city jail in anticipation of the upcoming trial) that night. She told her about the hacksaw blade and offered to share the opportunity it represented. When Jeannie wondered what that meant, Mom snapped the blade into two equal pieces of about five inches each and handed one over. Jeannie tentatively accepted.

Without delay (and with essentially no help or pre-planning) Mom began her own escape. Years later, I asked about her motivations and apparent disregard of the consequences. She replied, "I think it's human nature to want to be free, to want to escape. At least it gives you something to do." That "something to do" was sawing. Lots and lots of noisy sawing. However, unlike Country Boy, Mom took great precautions to keep her escape on the down low and on track.

She concentrated on an overhead bar in her cell and only sawed, very slowly and quietly, late at night or when other noisy activities or projects were going on in the jail. It was slow going. She wrapped the blade in a sock to protect her hands, and to conceal the cut she mixed the metal sawdust with toothpaste and used it as filler. Days passed, then weeks. Then one day Jeannie came to Mom with a declaration.

"I'm not going. I can't do it."

Mom asked her why with a facial expression.

Jeannie replied, "My mom is old. She needs me. I want to be able to see her again. I just can't do it."

"Okay, I understand."

Jeannie and Mom embraced through the bars and that was all there was to it. But unknown to Mom at the time, Jeannie, out of fear of being caught with contraband or in the commission of an escape, had decided to inform the guards of the existence of her and Mom's hacksaw blades and their impromptu escape plans. Considering the previous recent escape, they took the information seriously.

The next morning, Valdosta police department guards removed all the prisoners from their cells and scoured them for any indication of an escape attempt. Officers placed mattresses across each inmate's barred cell ceiling so they could crawl along, searching for any sign of a breach. Miraculously, nothing was found and all the prisoners, including Mom, were returned to their same cells that very evening.

Incredibly, all Mom's belongings remained untouched, including, most important, the bottle of conditioner that contained the piece of the hacksaw blade. As a hedge against the officers possibly changing their minds and deciding to confiscate everything—it had happened before— she decided to use some of the self-care products given to her by friends and family. One such product was a bottle of brunette hair dye Bummy had given Mom the week before. Mom had bleached her hair blonde for years, but Bummy, as well as Mom's attorney, had encouraged her to change her hair back to her natural dark brown. After dyeing her hair, she kept it wrapped in a towel for the rest of the evening until lights out.

Mom knew something unusual had instigated the shakedown but had no clue at the time it was the result of Jeannie's information. She merely continued, that very night, to finish the final little bit of sawing needed to cut through the single bar that would allow her head to pass between, for she remembered reading that where one's head could pass, the body could follow. A few strokes were all it took—she was nearly through and the bar was hanging on by a thread, so she thought to test its strength with a little wiggle—and to her utter surprise it came completely loose in her hand with no way to be replaced for a later opportunity. This was unexpected, as she had not planned on this particular night being the one, but there was no going back. She knew it was now or never.

Mom quickly and quietly gathered a few of her belongings that would fit in her pockets as well as a small number of bills and small change that still remained and climbed through the new gap in the ceiling of her cell. It was a tight squeeze, but not as close as she had anticipated. The brief hunger strike she had recently employed to protest her treatment had paid off. A short crawl brought her to the main hallway where she slid down the seven-foot cell wall. On her feet once again, Mom saw what she had perceived weeks ago as a security weakness: a low window, partially open for ventilation, its glass broken, conveniently located adjacent to the hallway. As an unexpected bonus, there were a couple of boxes filled with cleaning supplies stacked nearby. She carefully rearranged these as a makeshift ladder and silently as a cat climbed through the window to the relative freedom of the outer courtyard.

The Valdosta city jail was obviously not a high-security prison. Mom had gotten outside the main building with relative ease but did not know what awaited her there. As it turned out, the only obstacle that remained was a common six-foot chain-link fence with no razor wire or anything else. She scaled it without incident and crossed the police motor-pool parking lot, careful to avoid the lights as much as possible. The cool night air was invigorating as she headed down the dark street toward a brightly-lit convenience store she noticed in the distance. The night was dead still and quiet at this hour. No sign of anything amiss. So far, so good. She breathed a tad easier.

Ten minutes into her first taste of freedom in months found Mom staring at a payphone mounted near the main entrance of the convenience store. No one was anywhere in sight. Searching her pockets for change, she was about to deposit the coins and make a call when a Valdosta police department cruiser pulled up and parked, the cop inside looking her way. She felt totally exposed and vulnerable to his scrutiny. Following a sudden impulse from deep inside, she calmly returned the change to her pocket and casually walked over to the cruiser's driver's side. The cop rolled down his window. Her heart skipped a beat and the breath caught in her throat as she instantly recognized him as the officer who had brought her breakfast every weekday morning for the past several months of her incarceration.

Committed, she took a deep breath in an attempt to calm her nerves and leaned in close, a shy smile on her face.

"Excuse me, officer. Sorry to trouble you. Could I borrow a little change for the phone? My car broke down and I need to make a call to get a ride home."

Dozens of thoughts swarmed her brain and threatened to paralyze her. Would she be recognized? Had her escape been discovered yet? Oh God, please don't let it end here!

Officer Miller began to dig through his pockets, searching for change to help the lady out. "Here you go," he said, handing over a few coins. "Have a good night."

"Thank you, officer." Mom smiled at him warmly. The new brunette hairdo must have been enough. Mom turned and went to make her call. She dialed Baga's number. The cop drove off just as her call was answered.

"Hello?" a somewhat irritated voice answered. It was Baga, and he was not pleased at the hour of the call.

"Hi, Daddy."

"Oh, Christ…. Judy?" No doubt he was surprised.

"I'm out…. I love you, Daddy!" Mom was having a difficult time keeping her emotions in check. "How's Mama? How's my baby?"

"They're fine." The call lapsed into silence. Mom waited for his inevitable words of condemnation, only they did not come. Baga continued, his voice low and solemn. "Judy?"

"Yes, Daddy?"

"I love you."

"I love you too, Daddy."

"Judy?"

"Yes?"

"Run … run far and stay long."

With those parting words echoing in her ears, Mom hung up and went inside the store and bought a cup of coffee. A tenth of her money vanished with that one small purchase. She drank the coffee and pondered her next move. The events of the night made it difficult to concentrate. The only thing that she was sure of was the need to get out of town, put as much distance between herself and Valdosta, Georgia, as possible. And the sooner she could accomplish it, the better. But how?

A bitter realization had begun to sink in. Mom was technically free, but she could not think of a single person that would be able to help her capitalize on that freedom and make a clean getaway. Any family member's home would be hot as a firecracker come morning when her escape was discovered. Ditto any close friends. An APB would also prevent her borrowing a car from anyone but a stranger, so that option was off the table as well. And of course using public transportation of any sort was the quickest path to disaster, regardless of any disguise she could muster, as she had no identification of any kind. Her options were limited and dwindling fast. Resisting panic, she thought it might help her think of a plan if she just started walking, so that is what she did.

A soft glow on the eastern horizon that signaled the coming dawn gradually grew brighter as Mom made her way in the general direction of Interstate 75, which was the main north-south highway in the area. She reached it later that morning without incident. As usual, several motels and gas stations were clustered strategically around the exit. She headed toward the nearest motel.

It had been a long walk but not an unpleasant one. The weather was fair and it felt good to breathe the fresh outside air and get some exercise after months of captivity. As an added bonus, there had been no sign of her escape as far as she could tell; no police cruisers had appeared during her walk. Could the good luck continue?

Crossing into the motel's parking lot, Mom noticed two 50-something salesmen types shouldering duffel bags and heading toward a car. There was no time for a plan. Desperate, summoning all the charm at her disposal, she approached with a smile and a seductive feminine swagger and not much else. A deep Southern accent sprouted from nowhere.

"Hey, where y'all headin'?

"South…. Florida…. Tampa Bay," answered the guy just about to open the driver's side door.

"Could I catch a ride with ya'll? I was goin' to my sister's. She's havin' a baby and my car broke down and I've been lookin' for a ride. I just don't know who I can trust."

Before they had a chance to think it over, Mom strutted in closer and offered her hand and an even bigger smile. It probably didn't hurt that she had also adjusted her blouse to bare a substantial amount of cleavage just prior to her approach. The driver could not resist and Mom got a ride out of town.

By the following afternoon, after a series of rides, Mom found herself walking the beach of Anna Maria Island just south of Tampa Bay. She had had to ditch the salesmen in Tampa, where she had then hitched a ride with a south-bound trucker. He took her as far as Bradenton, but his route was heading inland from there and she decided to stick to the coast. From that point, it was nothing to catch a ride to the beach for there were always people heading that way. Valdosta seemed a lifetime away.

Everything had happened so fast, almost like a dream. Forty-eight hours earlier she had been a caged prisoner, now she was free and had nothing and no one to answer to. There was no doubt in her mind that she would have to go it alone for quite some time and that contacting any family or friends would be disastrous. It was both inhibiting and exhilarating at the same time. As she strolled along and mulled everything over, the afternoon wore on and the beach became more and more deserted. This did not bother her; she quite enjoyed the solitude after being crammed in a cage for months. On impulse, she crossed Gulf Boulevard to a nearby convenience store with the intention of buying a beer in celebration of her freedom. Hell, maybe a six-pack would be more appropriate!

She decided on Heineken and, eyeing the other customers for any signs of trouble—this had become habit overnight—she set the six-pack on the counter and began to dig for the little plastic baggie that held her dwindling supply of cash, which was now mostly assorted change. It was right at that moment, looking down, that she noticed something incredible. In fact, she had to take another hard look, a double-take, before she realized what was lying on the floor at her feet.

It was a Florida driver's license, picturing a woman about her age with long dark hair. Mom swiftly snatched it up before anyone noticed. Quickly, without so much as a second glance, she slipped it in her back pocket and resumed paying for the beer. Not much money was left, but she was so excited by the possibilities of her find that being nearly broke did not seem all that bad. She crossed back over to the beach before opening a beer and taking a good look at her newfound prize.

Mom could not believe her good fortune. So many personal details of the woman whose license she had found matched perfectly, or were at least compatible, with her own. The name on the license was Rachel McVey. Like Mom, Rachel had medium-long brunette hair, brown eyes, and her age, height, and weight were almost an exact match. It was a small miracle. Identification gave a smart fugitive a definite edge. Sipping a beer, she wandered on, praising her good fortune, and thought it might even be nice to sleep out on the beach in the sand.

The sun was quite low when Mom came upon a solitary figure lounging on the seawall of a nearby restaurant. The young man looked about as lonely as she felt. She headed in his general direction with her beer in one hand and an unopened cold one in the other. His eyes studied her as she approached.

When she got close, she said, "Hi, like a beer?" She held it up as if she knew it would not be refused.

"Sure." He took the beer, unscrewed the cap, and took a big swig in a single deft motion. "I'm Johnny."

"Rachel," Mom answered. She liked the name, felt it suited her.

"Nice to meet you," he replied. And quite casually, he reached inside his shirt pocket and produced a fat joint. Mom gave him a big smile of encouragement as he fired up. Things were getting better all the time.

They spent the next half-hour finishing the smoke and enjoying the best of what Anna Maria Island is known for—serene sugar-sand beaches and laid-back people. A gentle breeze rustled the palm trees while the surf whooshed softly through the sand as they talked. A magic spell was cast. Mom felt at home for the first time since her escape. She was feeling more and more optimistic things would somehow work out in the end and she resumed her normally overall positive outlook on life. I'm sure the joint helped, as she had not smoked in months and it must have hit her hard, but in a good way.

Johnny soon explained that he was a commercial fisherman from a fishing village located just across the Intracoastal Waterway from Anna Maria and he offered to show her around the next day. The place was called Cortez, with a population of around 3,000, founded in the 1880s and home to an eclectic mix of artists, commercial fishermen, hard drinkers, and snowbirds, not necessarily in that order. Not surprisingly, due to the nature of men who make their living from the sea, many of its residents were born rebels, very private, suspicious of outsiders, and predisposed against authority. All big positives for someone on the run. Additionally—Mom did not know it at the time—the tiny village had already spawned more than its share of marijuana smugglers over the years.

Call it happenstance or call it luck, but Mom had somehow stumbled upon the nearly ideal place for a fugitive from the law.

14

Cortez

Cortez was truly a gem for someone on the lam such as Mom. She was an attractive single woman, 40 years old but looked younger, no apparent baggage, a quick smile, and an easy-going, can-do attitude. Her arrival in the tiny village was like a strong current—hardly visible on the surface, but nearly overpowering once in the water and under its influence.

Johnny, true to his word, made it his mission to show "Rachel" around and introduce her to the Cortez gentry, of which he was a respected member. His family, the Guthries, had been fixtures in Cortez for generations dating back to the mid–1800s, and his elder brother "Junior" Guthrie was none other than a famous marijuana smuggler of the 1970s who still retained a folk-hero status among many of the residents of Cortez. At the time of Mom's arrival, Junior was in federal prison serving time for marijuana smuggling, but his legendary persona permeated almost every aspect of life in Cortez. Most of Cortez's residents were either fishermen, relatives of fishermen, or those that earned their living catering to some aspect of the industry.

Cortez fishermen, like many of their contemporaries around the world, had multiple ties other than family which brought them together in ways that are a veritable throwback to a forgotten time. The hard work commercial fishing entails coupled with the uncertainty of any profit would discourage most people, but not fishermen. They thrive on a particular blend of two variables—the freedom of the water combined with the chance of a big payday—and I can say from firsthand experience it is an addictive pursuit, much like gambling. And like gambling, some fishermen do occasionally hit it big. A boatload of fish can be worth many tens of thousands of dollars and the memory of a colossal haul can linger as a pleasant daydream in a fisherman's mind for years. And that's just the tip of the iceberg. Fishermen typically spend long hours in relative isolation from the world with nobody but their fellow crewmembers as company for days on end. Personalities must be compatible or there could be hell to pay. Trust also plays a big role. Fishermen have to trust each other with their physical safety when working around dangerous equipment, which is nearly constant, and they must be able to trust each other with secrets. A fisherman that locates a particularly good spot where fish are plentiful (a "honey-hole") is apt to guard that secret with his life and it's not uncommon for fishing boat captains to elaborately encode their "numbers" (the coordinates of the exact location of honey-holes) to prevent others from discovering the spots. I've heard of fishing boats leaving in the middle of the night without lights and making VHF radio calls that publicly announce a false position just to avoid detection and maintain secrecy. Anything that can be imagined has probably been done at one time or the other. It's no wonder that they have a well-deserved reputation for being close-knit and tight-lipped.

In addition to the fishermen's lust for the big catch is an almost equal tradition of ideology based on mythology, some ancient, some modern. And none is more captivating than the mythical "Square Grouper," which fishermen and non-fishermen alike have been known to encounter, floating at sea or washed up on the beach. Bales of marijuana, the Square Grouper, have been known to be washed overboard during a smuggling transfer or purposely ditched from a plane or boat at sea when authorities are closing in. They're not fish, of course, but a fabulous catch all the same, and it would be a poor example of a Cortez fisherman that did not maintain a close and constant lookout for that ever-elusive and most coveted fish in the ocean.

Mom, no stranger to Square Groupers (and the de facto mother of many herself), took to commercial fishing like a fish takes to water. It just made sense, because first and foremost, Mom loved to fish. She'd spent many a lazy afternoon on the banks of Lake Alison fishing for catfish with a cane pole in one hand and a joint in the other. Second, and perhaps more important, she had to do something to make a living. She could not risk any contact with friends or family and therefore had no source of money other than what she could earn herself. So, after she and Johnny had made the initial rounds of introductions with some of the good people of Cortez, he and other villagers began her education in the ancient art of commercial fishing of which there were many varieties and nuances.

After Johnny, some of the first villagers Mom befriended were a sixth generation fisherman named Don and his wife, a talented artist named Jackie. Don had begun his fishing career as a boy on his father's boat and by the time he grew up he had fished using just about every method known to man. At the time he met Mom he favored a method that utilized a small and fast outboard-powered boat and an 800-yard gill net that was used to "strike" fish. The technique required the fisherman to first locate an area where there were signs of a large school of fish, such as diving sea birds or jumping fish. Stealth was paramount, as it was important to get as close as possible to the school without spooking the fish. His engine idling low and keeping his approach slow and quiet, a fisherman must close in on his quarry, then pounce, hard and fast. This was accomplished by throwing the "let-go" (a weight on the end of a line attached to the leading edge of the net) off the stern of the boat and gunning the engine to quickly bring the boat up to full speed and drive like mad to encircle the fish as rapidly as possible. As the boat circled the fish, the net would smoothly deploy off the stern to surround the school with an impenetrable wall of mesh. Small floats would keep the top of the net positioned at the waterline while small lead weights kept the net held to the sea floor. Once the fish were corralled, the balance of the net would be deployed in the center for extra catching potential. Then the fisherman would wait—let the net "soak," so to speak. Maybe 20 minutes or so later, with one man at the cork (float) line and one man at the lead line, the net would be slowly and laboriously hauled in by hand, and if there were any fish in the net they'd be "shucked" (removed) and thrown into a waiting wooden box that typically held 500 pounds of fish when full. A lucky strike could easily fill one or more boxes, but many often resulted in much less.

The fish most commonly targeted in the Cortez area of Manatee County, Florida, was the freshwater mullet. Manatee County mullet are a variety that grow to a size unmatched anywhere in the world and are prized not only for their flesh but also for their red roe which are sold to overseas Asian markets, especially the Japanese. Most Cortez fishermen target mullet, but in reality are more than happy to catch any fish that they can sell. Johnny and Don took Mom fishing a couple of times and she caught the fishing bug. The only problem was that Mom had no boat, no net, and practically no experience. But that didn't deter her for a moment.

Mom saw an ancient, beat-up skiff crusted with barnacles and flaky blue paint sitting in a fisherman's front yard. It looked as if it hadn't been moved in generations. Without a second's consideration as to the seaworthiness of the vessel, she knocked on the fisherman's front door and promptly made a deal to buy the wreck cheap, as in "I have no money down, but I'll pay you in a couple weeks" cheap. As an added bonus, the skiff was so small it really couldn't handle a motor even if she had one, so that problem became obsolete. Now it was just a matter of obtaining a net. That's where Don, a big-hearted guy with a sense of humor to match, stepped up and loaned his new friend Rachel an old net he wasn't using. I'm sure he must have found the thought of her fishing that derelict skiff very amusing.

But Mom had a problem. How could she strike fish without a motor? It was simply not feasible to paddle or pole around searching for fish. There had to be another way or else she was finished before she started. She asked around, speaking to anyone and everyone, looking for advice. Many of the fishermen weren't eager to help the newbie as their natural cliquishness caused them to clam up, but Mom persisted. Still, a week or so later found her no closer to a solution to the problem and her fishing venture was close to going belly up when, for the second time in as many weeks, big Don came to the rescue.

"Hey Rachel, what ya gotta do is go wing-dinging down at the beach."

"Wing-a what?" she asked, perplexed.

"Wing-ding. You just gotta get your boat down to the beach and … well…" He trailed off in silence as he saw that he had lost Mom somewhere back at the "ding." "Never mind. I'll show ya tomorrow if the surf's calm enough. Ya got your boat ready? We'll need a coupla paddles."

"I've got one," Mom said, perking up considerably with the resurrection of her fledgling fishing enterprise.

"Good, you'll need it. I'll bring mine. Meet me at my house tomorrow morning around 5:30. Me and Jackie'll be waiting for ya with coffee. Be sure and get some sleep, big day tomorrow."

Don wasn't kidding. Wing-dinging from the beach in a tiny boat without a motor would be physically challenging for anyone, even a burly fisherman. For Mom, it would be tougher still, but she was determined to learn and she did. And this was how they did it.

The location of the wing-ding was on Anna Maria Island (only a couple of miles from Cortez) and had been chosen by Mom because it was conveniently located just a few yards from the small cottage where she was staying. Wing-dinging, like most all commercial fishing, was a process. First, they had to launch her net-laden skiff in the ocean's surf, right off the beach. It wasn't easy and timing was important as it required wading into the surf while dragging the boat by its painter until it was in deep enough water to float, all the while struggling against the waves that were constantly pushing the boat ashore. They chose a time in between the waves to hop aboard, throw the let-go up on the beach, snatch their paddles, and row like hell to clear the worst of the surf. The heavy net made their efforts hard and the headway very slow. In anything but low surf it would have been impossible.

The first 50 yards were the toughest, but as they made their way offshore the going became easier as the waves lost force and the net load continually diminished as it deployed into the sea. The objective at this point was straightforward. They must set out the entire 800-yard net in a large, continually contracting curlicue formation with the curlicue facing in the direction they reasoned the fish would be coming from depending on the season. This was because the wing-ding relied on the fact that fish commonly swim parallel to the beach (especially when migrating) and when fish encountered a net they instinctively turned out to sea to swim around it. But their escape would not be that simple, for the fish would inevitably follow the net as they wound into the heart of the circular maze. Once there, disoriented, most fish could not find their way out and were caught. Passive net-fishing at its finest. Don, the son-of-a-son-of-a-son-of-a-son of a fisherman, sure knew his stuff. And now Mom did too, at least a little bit.

Mom fished that spot (the fishermen eventually called it Rachel's Rocks because of a small rock formation that became visible through the surf at low tide) often during the entire time she was in Cortez and caught a lot of fish with the wing-ding. She was thrilled with the opportunity to earn a little money commercial fishing, even on a small scale. Her needs were few and there were other benefits as well. Fishing was the quintessential low-key job … how many jobs require no I.D., no Social Security number, no interview, and no boss? And she was able to eat some of her catch even though most of the fish she caught were salable. Mullet, redfish, jack, and snook were frequent catches as well as delicious stone crabs, since they were attracted to the helpless fish in the net and became ensnared themselves when they ventured too close. However, of all the fish, pompano were a favorite target of Mom's as they were both plentiful during their migration and fetched the highest price when she sold her catch at the local Star Fish Company. Mr. G, Star's owner, had the distinction of owning more cats than Mom had ever seen in one place in all her life. He must have had at least 100, maybe more. Go figure.

Cortez was indeed an unusual place that seemed to be a magnet for unusual people and Mom was not the only eccentric character in the mix. There was Stevie G, a Guthrie brother and hard-partying fisherman extraordinaire with a quick wit and a quick smile to match. He was called Stevie G so as not to be confused in conversation with the other Stevie in the village, Stevie Fine. Then there was Mickey. Mickey was an ex-con with a deep-seated grudge against cops—in fact, he hated them with a vengeance—and a pair of pit bulls that accompanied him everywhere he went. Built like a Viking warrior, with blonde hair and ice-blue eyes, Mickey spent almost every hour of his day working out at the beach and most of his evening violently arguing with his lookalike girlfriend Suzie. It was a good thing they tended to make up later in the night with equal passion or else they might have easily killed one another. And finally, I must mention Randy. He was a transplanted Northerner that found Cortez by accident while on vacation and became a blue-crabber. He had the dubious distinction of being one of the hardest working yet unluckiest fishermen in Cortez. His luck was just awful, but boy, did he work hard.

A funny thing I noticed when I eventually wound up in Cortez myself quite some time later and got to know all of these people and a few more besides: Most of them had names that ended with the long "e" sound, and if your name didn't, it would be added anyway when you were accepted as one of them. Maybe it was a fishing thing?

Anyway, while Mom was busy settling into the Cortez fishing lifestyle, things were really heating up back home in north Florida and south Georgia. The police hunt for Mom had intensified significantly. Federal agents increased their presence in all our lives with weekly threatening phone calls and unannounced personal visits. They would often drop by at Baga and Bummy's house around dinnertime. They'd be sitting on the front porch swing of the White Springs house at 6 a.m.

having a conversation until I woke up and went out to see who was there. They pulled me over several times and detained me on the side of the road for half an hour or more, no reason given, then let me go my way without any explanation. On the surface they were polite and their manners civil, but underneath I sensed an ill-concealed malevolence. They were still pissed off and I'm sure the Pitz continually stoked the fire to get Mom recaptured. I shuddered to think what would happen if Mom was ever under his control again. The crowning glory of their manhunt was the announcement that Mom had been placed on the U.S. Federal Marshal's 15 Most Wanted List. She was the only woman thus honored.

In truth, none of us had been contacted by Mom and therefore we did not know her location any more than the cops did. But our denials fell on deaf ears. Agents warned us that we would face serious charges if we didn't turn her in and threatened us with long prison sentences practically every time they opened their mouths. They badgered, we denied. It was like a broken record on both our sides, a true Mexican stand-off. Mom had taken Baga's advice to heart and was too smart to make the stupid mistake of contacting friends or family. We were bulletproof.

As the months passed, the commotion caused by Mom's escape gradually diminished and our family hunkered down in a sort of bunker mentality. Baga and Aunt Bonnie did the best they could to help their lawyers prepare a hopeless defense, which in reality only amounted to an attempt to receive as lenient a prison sentence as possible. Bummy's alcoholism escalated, but thankfully baby Morgana had long since gone to live with Aunt Nancy and that in itself was a big relief for me. I was flat broke and worried, my world shaken to the core, and my baby sister was a major concern. Nancy was a true lifesaver and ended up becoming Morgana's surrogate mother, and a great one to boot. Although I loved her dearly for a multitude of reasons, she will always have an extra-special place in my heart for that reason alone.

In the meantime, I had transformed the family house in White Springs into Rock 'n' Roll Central. Since my ninth birthday when Nancy had given me my first guitar, a 1952 acoustic-electric Gibson, music had always been a major part of my heart and my soul and, like Mr. Gaulding's beloved boat was to him, music became my refuge. Before the bust my band had only been around for rehearsals; now the band lived at the house 24/7. We wrote songs and jammed night and day, pausing only to eat, sleep and party. All of us were pretty broke and had to pool our money for food and gas, sticks and strings. It was a crazy time with quite a few people (mostly musicians, musician wannabees, and music fans) coming and going. In truth, those days sort of reminded me of the way it was at the height of Mom's shenanigans. And who knows, maybe it was all a needed distraction from the hard realities of the past year, a harmless and healthy way of hanging on to sanity and avoiding becoming a bitter person. Lots of innocent fun, good music and … cops. In the band.

Yes, cops. Well, to be more accurate, it was just one cop. Call it a sixth sense, call it whatever, but I will never be convinced otherwise. I am sure I ended up with a cop in my band. Was he FBI or GBI or a federal marshal? Heck, I never found out. He didn't last long and I realize I never knew his real name, but he was a nice guy and played a mean guitar. I knew him only as Michael Garcia.

Mike answered an ad I had placed in a musician's referral newspaper looking for a guitarist. He called early one morning (he was actually the very first to respond) and I invited him to jam with the band that same night. Looking back, I should have known there was something fishy going on. How many musicians are early risers? Anyway, he showed up on time (another red flag) with a Fender Stratocaster in one hand and a Twin Reverb Combo amp in the other. He was quite a few years older than we were, maybe late 20s or early 30s, Hispanic, and very friendly. When I introduced him to the rest of the band, he made a point to ask their last names as well. That should have been enough to set my internal alarms off, but he had set up his rig in record time and started to play and whoa! The music blew us away. This guy could rock!

We launched into a few covers that we all were familiar with and right away I could tell Mike was a pro. We played some Zeppelin, we played some AC/DC, and we even rocked some Police. Everything was sounding so good we got caught up in the moment and jammed for more than an hour straight. Any doubts I might have had about his true nature were lost in the whirlwind of the music. When we finally stopped for a break, Jud, my bass guitarist and best friend, retrieved a six-pack from the kitchen and passed the beer around. Mike drank with us, but when our drummer whipped out a joint, he declined. At that time in my life I had never smoked anything, cigarettes, marijuana, nothing, and neither had Jud, so our drummer smoked alone. I'm glad to this day I didn't smoke, for I have no idea what would have happened if I had. I think it's possible the cops could have used it against me. Who knows what Mike thought? I wonder if he felt I was on to him.

We rocked the rest of the night away and never sounded better. Mike was a hot guitar player for sure. He was older and didn't have the look, but man, was he a player and that trumped everything. In fact, he was so good that when we stopped for another break I asked the band right in front of him if they thought he was the guitarist for us. Everyone agreed that he was. I told Mike right then and there that the slot was his if he wanted it.

"Hell yeah!" he bellowed, raising his beer high. To seal the deal we all clinked bottles in a raucous band toast.

Thus began Mike's stint in the band. By the time he left late that night we had played nearly all our covers and had introduced him to several of our original tunes. We had also consumed an ocean of beer. Although Mike had apparently kept pace with us in every way, including the drinking, he seemed to be the only one that was not at least a little drunk. He can sure hold his booze, I thought to myself as he drove away. At least he wouldn't need babysitting at gigs and that was a big plus. It never even crossed my mind that he might not have imbibed as much as it appeared.

Mike had left his amp in our rehearsal room so all he had with him when he arrived the next evening was his guitar in one hand and a case of beer in the other. And shazam! We were tuned up and rocking like gangbusters in no time. Like the night before, everything clicked musically and sounded great and before long a few neighbors dropped in, and then a few more until we had a full-blown party. As I looked around I realized I didn't know half the people wandering around the house, but since nobody was getting too rambunctious I allowed the carnival to continue. Again reminiscing with the advantage of hindsight, I'm sure there were plenty of cops at the party that night.

It went on like that for the next two or three weeks. We rocked and partied almost every night and Mike pretty much held his own in every way as he got to know us better. Occasionally, usually during a break, he would get one or another of us aside and pick our brains, asking about school, friends, and family. All in all, pretty mundane stuff. Jud and Chris and Pryor, having nothing to hide, let it all hang out. But

when it came to me I had little to say, and not because I was hiding anything. I was still shell-shocked from the recent upheavals in my life and
talking about them to a relative stranger (even a fellow musician) did
not interest me. I remained steadfastly focused on the music.

Of course, music was what drove us and brought us all together
and that was where the center of all our conversations began. Mike knew
his stuff and dazzled us on a nightly basis. He knew music, both the
older stuff and the newest cutting-edge material. He knew guitars, amps
and effects and could equalize a sound system with the best of us. It was
obvious that he was a consummate musician, but beyond that superficial
observation we really didn't know him at all. He never spoke of family
or friends, nor did he ever specifically come down on what he actually
did for a living, even when Jud, the most amiable among us, asked him
point blank. He merely muttered something about "some savings" and
let it go at that. If his expensive rig was any indication, it was some hum-
dinger of a savings.

The oddest thing, however, was Mike's reticence when it came to
telling us anything about his former bands. Surely a player of his age
and caliber would have had quite a history which would have been very
interesting to us young players with our limited experience. We had
barely played a dozen shows between us and wanted to hear as much
as we could about what we might encounter at a real bar gig. But no
dice. Mike just wouldn't dish, so we sucked up our disappointment and
rocked on. Our sets were getting tight and I knew it would not be long
before we were ready to hit a stage with the new lineup. It surely would
have been great if that had happened, but it did not. Jud was the first to
know why.

"Hey David, come down here, would ya?" I heard Jud call one
morning from the band room. I knew my friend well and could hear
distress in his voice. I hustled down the stairs as fast as I dared and
joined him.

"What's up?" I asked.

"Look," Jud said, pointing to a small clearing among the amps and
speakers where Mike's equipment used to be, "it's gone."

I quickly surveyed the room, worried that some of our gear might
be missing as well, but it was all there. Only Mike's was gone.

"When did he pick it up?" I wondered aloud. Jud answered with a
shrug and a shake of his head. We asked the rest of the band and no one

had seen a thing. We figured that Mike had either taken his rig unnoticed after the last rehearsal or had come by sometime later and left without a word. Either option was a possibility as the house was very large and we weren't exactly standing a close guard or expecting such a move.

"Maybe he needed it..." Jud speculated, trailing off in silence.

I shook my head. "He's gone. He's not coming back. If he was he would have said something." I knew in my heart I was right. We never saw him again. Upon much reflection and with the benefit of good ole hindsight I am very confident in my opinion that Michael "Mike" Garcia (or whatever his real name was) was an undercover agent sent to find out what he could about Mom's life on the run and what, if anything, I knew about it.

Mom's location at that time was still a mystery to me and I missed her terribly. I also missed my baby sister Morgana and my thoughts often dwelled on the suffering I continued to see written on the faces of so much of my family. My band became even more of a haven. I lived for music alone. But one way or another, I could sense a change coming, a watershed moment on the verge of revelation. I waited, expectant, until one morning I woke up convinced that I had to leave. Get the hell out of Dodge, as the old saying goes. Leave the house, leave the band, and maybe leave Florida altogether. So that is exactly what I did.

I bid my band a sorrowful farewell, which was the hardest part. Making music is an emotionally charged endeavor if you play it with all your heart and soul as I did. We spoke of reuniting in the future, not sure if it would ever be possible. I think it was more about making the break as easy as it could be. I was resolute as I drove off with nothing but a couple of duffels, two guitars, and the rest of my musical gear. On my way out of Florida I stopped by Bummy and Baga's to bid them adieu. That goodbye was even tougher.

My grandparents and I had always been exceptionally close, as over the years they had raised me every bit as much as Mom. Curiously, they did not question my decision to leave; in fact, they sort of encouraged it. We had a long discussion over dinner where they basically told me that they would also leave if they were younger and circumstances were different. But they had my Aunt Blue to take care of and Baga was still under the gun with all his legal troubles, not to mention the sad truth that Bummy's drinking, always problematic, had assumed epic proportions since the arrests. I relished their company and enjoyed Bummy's cooking more than ever that evening as I knew it was likely to be some time before I saw them again. I went to bed that night with a heavy heart but more determined than ever to go.

Early the next morning after breakfast we said our tearful goodbyes and I hit the road. At first I was not sure where I would go, but when I came to the Interstate 10 exchange I felt a strong urge to head west so that was exactly what I did. Once on I-10 it wasn't long before I decided to go all the way to California. It was like I just had to take my adventure as far as I could go and drive as long as possible without spilling into the ocean. I think I chose California because I knew there were plenty of musicians and bands there that might be looking for a singer and guitarist such as me. Besides, I had been following the hard rock scene in various magazines for several years and the West Coast seemed to be the epicenter of the action.

I arrived in Los Angeles only a few days later and began the search for my new band. There were plenty of singers and guitar players in LA—in fact, too many—but very few good ones, at least when it came to singers, so I had my choice of several bands. However, after a few weeks I found the LA scene too crazy for me. But it wasn't the music scene at all, it was everything else. Rent was sky high (even back then), the crowds were stifling and the air was unclean. I just could not make myself at home in that city. The straw that broke the camel's back was the traffic. I'd been all over Europe and visited most of its great cities and nothing came close to the snarl of LA's roads. So I left, heading north, and eventually wound up in Sacramento.

I thought Sacramento was perfect. It was conveniently situated between the mountains and the ocean and just large enough to have a thriving music scene of its own. As in LA, I soon found several bands that were looking for a player like me and after a few mutual auditions I joined a group that had a laid-back but solid rhythm section and a brilliant lead guitarist with a large gaudy tattoo of a flying penis on his chest. Thank God he kept it covered most of the time he wasn't drunk!

I soon rented a small house that was more affordable than most because it had only a swamp cooler for air conditioning, but it was cozy and clean. Now that I was settled in a bit, I checked in with family. When I called Melanie to see how she was doing I could tell she was struggling much as I had and I felt a change might do her some good as it had me.

My little house had a spare bedroom so I invited her to come on out to California. She jumped at the chance.

It had been only a few weeks since I left home. I had reunited with Melanie and was wondering how Morgana was doing and I began to seriously think about the possibility of raising her myself but I knew that would take some serious planning. I had a new band and some new friends and the cops were not breathing down my back as before. Was it possible that I had thrown them off track by my sudden and unannounced departure? I wondered for the umpteenth time where Mom was and what she was doing. I laid awake many nights wondering if I would ever see her again and prayed she was okay. Little did I know that while I was singing my heart out and trying to make the most of my fresh start in California, she had already initiated a plan that would ultimately bring us together again in circumstances far more perilous than any we had experienced before.

15

Coming Up for Air

The Sacramento summer night was warm and muggy and reminded me of Florida. It was nearly 1 a.m. and my band and I had just finished our last smokin' set of hard rock tunes at a club off M Street near the downtown business district. As is normally the case after a show, we were both exhausted and hyped up. A good gig always had that effect on me and it hasn't changed in all the years I have been playing. So, with a contented smile on my face and my beloved Gibson in my right hand, I had knelt down to open my guitar case when I heard a woman's voice over my shoulder.

"David Michael?"

Still kneeling, I turned and looked up at her. She was extremely petite and about Mom's age, with long dark hair and melancholy eyes that appeared to have seen more than their share of life's disappointments. Her floor-length, long-sleeved, old-fashioned dress was quite bizarre for a rock club and she certainly looked out of place, but the directness of her gaze assured me that she was not there by accident.

"Yes?" I answered as I stood, a funny feeling beginning to worm its way into my gut.

"I'm Ellen." She extended a tiny hand for me to shake. "Is there someplace we can go where we can speak in private?" Her eyes briefly panned the club as if to add emphasis to the question. Meanwhile, the funny feeling grew stronger and told me to follow her lead.

"Let's step outside," I suggested. And without waiting to see if she was following me or not I headed for the door. Once outside I took a deep breath of the balmy air and turned around. She was just a few steps behind me and got straight to the point.

"Your mom sent me."

What felt almost like a powerful jolt of electricity shot through my entire body as her words sank in. And as unbelievable as they were I knew she was telling me the truth. I stood frozen, powerless to move as my mind raced with a thousand thoughts, a thousand questions. What felt like an eternity, but was probably only a minute later, I managed another deep breath and exhaled a feeble "oh."

Frankly, the news took me by such surprise that I really did not have a clue as to what to say, and even less of an idea of what I should do with Ellen's sudden revelation. As strange as it may seem I had not ever considered the possibility that Mom would make contact, and now that she had I was caught as flat-footed as a used up boxer who had taken one too many punches in a championship fight. I suddenly became very tired.

"Where is she?" I asked, using my library voice.

Ellen looked relieved. "Not far. I'll take you to her. She's going to be so excited. She can't wait to see you."

I knew right then I had to go with Ellen to see Mom, even if only for a minute. I just had to know she was all right. "Okay. Let me load up my gear and I'll follow you. Wait for me."

I didn't wait for her response as I turned and headed back inside, yet my mind churned with conflicting thoughts, some good, some bad, and for the first time in months I thought about cops and wondered if they were watching me at that very moment. I felt paranoid but I knew feeling that way did not necessarily mean the cops were near.

It was a valid worry, I reasoned. Mom was on the lam and God only knew what federal most wanted list she was featured on now. Furthermore, the cops had warned me dozens of times that if I ever learned of her whereabouts I must turn her in or face the consequences. On the other hand, despite all the dire warnings I'd received I actually believed them to be idle threats designed to get me to turn in my mother. I could never so much as contemplate such an unconscionable action, much less carry it out. In my mind that sort of betrayal would be right at home in Nazi Germany. I would have no part of it.

As I packed my guitars and loaded my musical gear I rationalized my way out of the dilemma of whether or not I should even meet her. It was so simple and pure on the face of it. I figured we would have a nice visit and then go our separate ways. That was all. I missed her terribly and wanted to see with my own eyes that she was okay. I wanted to tell her I loved her and I was glad she was not rotting away in some prison cell under the control of a demented madman. I wanted to let her know that Morgana was in the best of hands with Aunt Nancy. My motivations were simple, understandable, and ultimately harmless, I told myself. Boy, was I wrong. Understandable, maybe, but in retrospect I realize that I must have been too young to fully appreciate the complex emotions that were ripping me apart in much the same way our family had been torn asunder. Things could never be the same and a little family reunion would not change that unfortunate fact.

Ellen was still waiting outside and we left the club in my car, detouring briefly to pick up Melanie prior to the rendezvous with Mom. Ellen was surprised. Mom had not been aware that Melanie was living with me in California. When we arrived at our destination, a dimly-lit parking lot between a 24-hour Denny's restaurant and a vacant field, Mom stepped out of a faded compact car and into our arms. It was a tearful and joyous reunion. Mom had a suntan and had lost a little weight and looked good. She asked about Morgana and I could see that she was still extremely traumatized by the separation. Melanie could not stop crying and never left Mom's arms. It seemed that wild horses would not be able to separate them. I did my best to give Mom an abbreviated update on family happenings since her escape. She listened quietly, nodding her head from time to time in understanding and asking only a few questions. And when I finished she asked the $64,000 question.

"I came here to get you. So are you coming with me?" She looked questioningly at me, then settled her eyes on Melanie who was still sobbing gently in her arms. For an answer, Melanie pulled Mom closer and nodded enthusiastically. I expected nothing less from her. Mom then focused her attention on me.

I too was caught up in the moment, my emotions laid bare and my juvenile reasoning obviously impaired, because how else could I have expected a different outcome than the one that eventually befell me? Deep down I surely must have known that going with Mom could only end badly, but instead of using my head I used my heart.

"Of course I am!" I said as I wrapped my long arms around both Mom and Melanie at the same time. My fate was sealed, and by noon the following day the three of us, with Ellen in tow, were on the road to Phoenix.

We had decided on Phoenix because it was a relatively short drive and we needed to ditch Ellen's piece of crap car and get something suitable to take us to our eventual destination, Cortez. On the way to Phoenix Mom sold me on the place, and even if she hadn't I was game for just about anything at that point because once I am in, I'm all in. I rarely do anything half-hearted.

Shortly after our arrival in Phoenix we lucked out and found a full-size Dodge van. Its main attributes were that it was cheap (only $1,300) and had a strong 318-V8 engine along with decent tires. Its drawbacks were many. It had no air conditioning, no radio, and had a smashed-in passenger side front quarter panel as a result of a previous accident. Worst of all, its color was a garish orange that practically bruised the eyes of anyone who dared to look at it too long. I named the van "Orange Crush" after the soda of the same name and eerily similar color. Shortly after its purchase and according to plan, Ellen said her goodbyes and left, but not before promising to get in touch with Mom sometime later once we were back in Florida.

While in Phoenix we also picked up some camping gear, an ice chest, and a beat-up secondhand boom box that utilized a wire coat hanger as an antenna. Thus equipped, we hit the road again with soaring spirits and music from the radio providing an aural backdrop to the stunning scenery of northern Arizona and the Painted Desert. We were eager to catch up on events since Mom's escape so there was no shortage of conversation.

Though we were "roughing it" the entire trip, I remember it fondly. We camped in beautiful off-the-grid locations in Colorado, Kentucky and north Georgia before finally arriving in Cortez a week later. Orange Crush sure wasn't pretty to look at, but it had proved its worth by simply not breaking down and leaving us broke and stranded on the side of the road.

As we drove down the last stretch of road flanked on both sides by mangroves that bordered Cortez and served as its unofficial "city limits," Melanie and I settled on our new aliases. I would become "Nick," while Melanie would simply use her true middle name, "Desiree." We felt that would be best as it would be easy for her to remember and keep straight. Little did I know at the time that "Nick" would eventually morph into its Cortez counterpart "Nikki" because of the fisherman's penchant for adding the long "e" sound at the end of your name once you were accepted into the community. So Nikki I became. Fortunately, Melanie did not have to worry about her name. No one ever figured out how to successfully add the long "e" sound to the end of Desiree, pronounced (Deh-za-ray).

Since we had arrived flat broke Mom and I wasted no time getting to work, and in Cortez that of course meant fishing. And even though I was an experienced angler when it came to rods and reels and recreational fishing, I had a lot to learn when it came to commercial fishing. Mom began my education in the art by showing me what she knew best, the good ole wing-ding off Rachel's Rocks. For my part, I learned quickly and soon became proficient with the nets and techniques and we often caught a fair number of salable fish and edible crabs for our personal consumption. However, I soon realized that our tiny boat was not only dangerous for two people, it was a barrier to catching enough fish to make any real money. I felt it was imperative to find something larger and with a motor as well. So with that goal in mind I set out to find a job and put my fledgling commercial fishing skills to the test. And as luck would have it I found a position no one else in their right mind would accept—night skiff fishing with perhaps both the luckiest and most sullen man in Cortez. His name was Ed, and no one called him Eddie either, because he commonly fished alone and possibly did not fraternize with the villagers enough to earn the long "e" sound at the end of his name. Or maybe it was his grim and brooding demeanor. Heck, what did I know anyway?

What I did learn I found out the hard way. Ed was a demanding taskmaster and a tireless fisherman. We would start fishing at sundown and fish all night. Ed had good equipment, a 26-foot mullet boat with a top-of-the-line Yamaha outboard and two 14-foot skiffs, each with a well-maintained 800-yard gill net in the stern. Ed's fishing strategy was to drive up reasonably close to a school of mullet in his large boat (but not close enough to scare the fish) and then take to the skiffs to quietly surround them using only poles for propulsion. It was a tried and true fishing technique, but one that required a fisherman who was expert in poling a skiff and I, a greenhorn, wasn't. Every time I accidentally banged my pole a little too loud on the side of my skiff Ed would give me a look like he was the devil himself, thirsting for my blood. Luckily for me, if the set was a successful one and we caught fish he would overlook my earlier blunder. But if the set was a bust he'd heartily cuss me for scaring the fish whether there were any there in the first place or not. Yet Ed was a pretty good fisherman and we generally caught a lot of mullet and I earned decent money working for him. But it was not fun, not at all.

If I didn't know any better I would have supposed that Ed would be among the happiest of men. Why? Well, he was one of the few people I have ever known to win the lottery not just once, but twice. He did not win millions, only tens of thousands of dollars, yet I would have thought that should have been more than enough to put an occasional smile on his face. Not Ed.

My stint with Ed ended abruptly one day when we actually went fishing in broad daylight, an extremely rare event on his boat. We were traveling around 30 knots, rounding a point just south of Longboat Key when ... BAM! We slammed into an underwater finger of a sandbar and decelerated to a complete stop almost instantly. If I hadn't been busy sorting fish with the fish box in front of me I surely would have flown clear of the boat. As it was I only suffered a minor scare and a body-tingling jolt. Ed, with his hands on the steering wheel, fared even better. The boat's batteries, however, had not. The collision had caused them to jump from the battery box and now their cables were crossed and arcing with fiery current. Ed immediately killed the engine and hollered for the nearby fire extinguisher which I had already moved to retrieve. He snatched it from my hand and attempted a burst but it must have been defunct as nothing came out. Then, before I knew it, Ed reached into the battery box and tried to wrestle the batteries back into position using their cables as makeshift handles. The instant he touched them he recoiled with a guttural groan of agony and held his right hand up to examine. To my horror, the bones in his fingers were visible where the cable had burned a half-inch furrow through his flesh. It had only taken a second. Thankfully, there was no blood as the wound had also been instantly cauterized by the heat and current. Ed, for once, didn't have anything bad to say. He was clearly in shock and I knew I had to get help because we were stranded, high and dry on the sandbar with a falling tide.

I whipped off my shirt and tightly wound it around Ed's hand. Then I went for the VHF radio with the intention of calling for some help. But as I switched on the radio and began to raise the mic to my lips, I saw a fishing boat heading in our general direction and decided on the spot to try and flag it down, knowing that fishermen commonly kept their radios turned off to avoid scaring fish. Stepping to the gunwale, I urgently waved my arms at the other boat and to my surprise it instantly changed course and slowed as it began to approach our position. It was at that point I began to notice that the approaching vessel looked familiar, and as it neared the boat's captain came into clearer focus as well. It was Don! I couldn't believe it! What were the odds he'd be along right at the perfect moment for our rescue?

"You need a hand, Nikki?" he called out over the whooshing water and idling engine. His eyes peered into the water around our hull because he obviously thought we were only grounded.

"Hell yes, we do!" I hollered back. "Ed's hurt. We need a ride."

Don sure saved our bacon that day, and for months afterward we marveled at the unusual coincidence of his being at just the right place at the right time. I never questioned it beyond being thankful for the lucky break for Ed's sake and I chalked it up to just another example of one of life's little mysteries. In bed that night I played the whole event over in my mind and decided I had had enough fishing with Ed. I quit the next day.

I had saved a few hundred dollars by that time and Mom had some money as well. Quite a bit more than me, in fact. Only she had not earned it fishing. Despite the fact that she was well into her 40s in a young woman's game, she had been working as an exotic dancer at a local strip club. Her dancing name was Angel and her entrance song was Juice Newton's "Angel of the Morning." I must admit right here that I was embarrassed by her dancing, especially when both Stevies, Don, and a few other fishermen occasionally teased me good-naturedly about her doing it and often made breast implant jokes in my company. But I suppose it was a logical choice for her in many ways because commercial fishing and stripping actually had many things in common. Both occupations often attracted people on the fringes of society who needed to make a quick buck without the pesky adherence to formalities such as formal IDs, Social Security cards, tax forms, and job references. Everybody tended to mind their own business and ask few questions. I guess it was a win-win when it came down to it—she did what she had to do and I did what I had to do. Mom and I pooled our resources and bought a $400 mullet boat and were back in business, this time on our own terms.

The boat was only 22 feet long and nothing fancy. It even lacked a motor, a big problem I immediately set out to solve. The answer came when I worked out a deal with Randy, the bad-luck blue crabber the indigenous fisherman often referred to as "that damned Yankee" behind his back since he was from Ohio and had only taken up fishing late in life. My deal with Randy was a simple trade: I would work as his helper in exchange for a crappy, hard-to-start 40-horsepower Evinrude outboard. The motor truly was a piece of crap but it was better than no motor at all, and besides, I had no money left after chipping in half for the boat and buying a few other much needed fishing accessories including a $25 saltwater products license which would allow Mom and I to sell our catch directly to a fish house instead of using a go-between as we had been doing previously. We were officially in business!

I'm sure we were an amusing sight to behold in the eyes of the other fishermen—two greenhorns, mother and son, in a shoddy-looking boat with a sputtering motor and worn out net—but we weren't about to let our lack of experience or quality equipment stop us. On the contrary, we were gung ho and went all out. The first week was the toughest, as we needed a little time to get used to the boat and develop routines for the various on-board tasks. But by the end of the third week we had become good enough to consistently catch enough fish to pay for our expenses (mostly gas and oil) and put a few bucks in our pockets as well. Don't get me wrong…. I'm not saying we caught fish every time we went out. After all, this was fishing and that meant there were no guarantees. Sometimes we would strike a large school of fish and catch practically nothing. In those instances I figured we must have been too slow with our puttering motor. Other strikes sometimes resulted in a big catch, but of the wrong species of fish, such as chad which sold for only a few cents per pound. On those occasions we would work hard all day and barely cover expenses. Worst of all, some strikes netted us hundreds of stingrays. That was always a real bummer! They were very hard to shuck from the net while avoiding their barbed stingers which could inflict a nasty and very painful sting. On the whole, that scenario resulted in a lot of painstaking work with nothing to sell afterward. No fish house would buy rays. Without a doubt, commercial fishing was a mixed bag; we could be down in a trough one moment and up on a crest the next. Sort of like the waves and the sea itself and that was fine with me, especially when we did make the rare big catch. Not surprisingly, our first big catch turned out to be the most memorable one as well, or at least it was for me.

It all went down shortly after our second week in our "new" boat. Mom and I had set a wing-ding off Rachel's Rocks and had allowed the net to soak for a few hours. Starting at the seaward curlicue end, we'd begun taking in the net, Mom on the cork line and me on the heavier lead line. The catch wasn't looking good. The first 400 yards (usually the section that caught the most fish in a wing-ding) yielded only a couple dozen crabs and a few marketable fish, but none of our prized pompano. The next 300 yards netted fewer still and it had begun to look like a total bust. But then, as we got down to the last 25 yards—so close to shore that our stern was nearly on the rocks and the surf threatened to fling us on the beach—we noticed that the net had suddenly become massively heavy. At first I assumed the net was hung up on the rocks and we would have to cut it free, but when I took a second hard look into the frothy water between the waves I was shocked to see the blunt grey head and coal black eyes of a very large shark.

"Whoa, that's a biggie!" I exclaimed, instinctively leaning away from the water and the shark. I wasn't sure how well it was caught or even if it could jump into the boat if it chose. Due to the shark's weight, our stern was low with only a foot of freeboard at most. "Check him out! I wonder what he's worth."

Mom came over to my side and together we carefully peered over the transom to study the shark closer. I realized then that I needn't have worried about it jumping into our boat, for although it was still very much alive it was not green and I knew why. Multiple layers of net had the shark as trussed up as a Thanksgiving turkey and it could not move, much less swim, which sharks must constantly do in order to force enough water through their gills to provide sufficient oxygen. Gazing down into the surf, I wondered what would be the best way to cut the shark loose and whether I should concentrate on the thinner nylon mesh or just go for the lead and cork lines. Mom, however, had already made up her mind.

"Okay, let's get him into the boat," she said in her matter-of-fact voice.

"Yeah ... sure, Mom," I sarcastically replied as I scrutinized the shark again from its blunt head to the tip of its pointy tail fin. "Really? It looks big enough to eat our boat if we bring it aboard." I was joking, of course, but the shark did appear to be only a couple feet shy of half the length of our 22-foot boat. I should have known better than to argue with Mom once she had made up her mind. Stubbornness runs deep in our family.

Without waiting to see whether I agreed or not she reached down into the water and grabbed the shark's tail with both hands and started pulling with all her might. The shark didn't budge. "Come on, give me a hand!" She braced her feet against the gunwale and grunted with effort as the tip of the tail cleared the water. "Here he comes!"

A tail out of the water did not mean much in my eyes, yet I noticed that the shark was not fighting too much and seemed to lack real spunk. Being tangled in the net for several hours had given us an edge, I realized, and if we could just get half the shark's body into the boat we might be able to flip the other half in after it. So, like Mom, I focused on the end without the gaping mouth and rows of razor sharp teeth and grabbed the shark behind its rear dorsal fin and together we tugged in unison. Since most of the shark was still in the water it wasn't too difficult at first and together we had a good four feet of pissed-off shark in the boat in no time, however, as more of the shark's body cleared the water, it began to thrash harder and it appeared as though we would lose the fight. But then my fisherman's lust for the catch kicked in and I switched into high gear.

Leaving Mom alone with the tail, I quickly maneuvered to a spot a few feet from the snapping jaws where I could grab the net's main lines yet still remain safe while I worked to get the business end of the shark aboard. The lines conveniently functioned like handles and gave me the additional leverage I needed as I pulled and struggled in a fierce tug-of-war while Mom tenaciously clung to the tail like her life depended upon it. Inch by inch we dragged the thrashing shark aboard until suddenly its last remaining pectoral fin cleared the gunwale and it flopped entirely into our boat. Utterly exhausted, we stared down at the violently thrashing shark and I estimated its length using our poling oar as a guide. The shark was easily between eight and nine feet long. How much it weighed I had no idea. It was an exceedingly narrow species of shark, I ruminated as I estimated its weight. How much would it fetch once we got it back to Mister G's docks? Sharks sold for 55 cents a pound and I was elated by the good luck of such a nice day's work. Mom was too by the look on her face. The only thing was, we weren't nearly finished and it was going to be a very long day and an even longer night before it was all over. Why? Well, the other shark, of course.

Yes, there was another shark in our net, a veritable twin of the first, hopelessly entangled fewer than five yards from its brethren. And with a sigh of resignation to the task at hand we dove right into the fight with the same battle plan that had worked for us before. I guess there's a lot of truth to the old saying that practice makes perfect because we landed the second shark in less than an hour, despite our weariness. All I wanted to do at that point was haul in the last few yards of our net and make a beeline for the Cortez docks. Eight hours of sleep and a bowl of Wheaties and I'd be good as new. Seconds after the net was shipped I cranked our pathetic outboard and we sputtered off at full speed towards home, Mom in command at the helm.

But the day was not nearly finished with us, for while Mom and I had been having all the fun with our shark fishing a fair bit of squally weather had steadily crept down the coast and was now situated several miles north of us directly over the primary inlet we used to enter Sarasota Bay from the open sea. Still three or four miles out, as we approached the inlet it became increasingly clear to me that we would very likely have a rendezvous with the nasty squall line right at our point of entry at the inlet. Now, as a point of fact I don't mind rain and wind and I truly rather enjoy that sort of weather, but the ugly black thunderhead that sat over the inlet spitting lightning every 15 seconds was not your run-of-the-mill afternoon sun shower. And the closer we got the more exposed I felt as we were in an open boat with no protection. I mean nothing. No awning, no T-top, not even a VHF radio antennae higher than my head. I felt like a human lightning rod. Ominously, as if to punctuate my thoughts, the windy outflow of the storm reached us and rippled the water as an especially loud peal of thunder crashed in our ears.

"Let's turn around and take Egmont," I suggested, referring to the alternate way back to Cortez by way of Egmont Key. "It looks clear that way." It would be a much longer trip, for sure, but also a safer one. I gazed longingly to the south.

Mom pressed on directly toward the pass and the squall. "No, I want to get these sharks back to the dock before dark. We'll be okay. The storm won't be that bad."

"It will be in a few minutes!" I hollered as another lightning bolt flashed and the loudest peal of thunder yet practically drowned out my words.

"We'll be okay," Mom repeated, calm as a clam. And as I saw her there at the wheel I knew that there would be no changing her mind. Captain Rachel was in command and nothing was going to stop her from getting back to the docks before dark. And I thought I knew why. She wanted to unload the sharks in prime time when the docks were buzzing with action to prove she was just as good a fisherwoman as any of the men and if we came in after dark that wouldn't happen. Heck, I too would have liked to see the look on everyone's faces when we docked with the two big sharks, but my ego would just have to wait for a better time and I knew that that time was not now. I gave up my protest. Mom and I had already butted heads and had a few power struggles previously concerning who was captain of the boat and she usually won. So, Captain Rachel maintained her course and speed. I took one last long look behind us towards Egmont and then studied the beach off our port side for a single long minute. How far off was it? One mile? Five? I knew it was tricky to tell the distance over water, yet I wasn't overly concerned. I was a very strong swimmer and knew I could float if I got tired. Right then I made a stupid decision.

Without further thought, I stripped off my shirt and shoes and with a smart-ass "See you later, Mom!" I dove over the side of the boat and hit the water smoothly in a streamlined dive, then rapidly transitioned into a fluid American crawl heading for the beach. As I swam I listened carefully to the sound of the motor and expected to momentarily hear Mom throttle back and circle around to pick me up, but all I heard was the motor's steady drone diminishing slowly as she drew further away. With a peculiar mix of alarm and thrill I grasped the fact that she wasn't going to turn back and get me. I was on my own. Far from afraid, I was actually a little miffed. What was she thinking?

Then I remembered that it was I that had jumped overboard without warning. Maybe she hadn't yet noticed that I was no longer on the boat. Heck, in a couple more minutes it wouldn't matter anyway. I knew I would be nearly invisible in the water, low and lacking even a bright orange life preserver to aid with visibility. No, I wasn't worried and didn't really care one way or the other. I just needed to concentrate on swimming, and that's what I did for the next hour or so, pausing roughly every 15 minutes to rest for a few seconds. I was making good headway, of that I was sure. But how much? Was the current setting me back? These and other questions loomed with greater impact as my swim went on and on. I could see the shoreline just fine, but from the water it appeared much farther away than it had from the higher vantage point of the boat's deck. I also noticed that it was beginning to get dark, and that was when I made a crucial mental blunder. I started thinking about sharks.

Of course, the images of the two I had just caught were still very fresh in my mind and that didn't help. I vividly recalled their gaping maws, razor teeth and tremendous strength even in such a weakened condition. I wondered if I had been cut in the day's activities and was bleeding anywhere, however minor. I remembered how sharks are night feeders and imagined how I must appear to them in my present state, flapping around the water's surface like a wounded fish. And yes, I admit that several scenes of the movie *Jaws* nibbled at the edge of my psyche as well. As darkness fell the water became increasingly opaque to the point I could see nothing beyond an arm's reach. After sunset, it was all black. I felt like a sitting duck, and boy, did I regret leaving the boat. I was so pissed. Pissed at Mom. Royally pissed at myself. Fortunately, the anger gave me renewed energy and my stroke increased in rate and power. I figured the sooner I got to shore, the better; this was no pleasure swim. About an hour later I made it and collapsed on the shore like a beached whale. I had never been so tired in my entire life. I just laid there for what seemed like an eternity and by the time I walked back home Mom had already left to go dancing. When I saw Mom the next morning neither of us had much to say about the incident. She probably should have turned back to get me but I shouldn't have jumped overboard in the first place. What could I say? It was history. A little test of nerve that I could pass or fail, much like one that occurred only a few months later after Mom was involved in an accident.

If Orange Crush was an ugly van before, it was an outright Frankenstein monster after the crash where Mom wrapped it around a telephone pole after being hit broadside by another car. Luckily, there were no injuries and both Mom and the other driver were able to walk away unscathed. As further testament to the solid van, Mom was actually able to drive away in Orange Crush, but not before being cited by police and given a summons for a mandatory traffic court appearance. She had had Rachel's driver's license but no insurance, and that was the issue. Before long, Mom's court date arrived and I questioned whether or not it was wise to go, but she didn't blink. "Of course I'm going, why not?" I thought, well, if she isn't worried why should I be? So I decided to tag along.

We arrived early for the cattle call that passed for the Manatee County traffic court, and it was a good thing too, for the building was huge, a maze of passageways that could test the orienteering skills of Indiana Jones. And wouldn't you know, we got turned around and wandered down more than a few passages trying to find the one that led to our magistrate's courtroom. The problem was they all looked the same, that is, all of them but one, because that particular hallway had a very distinctive display case that first caught my eye, then froze my feet as we hurried past.

"Mom!" I hissed. We were alone, but I still tried to keep my voice down. She turned to see where I was staring.

Mom's U.S. Marshals most wanted poster (1984).

It was a typical large display case that contained a couple dozen miscellaneous informational documents and governmental notices, but that was not all. It also had a half dozen wanted posters prominently posted near its center, and one of them was Mom's. It was her United States Federal Marshals 15 most wanted poster, and together we gawked for nearly a minute in a mute blend of horror and amazement. All of a sudden I felt as vulnerable as I had during my night swim a few months earlier. Was I nuts? I was in a government building, a courthouse at that, with a most wanted fugitive! How many cops were within these walls at this very moment? Mom and I both were in deep water with circling sharks. It was a surreal moment and one I'll never forget.

Mom was the first to turn away. "Let's go, or we'll be late," she whispered over her shoulder. I snapped out of my silent reverie and glanced up and down the hallway. We were still alone but I was still disturbed.

Mom, on the other hand, appeared completely unperturbed, even going so far as to ask the next person we encountered for directions to the courtroom. We got in just in time and took our seats among the waiting throng. Forty-five minutes later Mom was called to the bench.

"Rachel McVey, case number CT-65774," a disembodied voice announced over the PA system.

My stomach did a little flip-flop as Mom stood and coolly approached the lectern and faced the magistrate. Would she be recognized? I couldn't see why not. The photo on the wanted poster down the hall was not flattering but did represent what she looked like to a reasonable degree and there she was, no disguise whatsoever, standing before a courtroom of people as well as several police bailiffs and the magistrate. Yet nothing happened. Nothing bad, anyway. I couldn't believe it.

In fact, the magistrate placed the only woman on the U.S. Marshals 15 most wanted list on three months probation along with an accompanying fine that had to be paid at each appearance to the county probation office. Rachel McVey smiled sweetly and thanked him and that was it. We walked out to Orange Crush in silence and drove away. I half expected blue lights to appear in our rearview mirror all the way back to Cortez. What a day that was!

So, Mom had her day in court and it had turned out well. However, the rest of our family was another matter, for we read the newspapers from time to time and knew they were still in dire jeopardy and their federal trial was slated to begin soon. Most of the charges had been upheld by the judge and the case against them appeared strong thanks in no small part to a very special witness for the prosecution. And I, for one, had little doubt who that could be.

It was a very sad thought.

16

Take Down—Part Deux

Baga was in the fight of his life and he knew it. His lawyer, Converse Bright, had reminded him repeatedly that the state had a mountain of circumstantial evidence against him as well as the pièce de résistance, a witness that tipped the scales irrevocably in favor of the prosecution. It was a grim thought. Baga had only joined Mom's smuggling operation because she needed help and his lifelong first impulse as a husband and a father was always to come to the assistance of those in need, especially his family. Now he was going down for that gut instinct. It was only a matter of how far.

Aunt Bonnie's position was not much better. Much of the same evidence against Baga, including the traitorous witness, was allied against her. Making matters worse was the fact that she was a mother with a young son, my cousin Logan. Because Bonnie had been out on bond since her arrest, Logan had been spared the torture of having his mother instantly disappear from his life like Mom had disappeared from Morgana's, but now that threat loomed large. I felt very bad for him because I knew how it felt to have your mom locked up. The only bright spot, if there was one at all, was that Bonnie faced fewer charges than Baga and therefore would not spend as much time behind bars in the likely event of a conviction. All in all, there was not much to look forward to except the mercy of the court.

The other co-defendants in the indictment, Jeannie Tumulty, her henchman John Parella, and catch-man Herman Witlow, would also be tried along with Baga and Bonnie in the same trial despite their attorney's best efforts filing motions to get their trials separated. It was common knowledge that the feds considered their case iron-clad and therefore wanted to save time and money by having only one trial.

The trial, held in the federal Middle District of Georgia, was presided over by Chief Justice Wilbur Owens, Jr. Judge Owens had been appointed by Nixon in 1972 and had a well-deserved reputation as an uncompromising hardline judge with a special enmity towards drug smuggling and drug crimes in general. Stated bluntly, he was about as close to an old-fashioned "hanging judge" as there could be. Of course there could be no hanging in their trial, but anyone convicted would be likely to receive the stiffest sentence allowed by law.

From the start, the trial was really more of a massacre than a trial. The state spent days methodically layering one piece of evidence upon the next until it had built a fortress that was all but impenetrable. The defense attorneys put up a valiant fight but were hampered by their sheer numbers. When one lawyer objected to a line of questioning or attacked a certain piece of evidence and was overruled or denied it tended to negatively reflect upon and impact all the others. And like an old-time gunfighter, Judge Owens was quick to shoot down defense objections and attacks. Most went in favor of the state.

I'm sure it didn't help that Mom, the explicit ringleader of the organization, was conspicuously absent from the trial and the feds still had to be more than a little pissed off as to the reason why. The media had not allowed the sensational nature of her escape to fade in the public eye. Every article was a reminder, a jab in the eye to a system that had allowed a horrible marijuana smuggler, a dangerous scourge of society, to escape. How could a cop, a prosecutor, or even a judge not take it personally? I felt sure the Pitz did. Why not the rest?

The prosecution onslaught continued unabated and mercilessly pummeled the beleaguered defense with everything it had. It told a story about fancy planes and tons of pot and how it came from Jamaica, landed in Florida and wound up in Georgia catch houses before eventually spreading nationwide. It told a story about the defendants being united in their goal of bringing marijuana into the country to sell for profit. This part was all-important and especially damning for it was a key factor of the dreaded conspiracy. And finally, it told a story about money, lots of it, like it was something to be reviled rather than glorified as it is in the good ole U.S. of A. And just in case all that wasn't enough, the prosecution announced their star witness, none other than Greg, dressed in a suit and tie and wearing a greasy smile.

It came as no surprise to anyone that Greg did what he did and said what he said, which was to essentially corroborate everything that had been previously presented by the prosecution while minimizing his own role and culpability in the operation. His testimony sealed the fate of all the defendants, as well as Mom's when and if she came to trial. Right after his testimony Greg ran into Bummy in the hallway outside the courtroom and, perhaps shamed, briefly looked her in the eye and, addressing her by a shortened version of her own name as he had done many times before, said, "Vi, it was nothing personal."

Well, it might not have been personal to him, a man who would walk free after ensuring that many of his former friends and co-conspirators, including the mother of his only child, went to prison, but I felt otherwise. It was a cowardly and selfish act that would define him forever.

Following Greg's testimony the prosecution rested its case in short order. Then it was the defense's turn at bat and it was a mess from the start. The chief problem was that because there were so many defendants the defense was uncoordinated and did not present much of a cohesive front. Of course, each attorney had the same ultimate goal, the acquittal of their client, but they also had somewhat different ideas how to achieve it. And in truth, after the prosecution's case it probably would not have mattered anyway. Judge Owens continued to sustain most of the pros-ecution's objections which allowed the defense few opportunities to score points for their clients. The embarrassment persisted until the last defense attorney finally rested. The prosecution's closing arguments were businesslike and stressed Greg's first-person testimony that placed each defendant, particularly Baga and Bonnie, squarely at the center of the criminal acts they were charged with. The defense's closing argument was lackluster at best. Converse Bright might as well have phoned in his summation; the jury just didn't buy it. All the defendants were found guilty. At the sentencing, Judge Owens lived up to his reputation and brought his gavel down hard. Aunt Bonnie was sentenced to ten years in the federal penitentiary, Baga 20. Bummy wailed as they were led out of the courtroom in handcuffs.

Mom and I heard of the outcome of the trial not long afterward but did not speak much about it. There simply wasn't much to say. I'm sure it worried Mom, yet she did not show it and was disinclined to dis-cuss anything that was negative, believing that bad things flowed from bad thoughts. I respected that and tried to follow her example, but the trial had driven home a feeling inside me that had begun not long after our arrival in Cortez. That is, I knew our situation was ultimately a hopeless one. It was only logical. We had no money to use to start over somewhere beyond the reach of the law, nor would it be feasible to live the rest of our lives on the lam. Maybe Mom could, but I couldn't see that for Melanie and myself. It was like we were involved in a game of chess with no possibility of a winning end game. Or even a stalemate. Pondering these thoughts, I wondered how long Cortez would remain a safe haven. How long until someone saw Mom's wanted poster and noticed her uncanny resemblance to newbie fisherwoman Rachel?

As it turned out, I did not have long to wait to learn the answer to at least the question of Cortez's viability as a place of refuge, and the answer came only a few months later in the form of a mysterious phone call in the middle of the night. Mom had answered the call with the usual "hello," listened in silence for half a minute, then uttered a simple "thank you" before hanging up. The call was mysterious for two reasons: the caller did not identify himself nor did Mom recognize the voice and the message imparted was startling: "Judy, the FBI is on to you and you've got to leave Cortez immediately. You may have a day or two, no more."

Mom was shocked, and when she told me what the caller had said, I was too. It was clearly a warning that had to be taken seriously. And because the caller had used Mom's real name as well as her location we had to assume the information was accurate. Undoubtedly the caller was a friend or else we would have already been arrested, but who was it? And why couldn't Mom recognize the voice? All of a sudden, the safe and friendly little fishing village we had come to know and love had become a dangerous place for us. Where could we go now? There were lots of questions with no answers. The only thing we knew for sure was that we had to leave, and leave soon.

I hardly slept the remainder of the night, my worried mind swirling with torturous thoughts, and was up before dawn ready for action. Since we needed money and had none, I knew what I had to do and headed for the nearest pawn shop. The only possessions of value I had at the time were my last two guitars and a pair of vintage Marshall amplifier stacks. In the hope of someday returning to redeem my cherished instruments I pawned them instead of selling them outright, keeping only my first guitar, my treasured birthday Gibson. I choked up as the pawnbroker laid the cash on the counter.

Now that we had a little cash to work with we really kicked into high gear. We packed our meager belongings (mostly just clothes) into Orange Crush and threw away everything else we did not intend to take with us. The idea was to leave nothing for the feds to trace or follow. I personally felt that that would be impossible considering the U.S. Marshals and FBI would surely turn Cortez upside down and question everyone at length. In my mind's eye I envisioned the swarming feds and their buzzing questions. "So, what does this Nikki look like? How about Desiree? Rachel? We have pictures of them … here, take a good look. His name is actually David Michael. But you know that, don't you? Her name is Melanie. And this is their mother, a marijuana smuggling drug-lord, head of the Haas Organization and the only woman on our most wanted list, Judy McNelis! Where did they live? How well did you know them? Were they your friends? Do you know you can go to jail if you harbor them? You are aware, aren't you, that there is a substantial reward for anyone that can provide us with information leading to their capture?"

I hoped that all our Cortez friends would weather the storm without too much abuse. They were good people and I hated to think they might be punished just for knowing and befriending us. And I took a modicum of comfort knowing that since we had never revealed our true identities to anyone, the villagers had the truth on their side. I prayed that it would be enough. So, with a full tank of gas and a general inclination to head south, Mom steered Orange Crush onto I-75 heading toward south Florida.

Mom didn't have a plan so I came up with one of my own. Spring break was in full swing in southeast Florida with tens of thousands of wild, partying college kids on every inch of beach and the hotels brimming with guests. I figured it would be easy to get lost in that kind of crowd. And when I explained my reasoning to Mom she went for it. Only a few hours later we arrived in Ft. Lauderdale.

It was jam-packed with college students just as I knew it would be and Melanie and I blended in perfectly, and although Mom was of course quite a bit older than us, she wasn't that conspicuous among the massive throng. Sadly, however, Orange Crush had to go. We knew it would be only a matter of time before an APB with our descriptions and that of our vehicle would be issued and if the van's unusual color wasn't enough to sink us, its distinctive caved-in body would. We solved the problem by renting a storage unit that didn't require ID and parked the van inside. It had served us well and never let us down except in the looks department and I said a silent goodbye. That was the last time I ever saw old Orange Crush and I sort of hated to see it go. To cover our tracks further we walked a few blocks from the storage facility, each of us carrying a suitcase and me with my guitar, before hailing a taxi and taking it to a weekly hotel a block from the Ft. Lauderdale strip. For the moment at least we felt invisible.

We spent the next several days unwinding, as much as we could, from the stress of our flight from Cortez. Melanie and I hung out at the beach most of the day while Mom tended to stay back in the room and read and watch TV. I think she knew she was the most recognizable of the three of us and therefore wanted to minimize her exposure. It was also around this time that we read an especially nasty newspaper article that had been written shortly after our flight from Cortez. The article had begun innocently enough by talking about Mom's stint as a topless dancer and then went on to talk about how the driver's license Mom found had actually belonged to a well-known attorney for the Manatee County commission. Thank God I didn't know that when Mom was in front of the judge in Manatee County traffic court—I would have been an absolute nervous wreck! Finally, the article ended by quoting a U.S. federal marshal who had spouted a huge pack of lies and innuendo, calling Mom a "black widow" (how original!) and saying she was suspected of multiple murders and a special task force had been assembled to "get her off the street." Were they kidding?! The marshal was totally full of crap, yet nevertheless we felt pretty sure that the feds had to be nipping at our heels. But what could we really do? Where could we go without money? I didn't think running again was much of an option, so I tried not to think about the future and mostly succeeded. After a long day at the beach I'd party at whatever nightclub I could find that charged a cheap cover and played rock music. Most nights, I usually went out alone because Melanie was underage, but one night after we had been in Ft. Lauderdale almost a week I decided to invite Mom along because I planned to play at an open mic night and I wanted her to see me perform. She accepted my invitation and we left together in a cab. Melanie stayed back at the hotel watching TV. That would turn out to be a fateful decision.

Once at the club, I signed up for my slot at the open mic and Mom and I had a few beers while we waited for my turn and watched the other performers. As usual for spring break, the place was packed to overflowing with a rowdy, drunk young crowd and by the time I finished my mini-set of three songs I was halfway there myself. Satisfied with my performance, I cased my beloved Gibson and suggested that we head back to the hotel and maybe pick up a bite of food on the way. Mom agreed, so we caught a cab and did just that, though once we arrived back at the hotel I noticed that something was different.

But exactly what was different I could not say. There was the usual assortment of vehicles in the parking lot and I could see the bluish-white light of televisions flashing through several curtained windows and the sign in front of the office continued to flash a neon "NO" in front of the word "VACANCY" just as it had all week. Nevertheless, something was wrong; I was sure of it. So sure that I flashed Mom a silent "hold on a minute" sign and told our driver to keep going. Instead, I had him stop at a nearby convenience store two blocks away and wait while Mom and I went inside.

"I think we're in trouble; something's not right at the hotel." My tone was low and insistent and Mom took my words seriously.

"What?"

I answered honestly. "I don't know, but something's wrong. I'm sure of it." Mom looked up at me quietly, gauging the moment as I hissed in an urgent whisper, "We need to get out of town right now, and I mean right this very minute!"

"But we can't leave Melanie…" Mom began, but I cut her off.

"Melanie's already busted Mom. We've got to go now," I pleaded.

For an answer, Mom shook her head and gave me the look I knew so well, as I had seen it many times before in my life. It was the look that said there was no way I could ever change her mind and I knew right then and there that it was all over. But then an idea occurred to me and I went for it.

"Okay, you're right. Stay here with the cab and I'll walk back and get Melanie and our clothes and meet you right back here in 15 minutes. And if I'm not back in 15 minutes, you get out of here and leave us because we've been caught. And please don't forget my guitar. Okay?"

Mom hesitated, so I insisted again in my most urgent and pleading voice, "Okay?"

"Okay," she said, clearly not happy in agreeing to my plan but accepting it anyway.

"Okay, see you in a few minutes." I hastily turned and walked away before she could change her mind and insist on coming with me. And once I got to the edge of the store parking lot I glanced back and saw her get back in the cab. So far, so good, I thought to myself. At least Mom will get away. A few steps more and I was swallowed by the night.

Walking back to the hotel that night was the weirdest feeling I had ever felt in my entire life, for I knew I was walking directly into a trap. I was 100 percent sure of it. It was a surreal feeling. My head said that everything was probably okay and that I was just being paranoid, but my gut told me the truth. The feds had the hotel completely surrounded and there was no way I would escape this mess. Yet something inside me decided to give it my best shot, so instead of approaching from the front I decided to stay under the cover of darkness and use the walled alley behind the hotel as a blind. I slunk down the alley as quietly as a panther, pleased that I was wearing the dark clothes I commonly favored when partying at night, and when I arrived at a spot directly in back of the hotel, my head once again tried to convince my gut that I had only imagined the danger and everything was going to turn out nifty. But my gut wasn't buying it. I took a deep breath and climbed over the block wall and landed silently on the other side. It was very dark on that side of the wall so I paused for a minute to let my eyes adjust, and as I surveyed the scene I didn't notice anything amiss. I had landed in a tiled courtyard and the hotel's main building was about 25 yards directly in front of me. With swift and sure steps I made a beeline for our door.

I was only ten feet or so from our door when I noticed in my peripheral vision a sudden press of movement close in on me from all sides, then seconds later I heard a chorus of loud, intense voices shouting the words I knew I was destined to hear before the night was over.

"FBI, FBI, GET DOWN ON THE GROUND, DOWN, DOWN, DOWN!!!"

I fell to the ground. I had been manhandled before by the feds and wanted to try to avoid getting hurt if I could help it. They reached me in seconds and while one held a gun to my temple and two others held my arms behind my back a fourth cuffed me. And when they were done they finished the punishment by jerking me roughly to my feet using my arms as handles. Boy, it was a good thing I didn't resist, as I probably would have gotten hurt because they were already pretty riled up for me being just a skinny, long-haired, unarmed Eagle Scout musician with no criminal record. I would hate to see them with a real bad guy.

"What's your name?" an agent shouted in my ear.

"I think you know my name," I replied nervously, "or else you wouldn't have me in cuffs with a gun to my head." I was not trying to mouth off; I just wanted the gun put back in its holster and I must have hit the nail right on the head because without another word they marched me off to a waiting car that was parked on the side of the hotel and put me in the back seat. Oh well, I thought. This had gone exactly as expected, no surprises whatsoever. No harm done. And in a strange way, I was actually relieved. It was as if a splinter had been extracted from a festering wound or a heavy load lifted from my shoulders, and the best part was the knowledge that Mom was still free and would make good her escape. At least I hadn't sacrificed myself for nothing. Or had I? Because I had hardly finished patting myself on the back before I noticed a familiar-looking car driving slowly up the street towards the hotel. Oh no, I thought, it can't be! Please don't let it be the cab with Mom inside! And as the car drew closer I began to see the driver and the passenger in the back seat come into focus and my heart sank with the realization. It was Mom!

The cab slowed as it drew even with the hotel and I could see Mom squinting through the window, most likely trying to figure out where I was or if she could discern anything useful. I was absolutely transfixed by the scene, helpless to do anything but endeavor to compel her to keep going by the force of my will alone. I focused all my mental energy and said a silent little prayer, "Oh God, please keep going, don't stop, just keep going, oh God, please … just … don't … stop."

The cab rolled to a slow stop right in front of the office. And up until it did, I hadn't noticed the feds taking any particular interest in the passing traffic in front of the hotel. But that all changed when the cab stopped. I saw several pairs of eyes flit over to study the driver and his female passenger, and then grow wide in obvious recognition. In three seconds flat a half dozen or more agents had the cab surrounded with drawn weapons and ordered the driver and Mom out with raised hands. And then it was all over. Mom was busted.

The entire scenario had played out in two minutes total, yet it had felt like an hour to me watching powerless and mute in the backseat of the FBI cruiser. I hoped they would put Mom in with me, but they placed her in another car instead. I would not see her again without a piece of glass or bars separating us for many years to come. Far different from the way I had felt only minutes before, I was now gripped by a pall of gloom. I barely paid attention as agents led the cabbie to the front of his car and started questioning him. I knew he would be fine since he didn't know that his passengers were wanted fugitives, but seeing him again triggered a thought from the edges of my consciousness. My guitar! It was still in the cab. I began kicking on the cruiser's window to get an agent's attention.

The kicking worked, and when the fed came to warn me against damaging federal property, I told him about my guitar and asked him to please retrieve it from the cab. He did and immediately put it in the trunk of the cruiser I was in. Later that night, on my way to the Miami federal building where I was initially held and questioned, the agents I was with assured me the guitar would be safe and returned to me when I bonded out or was otherwise released. They lied. When I was eventually released I tried to get my guitar back but the feds denied that they ever had it in the first place. It had essentially disappeared into thin air and I never saw my beloved guitar again.

17

Pawn Sacrifice

"Check," I declared as I attacked with my last remaining knight. In response to the move the former prime minister of the Turks and Caicos glanced sharply up at me through his wire-rimmed glasses and smiled devilishly.

"David Michael, you lied to me." His speech was crisp, his voice deep and rich with a British accent.

"How so?" I asked with exaggerated innocence, not looking up from the chessboard lying between us on the floor.

"You told me you were merely an average chess player, and that is clearly not so." His smile was contagious and I smiled too.

I looked him in the eye and chuckled. "Well, it's all relative, I'm sure."

"Yes, I agree," he answered as he moved his king from its original position. It was the move I knew he had to make in response to my attack, and now that his king was flushed from the pocket he could no longer perform a castle maneuver and his position was significantly weaker. I now had a slight edge and sometimes that was all that was required. Too bad all things in life were not as honest and straightforward as a good game of chess. The game was an excellent distraction and one that I desperately needed in my situation because I had been locked up for the first time in my life.

The ex-prime minister and I, along with 23 other men, shared a cell intended for only a dozen prisoners and our daily games were about the only thing that beat back my growing desperation and kept me sane. Although I was a federal prisoner, I had been jailed in the severely overcrowded Hillsborough County jail for over a month. The place was a filthy, squalid hell-hole where prisoners lived under 24-hour lockdown with glaring lights and unending noise. On my third day there I noticed an empty bed and took it. Later that night while I was sleeping I was hit in the head with a hardback notebook binder by some unknown assailant and woke up with a bloody ear. No wonder the bed was empty! From then on I slept on the grimy floor. Everyone shared a single stinking steel toilet that was bolted to the bare wall on one side of the cell. Most of my fellow cellmates were in for serious violent felonies that included second-degree murder, assault, and armed robbery, to name a few. There were also a couple of serious drug offenders and one child molester in the group. The ex-prime minister, who had been charged with some type of financial crime, and myself were the only federal prisoners. When I had first arrived and told the other men what I was in for they were dumbstruck.

"Whaddaya mean 'harboring a fugitive'?" they asked, busting a gut like I was the jail comedian put in the cell for their amusement. "And you say the fugitive was your momma? You gotta be kidding!"

Well, I wish I had been kidding, but I wasn't. After my arrest more than two months earlier I had been in a total of three lock-ups. The first two were in Miami-Dade County and were bad, but not as bad as Hillsborough County, where I had ended up. My court-appointed attorney, Chesney Larson, was of the opinion the feds had moved me to the worst jail they could find in order to try and break my spirit and get me to testify against someone. I not only agreed with him, I knew exactly who the feds were after, as the questions they asked me left no doubt. They wanted Aunt Nancy. Bad. And when my answers didn't help their efforts I was issued an orange jumpsuit (its color akin to Orange Crush) and put on a prisoner transport bus wearing waist chains, leg irons, and paper slippers. My destination? Why, Shithole Central, of course!

Being locked up sure gave me plenty of time to think about things and I came to several profound realizations in no time. Regrettably, the recurring theme centered on my stupidity. One, me sacrificing myself on the night I was arrested by going back to a place I knew was loaded with feds was just plain stupid and had counted for nothing. Melanie had already been arrested hours earlier and was not even at the hotel by the time I had arrived. Two, it had been a stupid decision to join Mom in the first place. I had been a free person and now I wasn't and joining Mom hadn't ultimately helped her in any meaningful way. And finally, I had been stupid not to immediately fire Mr. Larson as my attorney and replace him, because not only had I been rotting in a hideous cell for weeks and weeks, when I finally had the chance to make a legal move I took his advice and accepted the deal he had arranged with the federal district attorney on my behalf. Making an uninformed decision that would haunt me for the rest of my life based on incompetent legal advice, I pled guilty to federal felonies that were not even a crime in most states at the time: harboring a fugitive and conspiracy to harbor a fugitive. The judge sentenced me to three years' probation. I had given in because I was very tired and desperate, but at least I was out of jail.

Like so many times before, I should have followed the gut feeling I had when I first saw Mr. Larson, an immense man dressed in a banana-yellow suit and wearing a white tie with blood-red polka-dots. "He can't be serious," my gut screamed, "unless he's a real bad-ass lawyer, because you've got to be either that or a total flake to dress this way." I might just as well have taken the advice of Bozo the clown as Mr. Larson.

In retrospect I should have gone to trial and thrown myself on the

mercy of a jury that might have understood the complex emotions involved when a child is interacting with a parent. It's not a cut-and-dried situation and judgments easily become blurred. The "overt acts" listed in the indictment that led to my charges showed what a bad guy I was: I didn't call the feds and turn in Mom when I learned of her whereabouts and I pawned musical equipment to pay for communal necessities while we were on the lam. The "conspiracy" in the indictment was with Melanie because we acted together in not betraying Mom. What kind of son would betray his mother or father? Not me, for sure.

Free once again, I returned to Valdosta and lived at Bummy's. Baga and Bonnie had begun serving their time by then and it wasn't long before Mom followed suit. Rather than go to trial on the multitude of

Baga in charge of the prison library, ca. 1985.

charges she faced, she had pled guilty to reduced charges and was sentenced to 20 years. Her plea had been arranged by a good lawyer, a guy called "D–Day" because of his birthday. She was shipped out to California and began doing her time in the co-ed federal penitentiary at Pleasanton.

By all accounts Mom settled into prison life as well as anyone could have expected. She had a long sentence and tried to make the best of it. To this end, she managed to show off her gardening skills to prison officials and was eventually rewarded by being assigned the job of prison gardener. The years passed slowly and everyone in my immediate family suffered the pain of separation. Prison was still prison and Mom missed her family dearly, especially Morgana, but at least she had found an outlet with her flowers. Besides that, Mom had also found a friend, and an unusual one at that.

Mom's new friend and cellmate was Svetlana Ogorodnikova, a striking woman with bright blue eyes and a heavy accent who had immigrated to the United States from the USSR with her husband in the early 1970s and settled in

David Michael and Morgana, ca. 1985.

David Michael and Morgana, ca. 1987.

the Los Angeles area. She was locked up with Mom in Pleasanton because in 1984 she had pled guilty to federal espionage charges connected to the infamous Richard Miller spy case. The story is a remarkable one to say the least.

Richard Miller was a married Mormon FBI agent based in Los Angeles. His lackluster career had been characterized by most of his colleagues as one of incompetence. It was said he didn't even look the part of an FBI agent as he was often described as being portly and disheveled, which many considered manifestations of his ineptitude. Yet that did not prevent Miller from undertaking what he professed to be a private attempt to "turn" a woman he suspected of being a KGB operative into a double-agent working on the side of the FBI in the hope of resurrecting his ruined career. The woman Miller was referring to was Svetlana.

Lana (as she's called by Mom and other friends) had, according to the FBI, been what the KGB refers to as a "swallow," an attractive woman set "in flight" to subvert an opposing nation's agents through sex. However, Lana's attorneys contended that she had merely been an FBI informant and had had an affair with Miller in that role.

Oddly, it appears that the Richard Miller spy case actually came to the attention of the FBI through Miller himself when he presented it to his superiors and reportedly asked for their help to keep it going. But the case was wrought with contradictions. According to Miller, Lana told him the USSR would pay a lot of money for secret FBI intelligence files and had set up a clandestine meeting in Vienna between him and Soviet intelligence. He also reported that in order to further his investigation he played along and agreed to receive payments of cash and gold in exchange for classified documents. When pressed, Miller admitted to handing over a genuine classified FBI counterintelligence manual, and when his home was searched he was found to be in possession of many more classified documents. Obviously, something was going on. But what?

If Miller's story was true it gives rise to other troubling questions that no innocent FBI man would care to answer. Why hand over a real classified document instead of a fake? Why wait until the case was so far advanced before bringing it to the attention of his superiors? And last but definitely not least, why did he have so many other classified documents in his possession if he was only trying to set up a double agent?

Over the years, Lana has continued to insist that she was innocent of the charges that resulted in her being sentenced to 18 years in prison and serving nine. She has repeatedly stated that she was the victim of manufactured evidence and false media reports and that she only pled guilty out of fear of governmental reprisal or deportation. And there is evidence that supports her claims. One widely reported but later debunked report claimed that when she was arrested she was found to be in possession of secret writing implements, code books, and concealment devices. Other sources have since reported that the FBI's own internal investigation of the Richard Miller spy case was sloppy and tainted by the obvious fact that they were investigating one of their own. At the time, Miller was the first FBI agent in history to be indicted of espionage and many contend that the embarrassment he caused the FBI overshadowed the facts of the case. It seems a reasonable speculation to me.

Regardless of the actual truth, one fact remains resolute. The Richard Miller spy case and the part Lana played in it continues to capture the imagination of many people. Lana's story was featured on CBS's *60 Minutes* in a story titled "The Spy Who Couldn't Go Home" which was the most watched episode in the show's history. It was also included in subsequent highly-rated episodes of *60 Minutes* including the "Best of *60 Minutes* for the Decade of the 80s," "Mike Wallace Remembers 25 Years of *60 Minutes*," and "35 Years of *60 Minutes*."

Lana and Mom became true friends as they served their time together. I think it was because they had found in each other someone they could trust. Meanwhile, I spoke with Mom as often as I could and sent letters that contained pictures of me, Morgana, and Melanie, and together we all dreamed of the day she would be released and our little family could reunite. I knew our lives could never be quite the same after all the water under the bridge and the distance created by the many years of separation, but we were family and that was what mattered. It was something to hope for—something to pray for. Mom being locked up for so long was awful but the road ahead seemed clear and the worst was over, or so we thought. But we were wrong. Dead wrong. The cruelest trial yet was just around the corner.

18

A Fight to the Death

The devastating news arrived via a lawyer's phone call on an otherwise agreeable fall day as Mom went about her daily routine at Pleasanton. The attorney was sympathetic but his words had been brutally direct. Mom had been indicted in Palm Beach County, Florida, for the capital first-degree murder of her former drug pilot and friend Frank Maars. It was horrifying news for sure, but not altogether unexpected, because anyone that cared to follow the continuing legal troubles of the former "Haas Organization" conspirators knew that Jeannie had been indicted and convicted on the exact same charge only months before and had been sentenced to 25 years. Shocked, we had heard about her trial and followed it with morbid interest. Frank Maars' murder had been a mystery for years and it was unsettling to think that someone we all knew had anything to do with it. None of us were confident that the true story had yet been told, and however sad the final outcome was it had seemed the case had been closed. Now it appeared that the Palm Beach district attorney (aptly named Bludworth) wasn't finished and was thirsty for more blood, Mom's blood. I say this because he not only wanted Mom's conviction, he wanted her life. That much was crystal clear, because when the charges were filed against Mom the district attorney's office formally declared that it was seeking the death penalty in her case. My blood ran cold when I heard the news.

The thought of Mom being executed in Florida's electric chair, nicknamed "Old Sparky," terrified me like nothing had before in my entire life and I had recurring bad dreams for months as the opening day of her trial neared. Every night I went to bed with the dreadful vision in my mind only to wake up to the living nightmare the next morning. Mom being in prison was difficult for me to contemplate but it was something I could endure as there was always an end in sight, however distant. There would be no such reprieve if she was executed. If that happened I felt as though they might as well kill me too. I just wasn't sure I could carry on with my life knowing Mom died that way. The only thing that saved my sanity during this period was constant and fervent prayer. I simply begged Jesus for the justice I feared the court might not provide. My fears weren't unfounded either. History proved that Florida regularly used Old Sparky, and other statistics painted an ugly picture as well.

At the time of her trial's start in early February 1987, Palm Beach County's murder conviction rate was more than 98 percent, and that single fact all by itself scared the living hell out of my entire family. But that was not all. We knew the state would be prosecuting the case for the second time in two years using the same evidence that had been used successfully to convict Jeannie, and even though there was no physical or other forensic evidence involved, the state's prosecution team was well practiced and their witnesses well rehearsed. The state's confidence was obvious from the start as chief prosecutor Gay Broome, tall, dark-haired and grim-faced, dressed in a navy skirt and tailored jacket, stepped forward and ominously declared to the wide-eyed jury and enthralled spectators, "You are about to enter a world of drug smuggling, drug greed, and drug murder."

You could have heard a pin drop as Broome laid out the case against Mom, and it was elegantly simple. She contended that Mom had ordered a hitman, John Parella, to kill Frank Maars. She then calmly explained to the jury that Mom had ordered Frank's murder because she owed him more than $125,000 and Frank had stolen one of her planes in order to hold it as collateral until he was paid. "It was a fatal mistake," she told the jurors. That was the prosecution's case in a nutshell, she explained, and to drive it home to the jury Broome promised to call both the hitman and his accomplice to the stand. She retired to the prosecution's table with a smugly confident expression.

Mom's lead attorney was court-appointed Philip Butler, a stout bulldog of a lawyer who made up in tenacity what he lacked in physical stature. Butler was an experienced litigator and played to his strengths, namely, a candid courtroom style that was uncomplicated and straightforward. He kept his opening statement brief and concluded it by coming straight to the main point. "This is nothing more than a robbery and a murder planned, orchestrated and executed by a bad dude—John

Parella." He strode back to the defense table where Mom's hired attorney and chief defense strategist Randy Daar was busy taking notes. Randy was a green yet gifted defense lawyer from the famed San Francisco Tony Serra Law Firm and this was his first capital murder trial. Despite that, Mom had tremendous faith in him and actually wanted to fire Butler early on and appoint Randy as lead counsel but Judge Carlisle wouldn't allow it. A true professional, Randy accepted the supporting role and vowed to keep Butler on track. As Butler sat down, Randy turned to Mom and whispered, "Here we go." Then it was the prosecution's courtroom once again.

Prosecutor Broome did not introduce Parella to the court as Jeannie's ex-boyfriend and exclusive former business associate, which he had been. Instead, she presented him as a former Ft. Lauderdale bar manager, who had moonlighted as a strong-arm enforcer and bill collector for drug dealers. On the stand, Parella told the jury, "If somebody didn't pay their bill, I would try to get it." He then went on to testify that he killed Frank Maars on orders from Mom and Jeannie. "They wanted the pilot scared or killed, and it was leaning on killed," Parella told the jurors. Then Broome asked, "Were you surprised when Jeannie offered your services to kill the pilot?" "No," Parella replied. "That's what I was there for."

Well, he might have been there for that reason, but I know for a fact that John Parella was and always had been Jeannie's man, not Mom's. I never once saw him around without Jeannie being there also. Jeannie even called him by a pet name, "JP." Broome also tried to establish that Jeannie was Mom's smuggling partner. She wasn't. Mom merely supplied her with marijuana that she in turn sold through her own channels. Jeannie never had anything to do with the smuggling. That was exclusively Mom's gig.

Prompted by Broome, Parella's direct testimony went on to describe how he and Gary Childers murdered Frank in cold blood. He also testified that he and Gary had been promised $15,000 each for the job, but were never paid. Mom broke down and cried when Broome displayed photographs of Frank's dead body to the jurors.

Then it was the defense's turn to take a swing at Parella. Philip Butler hit the ground running by making it clear to jurors that Parella had a very good reason for testifying against Mom. "He [John Parella] can't be believed. He's been given something better than a million dollars;

he's been given his life back. He'd tell authorities whatever they want to hear so he would receive only one 15-year sentence and now he'll be on the streets in eight years."

But Butler didn't stop there. He went on to ask Parella probing questions that established that Gary, Mom's catch man and a friend of John's, had known that Frank Maars had just been paid by Mom and would therefore make a prime target for a robbery. Butler's cross examination ended with a series of questions about Parella's criminal past and he took most of them in stride, but one question in particular seemed to rankle Parella more than the others.

"Who's Robert Bazzano?" Butler asked.

"The person I shot," Parella answered, looking very nervous.

Butler turned his back to Parella and sat down. "No further questions at this time, your honor."

The following morning Prosecutor Broome resumed her attack and called Mom's former catch man Gary Childers to the stand, guiding him carefully through a story that closely mirrored Parella's. He also testified that he had overheard Mom and Jeannie discussing Frank's killing because he had decided to keep "their" plane. It was strange, but Gary had undergone hypnotism (supposedly to help his recollection of events) prior to his testimony. All the same, I was again struck by Gary's obvious lack (or suppression) of knowledge regarding the true nature of the business relationship between Jeannie and Mom. Why would Jeannie be concerned about the supposed theft of Mom's plane? Nevertheless, Broome kept fighting to try and establish a partnership between Mom and Jeannie that simply did not exist. When she had finished her direct, Butler went in with both guns blazing.

He immediately established that Gary, like Parella, had been given the same plea deal. Testify for the prosecution and get 15 years or go to jail for life for first-degree murder. Butler closed his cross of Gary by asking, "Did Judy ever tell you to kill Frank Maars?"

"No, sir," Gary answered.

Gary's involvement in Frank's murder did not surprise me, nor did his testimony against Mom. I had come to know him fairly well over the years and had always perceived him to be (unlike his older brother O.B.) more of a follower type of person, someone predisposed to going along with the crowd and taking the easy way out. Not really a bad guy or someone capable of being part of a murder, just weak of character.

However, the next witness for the prosecution not only came as a complete surprise to me, but it hurt, for I had known him well and we had been good friends for many years during my youth. When I first learned that he was taking the stand I did a double-take, thinking I had misheard. Would this nightmare never end? Jimbo was going to testify against Mom?

Jimmy LeMaster, known to my family and his friends as "Jimbo," had been a very close family friend for years and we all knew and loved him. A Vietnam veteran, he was a country boy at heart with an easy smile and Southern accent, born and raised in north Florida. Jimbo enjoyed partying, drinking, and picking, not necessarily in that order, and he had been my earliest musical mentor as well. I had learned a lot by watching him play guitar as I grew up. Mom and I had met Jimbo the day he accompanied his mother on a visit to the sewing shop and we all hit it off right away. He immediately became a fixture in our household. Jimbo had been a drifter since 'Nam and had spent many a night at our house, crashed on the couch or set up in a spare bedroom. He had been sort of like an older brother to me in many ways. At the height of Mom's smuggling, he had babysat a load of pot a few times at a stash house, hanging out, drinking beer and playing his guitar, just keeping an eye on things and serving as a deterrent to anyone wanting to steal the load. But that was all. I never once saw him in contact with Frank, Parella or Gary, or involved with anything critical to Mom's operation. He was way too easygoing and laid-back. I truly wondered what he could have to say about Frank's murder and I was about to find out. On the fourth day of the trial Jimbo took the stand.

Obviously not wanting to allow Butler to be the one to break the news of Jimbo's plea deal as he had the others, Broome began her direct by admitting that Jimbo had been granted immunity from any possible drug charges in exchange for his testimony against Mom. Okay, I thought, there's the motive for his testimony, but what could he add that had not already been said? A lot, as it turned out.

For more than two hours, Jimbo spewed the craziest, most damning testimony imaginable and placed himself at the center of a half-dozen pivotal events both before and after the murder. He recalled Frank stating before his murder, "I'm a dead man," and he put words in Mom's mouth that incriminated her on so many levels that his testimony actually surpassed that of Parella himself in terms of sheer content. Stated bluntly, I have to say that he made her sound like a gangster. It was like he was quoting lines from *The Godfather* and I felt sure that anyone who knew Mom could easily tell that his story was ridiculous, but the jury didn't know Mom. Maybe they'd buy his fairy tale. Hearing his testimony, I was in disbelief and sorely disappointed that Jimbo had allowed himself to fall into such a pathetic condition. Overall, I felt much more sorrow than anger toward him. He was a weak soul that had been victimized by the system.

I might have felt sorry for him, but Butler did not. He and Randy had been expecting Jimbo's nonsense and were not about to let him get away with it without a fight. He began by showing the jurors that much of Jimbo's testimony stemmed from recollections of conversations he didn't first recall until the week of the trial—more than six years after the murder!

"So, you're just flying down here on the plane," asked Butler incredulously, referring to a statement where Jimbo recalled Mom saying she wanted Frank dead, "and all of a sudden it just popped into your mind?" It was a valid question and the jury perked up for the answer. Jimbo shrugged his shoulders as he gave a slight nod and muttered a sheepish "yes."

Randy and Butler had repeatedly counter-attacked the state's case via its witnesses because that was practically the only avenue worth exploiting. At its best, the prosecution's case was flawed by its lack of tangible evidence, for there truly was no motive for Mom to commit murder other than the testimony of two admitted killers and one completely cowed country boy that had probably drunk a few too many beers in his day to adequately stand up for himself. Butler and Randy had scored a few points, but the fight was far from over and the prosecution still had the inherent edge that came with being the aggressor. It was like a football game where one team always had the ball and was playing offense. But after Jimbo's testimony the prosecution's momentum began to wane. Broome called several more minor witnesses and then rested her case. I was mildly surprised that Greg hadn't been sprung on the court at the last minute to spurt a mess of lies like Jimbo had. We later found out that Broome had planned to use him but changed her mind after weighing the overall pros and cons of using yet another tainted witness that the defense could impugn. The defense would have the floor the next morning and it was literally going to be a case of do or die.

Although Randy and Butler had been working together on Mom's defense the entire trial, it had not been entirely smooth sailing and they'd already had several serious clashes up to the halfway point, one encounter actually coming close to fisticuffs in the hallway right outside the courtroom. The tension between them was palpable. The first issue between them was that Randy simply did not believe that Butler was prepared to go to trial. To a large degree this belief stemmed from the fact that Butler had not interviewed Mom to any significant degree prior to the trial and did not feel the need to confer with her much during the trial. His style was bombastic, straightforward and take-no-prisoners, slash-and-burn and to hell with the consequences. It was effective and he had used it successfully in the past. Randy's approach was more nuanced, more adaptive. He was an intellectual people-person who could read a courtroom and exploit its changing atmosphere in real time. A strategist at heart, Randy took the time to interview Mom at length and learned a lot of useful information that greatly benefited the defense throughout the trial, often taking notes and conferring with Mom at the defense table while Butler waged a spirited pitched battle with the prosecution. Fortunately, the two lawyers worked out their differences and forged ahead.

Mom knew going in that her defense did not have much to work with, for, after all, how do you prove a negative? She was truly innocent of Frank's murder. So with that in mind Mom had decided early on that she would take the stand in her own defense despite the risks that presented. It was common knowledge in legal circles that a clever prosecutor could manipulate a defendant into making an incriminating statement even when he or she was innocent of the crime. It had happened many times before. Mom, however, threw caution to the wind and insisted that the truth would set her free. Oddly, this was an issue upon which both Butler and Randy agreed. I think they realized that the jury might appreciate a hearty dose of honesty after all the self-serving lies told by the self-confessed killers. The defense had to show the jurors the truth. First, Mom was a peaceful marijuana smuggler and nothing more. Second, she had no history of violence and was not someone who would order anyone's murder. Third, there was an explanation for the murder that made a lot more sense than the fairy tale told by the prosecution's witnesses. And lastly, Frank Maars had always been her friend. To help make this point, I was called to the stand on the sixth day of the trial as one of the very first witnesses for the defense.

When Butler asked me about the relationship between Mom and Frank I just told the simple, unvarnished truth: "I thought they got along real well." After a few more questions from Butler, it was Broome's turn to take a shot at me. She probed deeper, but I had nothing to hide and the jury could see it. Broome let me go after only a few questions.

Through the earlier testimony of my Aunt Roberta the jurors had learned of a birthday party Frank had attended with Mom less than a week before his murder. Roberta and I had been there and remembered it well. Strong drinks and tasty food were plentiful and Frank and many of the party-goers were quite tipsy and everyone had had a rollicking good time. Mom and Frank were laughing and cutting up as usual and on very friendly terms. That was just the way it was. I think the jurors were beginning to see the true picture but there was still a long way to go before they could discard the prosecution's damning case. Mom would have to do some heavy lifting herself and let the jury get to know her. The day after my testimony Butler called Mom to the stand and she was sworn in before a rapt courtroom.

Butler began with a line of questioning designed to let the jurors take a little peek inside Mom's smuggling operation while he focused on the relationship between Mom and Frank, especially during the two weeks leading up to the murder. Frank had given Mom a car and Mom had invited him to a party. The two were good friends and their relationship was solid. Mom and Greg were on the rocks romantically and Greg was forging ahead with his own smuggling plans. Jimbo had been recruited as a stash house babysitter because Gary couldn't be trusted anymore due to his cocaine habit. Mom's testimony all that morning was pretty mundane stuff, nothing spectacular. Just before the noon recess, Mom described how she paid Frank $25,000 just hours before he was murdered and Gary had known it.

When the court reconvened, the testimony ratcheted up a notch as Mom solemnly described how she first heard about Frank's murder from family friend and corporate attorney Ed Sawyer. "It was right after midnight. He calls me up and he says, 'I got some real bad news for you.' And any time anybody says that I get sort of a weak feeling, you know, and he says, 'Frank is dead.' And I don't know whether he said, 'Frank was killed,' whether he was shot, whether he was murdered, I don't have any idea what he said. All I remember is that he told me that he was dead and—"

"What did you do?" Butler interrupted.

Mom continued. "I cried, I cried, and then I, you know, he talked to me for a few minutes. I don't know what he said because I was just crying, and I thought about going over to Mother and Daddy's and telling them. I wanted to be with somebody. I felt like I was alone, and later ... Frank liked this record, a Moody Blues album, and I made a hot cup of tea, turned on the stereo, and cried. The next morning I went over and told Mother and Daddy..." Mom's voice trailed off.

Butler continued, "Judy, I have to ask you these questions: Did you ever ask or instruct anybody to kill Frank Maars?"

"Never, never."

"Did you ever promise to pay anybody to kill Frank Maars?"

Shaking her head as her gaze drifted from Butler to the jurors, Mom answered, "No, I never instructed anybody; I never promised anybody anything for murdering Frank. Frank had been a friend of mine and when Greg had taken off, Frank had been there and helped me a lot. Frank was an excellent pilot, he was good for my business, and he was a personal friend of mine."

"Did you ever want Frank Maars killed?

"Never, never, no, sir, never..." Mom answered, then shifted in her seat to look intently at the jurors as she took a deep breath and exhaled, quivering slightly with emotion and speaking in a stream of consciousness. "Okay. I am a totally ... all my life I have totally been a very non-violent person; I am a health food nut; I smoke pot, but I have never been violent. I have never wished anybody harm. I have never offered to hurt anybody. I have never threatened to hurt anybody, paid anybody to murder anybody, never in my life, never..." Drained, she shook her head.

"That's all I have for now, Judge," Butler declared. "Thank you."

Sitting there in the gallery, I studied the jurors. I knew Mom was telling the truth. I knew she was exactly as described, a totally nonviolent person. However, would the jurors agree? Could they see the truth? My thoughts crashed back to Earth as Broome stood, notes in hand, and stalked to the lectern.

I didn't know what to expect from her. Where would she begin? Would it be a personal attack based on Mom's admitted drug dealing or would she try to destroy her with some tidbit of damning information kept hidden for just this moment? Oddly, it was none of that, for Broome began by asking Mom, an admitted marijuana smuggler on trial for capital murder, about the prior conviction when she neglected to declare the $29,000 brought into LAX from Mexico all those years before. Bizarre, I thought. Of course a big-time pot smuggler had plenty of undeclared illegal cash. What was Broome's point? Where would she go next? The jurors appeared as baffled as I was.

Broome's next series of questions tried to establish that Jeannie was Mom's smuggling partner, yet backfired.

"Isn't it true that you and Jeannie went to the house together and weighed the marijuana, your first load to Georgia, and looked at the marijuana, see what you had...?"

"I am sure we did," Mom answered.

"You and Jeannie were involved in this business together, right?" Broome left the door wide open with the question.

"That was the first time that she bought a load of my herb, yes, but she wasn't involved in the smuggling."

"She was just involved in the selling, correct?"

"Yes, ma'am," answered Mom.

"But didn't you consult her on your problems?"

"No, ma'am. Well, possibly the problems we both had ... uh, romantically, with men." Several spectators in the courtroom chuckled at that.

Broome abandoned that line of questioning with a puzzled look lingering on her face as she flipped through her notes. I could hardly believe what I had just heard. Did the prosecutor just help Mom explain that Jeannie was just a pot dealer and not her smuggling partner? And if Jeannie was not involved with smuggling, why would she be concerned with Frank Maars and Mom's airplane, especially enough to conspire with Mom in a murder as the prosecution contended? It seemed to me that Broome's questions were helping Mom's defense. Were the jurors listening?

Broome continued to question Mom ineffectually for the remainder of the day. Her last questions established that Mom had already pled guilty to drug charges and had received a 20-year prison sentence which was five years more than the sentence imposed on both of the confessed killers of Frank Maars. Was that the message Broome wanted to convey? I thought it very weird. It just seemed to me that either her heart was not in the case or she was simply not a very effective prosecutor. Either way, I felt a tinge of optimism for the first time as Mom stepped down from the stand. Wearily, Judge Carlisle banged his gavel and dismissed the court for the day. Mom had survived her testimony and perhaps bolstered her defense, but the fight was far from over. The defense had one last witness to present, a final lifeline that had been discovered by a famous private eye. Later that night back in my hotel room I prayed like never before. Oh God, please save Mom from the clutches of Old Sparky!

19

The Hail Mary

"All rise," ordered the bailiff in a booming voice as Judge Carlisle scurried into the courtroom like a tall, wispy phantom in his long black robes and settled into his high-back chair. Well, this is it, I thought. Today will be the day that will make or break the case. Make or break Mom's life. Make or break mine. I was as tense as the high E string on my long-lost guitar and I felt like I was made of glass and could shatter at any moment. And if I was this wound up, what must Mom be going through right now?

No sooner had the thought crossed my mind when I noticed Mom had turned completely around in her seat and was flashing me an encouraging smile. It caught me by surprise and stiffened my upper lip and I vowed to concentrate on positive thoughts the rest of the day. I knew that would be what she wanted, scared or not. Electricity was in the air. I was sure something crucial was slated for that day as I had met a very interesting older lady in the hallway outside the courtroom while waiting for the doors to open. I had noticed her immediately as she confidently approached me with a warm smile and held out a hand.

"Hello, you must be David Michael." It was a statement, not a question. She obviously knew who I was although I was positive I had never met her before. "I'm Virginia Snyder." I took her hand and shook it.

"Nice to meet you," I said, liking her instantly. Besides her unguarded demeanor and open expression, she wore a cheerfully-colored blouse and skirt and had a large purse slung casually over her plump shoulder. She was short and had to tilt her head up sharply to look at me.

"All this must be very hard for you and your sisters," she observed. "I've met your mother and she's a good person. I'm praying for her."

"Me too." I didn't know what else to say and I got the vibe that maybe Virginia was a reporter that had been following the case. I wondered if Mom had done a phone interview or something.

"I think she's going to be okay," she said, looking me straight in the eyes.

That statement caught my attention. Virginia was serious and her words seemed to bear a peculiar sense of judgment. Kind of like those of a religious zealot but without the craziness.

She went on. "I'm a private investigator and I've been working on your mom's case. She's told me a lot about you and Melanie and Morgana and she loves you very much."

I was all ears then. Here was this grandmotherly-looking, kind-eyed little lady telling me she knew Mom and was a private eye to boot. She sure didn't look like any detective I'd ever envisioned, but I never doubted her for an instant and by this time my natural curiosity was piqued to the max so I began asking questions and she answered.

And boy, was she interesting!

Virginia was 66 years old when I met her and she had worked on more than 70 murder cases since opening her investigative agency in Delray Beach, Florida, in 1976. She had been a successful investigative newspaper reporter before becoming only the second woman in Florida to have her own Class A–licensed investigation agency. She did not carry a gun—she didn't believe in them. Instead, she believed that a private eye should gather information solely by using his or her wits, either outsmarting the bad guys or enlisting the help of witnesses by involving them in the case and thereby gaining their confidence and cooperation. She was unorthodox in other ways as well and went on to explain.

Virginia frequently used her unthreatening appearance as well as formidable acting chops to her advantage, time and again gaining access to restricted areas by posing as a distraught woman looking for her dog, a leash in her hand and tears in her eyes. The average security guard didn't have a clue and would often wave her through without a single question. Other times she would play a grieving wife and sit in her car on the street and pretend to be trying to catch her cheating husband as he exited a lover's home. Sympathizing with her story, neighbors would often volunteer their help and report to Virginia her mark's comings and goings and even offer to keep an eye on him themselves when she wasn't around. Still, as entertaining as her stories had been, I had found Virginia's motivations for her work to be even more intriguing.

She had told me that she was very selective when it came to deciding whether or not she would take a case and personally interviewed every potential client in depth before making the decision. Anyone wanting to use her to gain information to use against someone else in a malicious way would not be able to hire her. In short, I found Virginia to be a highly principled person who believed in our justice system but realized its flaws. She felt that justice was best served when attorneys had all the facts of a case at their disposal. "That's when the truth comes out," she said. "And guilty people usually don't hire private investigators."

When the courtroom doors finally opened to let us in that final day I pondered Virginia's words and hoped that the truth would come out in Mom's case and free us of our ordeal. I began a silent prayer to that effect and had barely finished before Butler approached the lectern and announced, "I call Robert Bazzano to the stand."

There it was, I thought, that name again. The one Butler had asked Parella about when he was on the stand. Who was this guy? Parella had said he knew Bazzano, but how? Well, everyone present in the courtroom was about to find out. Two bailiffs, one on each door, swung them open and in rolled Robert Bazzano. Yes, rolled, for he was in a wheelchair, paralyzed from the waist down. Instead of climbing the stairs to the stand he rolled up alongside and raised his hand. He was sworn in, ending with the customary "I do." Bazzano had medium-length straight black hair, a long black mustache, dark glasses, and looked deadly serious and eager to speak. The courtroom was transfixed.

Butler questioned Bazzano and quickly established a series of facts that John Parella had already admitted were true because they involved a previous unrelated case in which he was the defendant and had pled guilty to attempted murder. The first fact was that Bazzano had never met Mom nor had he ever heard of her at all. They were total strangers until that day in court. The second was that Bazzano knew Parella and they had last been together on the 29th of December 1979, which was exactly one year and a day before the murder of Frank Maars. The third was that Bazzano and Parella had met for the supposed purpose of a drug deal and Bazzano had $50,000 in cash with him for the buy. Butler waded in deeper.

"And who had set the drug purchase up?"

"John Parella."

"And did he notice you had the money with you at the time?"

"Yes, he did."

"Did he direct you to go to any certain location to consummate the drug deal?"

"He told me to take a ride with him. He rode with me in my vehicle."

"But he told you where to go?"

"Yes, sir."

"Who else was in the vehicle at the time?"

"Just he and myself."

"And did there come a time when he directed you to stop the vehicle?"

"Yes." Bazzano wiped his forehead with his white-sleeved forearm as if remembering a bad thought or some buried pain. "He asked me to pull over on the way to Oakland Park."

"In a rural section or populated?"

"Back then it was not populated."

"And did there come a time when Mr. Parella exited the vehicle?"

"Yes, he said he had to go out to take a leak."

"And did he in fact step away from the vehicle?"

"He stepped out of the vehicle."

"And then what happened?"

"He stepped back in." Bazzano's voice quavered.

"And...?" Butler probed gently.

"He shot me."

"How many times?"

"Three times in the head and twice in the body, so it was a total of five, but they all went through, all five weren't at the same time."

"Jesus Christ," one of the jurors said aloud as Butler continued.

"I don't follow you."

"He shot me three times. I dropped out of the van and he walked around the other side and shot me twice more."

"He shot you three times through the passenger door where he was outside?"

"No, he was sitting next to me. He'd stepped back into the van."

"Okay. He stepped back into the van, he shot you three times?"

"Yes, sir."

"What location of your body did those three shots go in?"

"Through my right eye and through my lungs and through my liver." Several spectators in the gallery gasped audibly.

"And what did you do then?"

"I went falling out of the vehicle to try to get away."

"And what did he do?"

"At the time the third bullet took out my back, which I am now paralyzed, so when I hit the ground there was no legs underneath me and he came around the other side of the vehicle and lowered himself over and fired two more times."

"Where did those bullets strike?"

"The top of the forehead, the side of the head." As he spoke, Bazzano touched each spot with the tip of his finger to pinpoint the exact spots. Several jurors shook their heads slowly in sympathy.

"How far away was John Parella when he did that?"

"As close as he could possibly get."

"Point blank range?"

"Yes, sir."

"What happened to the $50,000?"

"He took it."

"Was that the last time you ever saw John Parella?"

"Yes, sir."

"Are you aware of the fact that he entered into a plea bargain for the shooting that he did to you?"

"Yes, sir."

"Are you aware of the fact that he could be paroled within 13 months?"

"No," answered Bazzano, obviously surprised.

"That's all I have, Judge," said Butler.

Judge Carlisle looked toward the prosecution's table. "Cross."

Gay Broome rose and proceeded with an uninspired cross examination of Bazzano that lasted less than five minutes. It just seemed to me that she didn't have a direction and was ad-libbing as she went along. Her first line of questioning abruptly ended when she tried to get Bazzano to testify to hearsay. Butler objected and was sustained. Broome's final question exemplifies the overall oddness of her cross examination that had never made much sense.

"Mr. Bazzano, if you had to hire someone to kill someone for you, would you believe that John Parella would be a good candidate?"

"Judge, I object to that," Butler said. "That calls for his opinion."

"Sustained," said the judge.

Broome, shot down in flames yet again, called it a day. "I don't have any further questions."

After Broome returned to her table, Butler mopped up with a brief re-direct that didn't break much new ground other than to let the court know that Bazzano had spent four and a half months in the hospital after the shooting and had been pronounced dead on the operating table before miraculously pulling through. And thank God he did, because I felt Bazzano's testimony had been a game-changer. The defense had said all along that Parella had murdered Frank Maars as part of a robbery and now there was direct evidence that he had attempted exactly the same crime practically a year to the day prior. It was powerful stuff, pure courtroom magic. I felt it and I'm sure the jurors felt it. My optimism increased exponentially.

As expected, the lawyers presenting the closing arguments for both sides stuck to their respective guns and merely restated the cases they had already presented. Broome almost appeared to be on autopilot. Butler and Randy were as passionate as ever. When Judge Carlisle sent the jury to deliberate I said another prayer as I watched them go. Everyone had their own opinion as to how long they'd be out and I didn't dare speculate. Would it be hours? Days? A hung jury? The court was adjourned and everyone filed out.

Every minute the jury deliberated felt like a year, the pressure was so intense. Melanie, Bummy, Morgana, Nancy, Bonnie and Virginia Snyder … we were all camped out in the hallway outside the courtroom. I hardly dared to breathe. I imagined the jurors gathered in a room somewhere nearby with Mom's life in their hands. I prayed they would see the truth. An hour passed, then two, three. Oh well, I thought, it's going to be tomorrow or maybe even the next day. It doesn't matter, I told myself, as long as they get it right. But then all of a sudden I looked up and saw Randy walking toward us with a determined stride. "The jury's in," he declared.

A few minutes later everyone but the jury was back in the courtroom. My body was tingling with excitement and I was absolutely petrified. I wanted to both flee and stay. I couldn't bear to even think about what I would do if Mom was found guilty. My stomach flip-flopped like it contained a fish out of water and I might have passed out had the judge not intervened. "Let's get the jury," he said.

As the jurors filed in I couldn't help but stare at them. And lo and behold, three or four of them stared back at me! What could it mean? I couldn't help but think it was a good sign, for they had to know a guilty verdict would utterly destroy me and my family. Then I noticed what appeared to be a tiny marijuana leaf embroidered on the Izod-style shirt worn by one of the jurors, a young man in his 20s. Was it also a sign, or was I going crazy? It sure felt like it. Thankfully, I was snapped out of the daydream when Judge Carlisle enjoined, "Please be seated." The jurors sat. Then it was the moment of truth. "Okay. Have you reached a verdict?"

"We have."

"Can you give it to the bailiff, please?"

The jury foreman passed the paper to the bailiff, who in turn passed it to the clerk. My head felt like it was about to float off my shoulders. As the clerk began reading the legal mumbo-jumbo, "...of the Fifteenth Judicial Circuit, Criminal Division, in and for Palm Beach County, Florida, blah, blah, blah.... State of Florida versus Judy Haas..." the buzzing in my ears that had previously been background noise now reached a reverberating crescendo as the clerk's voice seemed to fade in and out, "...we, the jury, find as follows as to the Defendant in this case: Not guilty, so say we all..."

Hearing those two words caused a tidal wave of euphoria to wash over me with such force that for an indeterminable period of time it seemed I couldn't breathe and my heart raced with elation. My prayers had been answered! I stared toward heaven and threw my head back and mouthed a silent, "Thank you, God!" I know it may sound corny, but I truly believed that there had been a divine intervention that made sure justice was served. I think Mom summed up my feelings best when I heard her loudly proclaim, "Just thank God, thank Jesus Christ." Mom and I locked eyes and she beamed with happiness as Bonnie, Nancy and Bummy cried. The feeling was simply out of this world and we all hugged each other in jubilation. Then Judge Carlisle spoke up, sarcastically asking Mom, "I assume you want to withdraw your request of having Phil Butler fired as your attorney?" Mom just smiled at him as he turned his attention to the jury and began a rambling off-the-cuff statement.

"When you go home you will see this case had quite a bit of news coverage. Guaranteed you are going to go to a cocktail party or something and I know someone is going to say, 'How did that judge let that woman off? The woman was a drug smuggler and all that.' But none of those people have the right to say that because they weren't here. At best they read about it in the newspaper, but you are the ones that heard the evidence and never let anybody impugn your verdict because they weren't here; they don't know. But I guarantee that someone will say, 'How could that have happened? I agree or disagree with your verdict.'"

Judge Carlisle took a deep breath and continued. "I recognize that this case could have gone either way. There were some holes in the state's case and yet it was good enough to send to a jury, and you had to take it from there. Hey, you want to get a big banner and hang it up saying, 'I was on this jury,' well, you ought to; you ought to be proud of it. You come and do your thing, you tell it the way you see it and you don't have to take heat from anybody. I hope you enjoyed this. I think this is one of the greatest things in the world for people who do, in addition to being such a great protection for the public." With those final words the judge finally ran out of steam and dismissed the jurors who slowly filed out, smiling at all of us the whole time. I just thought all of them were the greatest people on Earth and smiled back.

Then came the time for goodbyes and everyone was allowed to give Mom a quick hug before she was shackled head to toe and led out of the courtroom. Then it was our turn, and when we exited the courthouse the media was right outside asking questions. When a reporter asked about the trial, Bummy said, "From the start, it was impressed upon us that in Florida the electric chair is a real possibility in a first-degree murder case, and let me tell you, it's an awful thing to face." I agreed wholeheartedly. We all knew that Florida was second only to Texas in the number of executions carried out. Then Bonnie was asked about the verdict and wasn't shy about offering her two cents. "Oh, let me tell you something," she began, overflowing with emotion, "that's the only verdict they could have come up with. What the government did was unconscionable. Judy spent 14 months in the county jail waiting to go to trial because the government wanted to make her out to be some demon queen drug smuggler." Not to be outdone, I took the opportunity to declare, "My mom wouldn't hurt a flea," and Melanie, standing at my side, agreed with a vehement nod. It was a good day, one I'll never forget.

Later that evening back at the hotel Randy dropped in to say farewell before flying back to San Francisco early the next morning. Of course, we had only met a week earlier and I didn't know him very well, but what I did know of him both impressed and inspired me. Here was this young lawyer that I knew had played a major role in Mom's defense and in doing so had saved her life, and mine as well. He was a real life super-hero to me and I didn't have the words to thank him, but he took everything in stride as if he did that sort of thing every day.

Randy had arrived just as I was about to take a night stroll along the beach, so I invited him along. We took off our shoes and talked as we made our way down the deserted beach, the sand and surf working their magic. It was fabulous stress relief after the ordeal of the trial and Randy was in the middle of telling me about law school (I was considering the possibility of becoming a lawyer myself) when we noticed a shark, about six feet long and freshly beached in the surf just ahead of us.

Without a word, we sprang into action. I grabbed the shark's tail and one pectoral fin while Randy got a grip on the opposite side and together we dragged the thrashing toothy creature into deeper water. By the time we had gotten it into thigh-deep water it had become quite rejuvenated and frisky enough for Randy and I to let go before beating a hasty retreat. Once free, the shark shot into the black depths and was gone. It wasn't a man-eater just because it was a shark, and Mom wasn't a killer just because she was a smuggler. Back on the beach, wet and exhausted, we just looked at each other and laughed. It was the perfect ending to an eventful day.

20

After the Gold Rush

The years after Mom's murder trial were sort of anticlimactic, but that was a good thing. Going through that kind of ordeal was something I would never want to experience again. Thankfully the nightmares I had suffered leading up to the trial disappeared after her acquittal and return to federal prison. Mom got her job back as prison gardener and her best friend Lana was still there. It was a kind of homecoming of sorts, still prison, of course, but without the threat of execution. Not too terrible considering everything Mom had already been through. Shortly after her arrival, Lana came to Mom and announced, her Russian accent as thick as ever, "Judy, today I introduce you to someone I think you will like. He is maybe only person here other than you that is not snitch." She did, and that was when Mom met Bruce Perlowin for the first time. He and Lana were a couple and together the three of them served their time as their friendships grew and strengthened. Not long afterward Mom even found herself a boyfriend, another pilot, as fate would have it, a man by the name of John Robertson. John had been imprisoned for his role in a famous Colombian cocaine smuggling ring dubbed "Air America." The romance with John and Mom's friendship with Lana and Bruce did a lot to help pass the time, and there was plenty of it. Mom and I wrote letters back and forth and she called from time to time as she served her 20-year sentence. Meanwhile, I did my best to live a life I could be proud of.

Only a few months after Mom's trial I met and married Christine, a magically beautiful girl I fell in love with the instant I met her. It was surreal, after all the craziness in my life I had had the incredible good fortune to find my soulmate. How lucky was that? We settled in St. Augustine, Florida, and I worked as a professional musician while Christine attended college. In the interim, the incarcerated members of my

Family reunion shortly after Mom's release from federal prison, ca. 1992. Clockwise from left: Melanie, Mom, David Michael, Morgana.

family were paroled. Aunt Bonnie was the first, then Baga. Then the day came that Mom was paroled. She had served almost eight years.

When she got out she went straight to south Florida and opened a small custom sewing and alterations shop and named it—what else?— "Violet's." Long gone were the days of big money and everything else that accompanied it. Mom was on parole, so she stuck to what my grandfather Baga called "the straight and narrow." Over the years, Violet's became a modest success and Mom's parole was eventu-

David Michael's musician promo photo, ca. 1990.

ally terminated. She then became just another middle-aged ex-con with a storied past and an infatuation with marijuana and, of course, her ever-present green thumb.

The years since her marijuana smuggling conviction had brought about great change in the country and Mom, being what she was and noticing the change along with everyone else, couldn't help but turn her attention to one of her first loves. Of course, smuggling was out of the question and completely unnecessary as well. This time she would become a legal marijuana grower and there was one place leading such activity. Mom closed Violet's and bought a ticket to California.

Once in California, Mom reunited with Aunt Bonnie, who had settled there in the years since her daughter, Leighton Meester, had become a famous television and movie actress. I was not privy to the details, but one way or another Mom somehow bought her way into some sort of quasi-partnership with a man who owned a legal marijuana dispensary in the Los Angeles area named the Green Mile. When I first heard about it I wasn't surprised and figured, what the heck, Mom's back in the industry she knows and loves and, thank God, this time it's legal. However, I made a mental note to myself to always maintain a safe distance from any of Mom's marijuana exploits, no matter how legal they were. And it was a good thing too, because Mom's Green Mile dispensary did take a bad turn some months later, and while I had nothing whatsoever to do with it and remained unscathed in the fiasco, my little sister Morgana was not so lucky.

Again, I was not aware of the details but know that Mom had some-

David Michael and Christine's elopement, 1996.

what recklessly gotten Morgana involved in a dispensary that, although legal, had technical issues with its operation that allowed it to be targeted by local cops that were capitalizing on the rapidly-changing marijuana industry at that particular time in California. Both Mom and Morgana were arrested on misdemeanor charges. I was really bummed when I heard about it. Unfortunately, I think Morgana made the crucial mistake of allowing Mom to make sure that all the technicalities of such a business were adhered to. And while I had always known Mom to be a clutch player who operated on impulse, made decisions on the fly and didn't fuss over details, Morgana did not know Mom nearly as well

Mom as a blonde, ca. late 1990s.

and therefore was not nearly as aware of potential trouble in that regard. In fact, I clearly remember a phone call with Morgana in the weeks before the Green Mile imploded and I'm sure she thought she was involved in a totally legal dispensary that had everything in complete legal order. I know she wouldn't have been involved otherwise. Thankfully, the charge was a misdemeanor and Morgana weathered the storm, yet the Green Mile was no more and Mom was back to square one.

However, as far as Mom was concerned, the genie was out of the bottle and there was no going back. State after state had legalized medical marijuana and several more had legalized recreational marijuana or had legalization pending. There would be a demand for knowledgeable growers like her and the future held tremendous promise.

21

Seedlings

Years after the Green Mile debacle I look back and see that it was only the beginning, only a step, a sort of milemarker in the inevitable path our country is traveling. And if I had had a crystal ball that allowed me to see into the future from the very start of all Mom's crazy exploits I wouldn't have believed we would ever reach the point where we find ourselves today. It just doesn't seem possible after all that has occurred. Mom spent so many years in prison for importing a commodity that is now well on its way to societal and political acceptance. So much has changed.

El Loco is gone now, taken by the AIDS epidemic of the late 1980s. In my mind I like to think of him as he was, flying with one hand on the yoke and the other holding a joint, flashing the lopsided grin he so often wore. Baga and Bummy are long gone as well, still together, I hope, in a place with no worries and no bad memories. I'll never forget the life lessons Baga taught me as well as our marathon chess matches. And what can I say about Bummy other than she was truly my second mother and the one person solely responsible for me becoming totally hooked on books since the age of five.

My wonderful Aunt Nancy—always so full of life that I still can't imagine her any other way—was taken from us so unexpectedly it serves as a testament to the underlying truth of the Billy Joel song "Only the Good Die Young." Her loss was a severe blow to all of us and especially Mom, as they were always so close, true sidekicks in everything.

Randy Daar is still in San Francisco protecting people's rights and saving lives. I truly believe that's what he was born to do. I simply cannot imagine a better lawyer exists anywhere in the world.

Bruce Perlowin, true to form, has not skipped a beat. He was released after serving nine years in prison and became the founder

Randy Daar, defense attorney extraordinaire, 2017.

and CEO of Hemp, Inc., a publicly-traded company that is now at the forefront of the burgeoning CBD and industrial hemp industry in the United States. His star is a rising one and I'm glad to see it. He, Lana, and Mom have remained close friends.

Morgana is now a successful jewelry designer in southern California and the long-time love of actor Charlie Hunnam. Melanie, a licensed cosmetologist, lives in south Florida with her two children.

As for myself, after more than 20

Melanie, 2017.

years as a U.S. Coast Guard–licensed ship's captain, I now plan on going to sea again only as captain of my own private sailboat with my family as my crew. I still play music professionally as frontman for the band Harvest Moon. Christine and I have been together 30 years and we now have two wonderful boys. Both are into music. My dad still lives in Arizona and now my family does too. I'm happy that my boys have gotten to know their grandfather.

Mom and I remain very close to this day

Mom, 2017.

David Michael and Christine, 2017.

and to me she is and always will be the same person she has always been. Complicated, no doubt about it. She's also a survivor that loves her family. And I suppose I'm one too.

The Cheyenne believe that all life is a circle, and so do I, for Mom's life has come full circle since that first Saturday night in Buckeye all those years ago. And if you might be wondering if she still has her green thumb … you bet she does!

Index